Richard & Sara

Best wishes

Russell

IMPERIAL DISGUISES

The Life Of Terence Keyes

GW00496632

Terence Keyes

IMPERIAL DISGUISES

THE LIFE OF TERENCE KEYES

Richard Whittingham

YouCaxton Publications
Oxford & Shrewsbury

ISBN 978-1-912419-58-6

Printed and bound in Great Britain.
Published by YouCaxton Publications 2019

Maps by Ellie Ashby
Photographs of present day St Petersburg by Maksym Alokhin

YCBN: 01

YouCaxton Publications

enquiries@youcaxton.co.uk

To Charlie Craddock with thanks

Contents

List of Illustrations

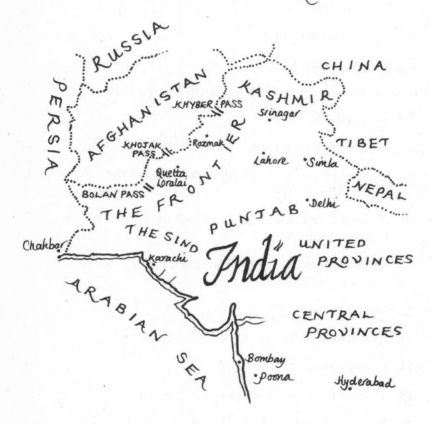

NORTHERN INDIA

RUSSIA

PERSIA

AFGHANISTAN

KHYBER PASS

KHOJAK PASS

Rozmak

Quetta
Loralai

BOLAN PASS

THE FRONTIER

THE SIND

Chahbar

Karachi

India

PUNJAB

Lahore

Srinagar

KASHMIR

CHINA

TIBET

Simla

NEPAL

Delhi

UNITED
PROVINCES

CENTRAL
PROVINCES

Bombay
Poona

Hyderabad

ARABIAN SEA

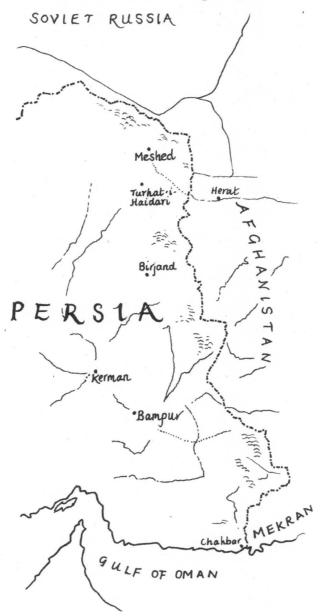

PERSIA'S EASTERN BORDER

SOVIET RUSSIA

Meshed

Turbat-i-
Haidari

Herat

A F G H A N I S T A N

Birjand

P E R S I A

Kerman

Bampur

Chahbar

MEKRAN

GULF OF OMAN

EUROPEAN RUSSIA
circa 1917

SWEDEN

Murmansk

FINLAND

Archangel

Helsingfors

Baltic
Sea

URAL MOUNTAINS

Tobolsk

Petrograd
Novgorod
ESTONIA
Riga
Kovno
Wilno
Vitebsk
LITHUANIA
Minsk
Warsaw
POLAND BELORUSSIA
Brest-
Litovsk Chernigov

Pskov

Vologda
Kostroma
Yaroslav
Nizhniy Novgorod
Smolensk
MOSCOW
Tula
Oral

Viatka

Volga

Perm

Kazan

Tiumen

Omsk

Ekaterinburg

Cheliabinsk

Ufa

Simbirsk

Samara

Lvov
GALICIA

Jassy

DNIEPER

Kiev
UKRAINE

Kharkiv
Poltava

Tambor
Saratov
Voronezh

Orenburg

Kishiner
Odessa

Rostov

DON

Tsaritsyn

Volga

ROMANIA

Bucharest

Sevastopol

BULGARIA

Black Sea

Ekaterinodar

Stavropol
Novorossisk

CENTRAL
ASIA

GEORGIA

Caspian

Khiva

Tiflis
AZERBAIJAN
ARMENIA

OTTOMAN
EMPIRE

Baku

Sea

Bukhara

PERSIA   0   miles   500

Chapter 1:

Early Years

The weather in Abbottabad is approaching its hottest by late May with average temperatures ranging between sixteen and twenty eight degrees centigrade. It was on 28 May 1877 that Terence Keyes was born and "first smelt the sweet Abbottabad air."[1] He was the fourth son of Sir Charles Patton and Katherine Jessie Keyes (always known as Kate). The town then was only twenty three years old and was a hill station affording respite from the heat of the plains. It has had military connections since its foundation and has been described as Pakistan's Aldershot.[2] It was this military connection accounted for the presence of Charles and Kate Keyes.

Quite how Charles and Kate Keyes came to be in the North West Frontier Provinces is set out in more detail in the Appendix. However, both of them came from families with long military antecedents in British India. Charles Keyes had a highly distinguished career being twice considered for a Victoria Cross and was a frequent participant in operations against the local tribes. His rank on retirement was Major General and he had a considerable influence upon Terence Keyes and his brothers. Terence Keyes was to follow his father in spending the best part of his adult life in India.

In 1878, Charles Keyes returned to England on leave together with Kate and his five young children. He did not return to India for three years. There is limited information about how he spent his time. Presumably, he would have returned to Ulster where had spent much of his boyhood but he probably mostly resided in London as Katherine Mary was born in Kensington on 5 November 1878. Time may also have been spent in Kent as his eldest son Norman was enrolled at Albion House a preparatory school in Sweyn Road, Margate run by a Mr Schimmelmann.

After three years, his leave came to an end. This presented a problem with what to do with his children and a decision was made to leave the five eldest with a country parson who became known to the children as "Uncle Edward." Kate spent a week at the vicarage and satisfied herself with the arrangements before departure. Uncle Edward was clearly well connected and spent much of his time fishing or shooting and the children accompanied him regularly. A regular visitor to the vicarage was an Admiral who may have encouraged Terence's second eldest brother Roger's nautical ambitions. However, conditions were Spartan in the extreme and the mood worsened when, in September 1883, Norman died at his uncle's house in Kensington of appendicitis.

Very little is known of Terence Keyes' childhood. There are no records of his reaction to being left in England when his parents returned to India in 1882 or to the sudden death of his eldest brother Norman in September 1883 when he was six. He almost certainly followed his brothers to Albion House. This was a small establishment with thirty five pupils in 1881 rising to thirty eight in 1891.[3] His eldest brother, Norman, had been put down for Wellington which would have indicated a likely military career, Roger having decided upon a Naval career went to HMS Britannia. In 1890, Terence was sent to Haileybury with its historic links to British India whereas Charles Valentine was sent to Eton.

He had a successful school career at Haileybury where he was Prefect and Head of Colvin House in 1893 and 1894 as well as featuring in the house Cricket Eleven in 1894.[4] He was small for his age and as a result, had to be accompanied by a fag at Lights Out because he could not reach the gas overhead pulleys. This lack of height prevented him from being accepted by the Artillery at Woolwich.[5] It was clearly a family trait as his brother Roger was only four feet ten inches and five stone at the age of thirteen.[6]

Fortunately for Keyes, the Royal Military Academy, Sandhurst was more forgiving and he was accepted for the following year (1895) apparently on the condition that he managed to grow somewhat in the interim. This led to him taking what amounted to a proto gap year. He travelled through Germany before ending in Russia where he found employment as the driver of a brewer's dray. Chiefly, he achieved his principal aim of growing sufficiently to be accepted at Sandhurst as a Queen's India Cadet.

Apparently, before departing for Germany, he had been contacted by military contacts of his father and given instructions to research areas of interest. Whilst this seems inherently unlikely, it is possible that with his family connections such an approach was made. Certainly, the Russian which he picked up served him in very good stead later in his career.[7]

Following Sandhurst, Keyes was commissioned in the King's Own Scottish Borderers, it being established practice at the time for an officer to commence his Indian career in a British regiment before being posted to an Indian one. Keyes' introduction to Indian service was a lively one as the KOSB were engaged in the Tyrah Expedition in 1897.

The expedition was brought about by the actions of a Muslim holy man, Sagidullah, the Lewani Faqir generally referred to by the British as "the Mad Mullah" although "Lewani" loosely translates as "intoxicated" indicating a degree of religious rather than alcoholic enthusiasm. He claimed that the British were seeking to spread Christianity to the area but had lost control of the Suez Canal and therefore could expect no reinforcements. The rebellion spread from the Swat Valley to neighbouring areas and, at one point, the British lost control of the Khyber Pass. This caused great consternation as it opened the plains of North India up to raiding by the hill tribes. It should also be viewed in the context of the ongoing tussle for control of South Asia between the Russians and British so that the rebels' breech loading rifles had been supplied by the Russians or their agents. This, at a stroke, reduced the advantage that the British had previously enjoyed in their encounters with the hill tribes.

The ongoing Anglo-Russian rivalry was the dominant strategic issue for the British in the late nineteenth century. The Russians had developed a railway system that spread well into Central Asia and which enabled them to establish effective dominance of the territories south towards Afghanistan. This, combined with the Russian opening up of Siberia and the commencement of the Trans-Siberian Railway in 1891, caused British nervousness about Russian ambitions. These were not far-fetched as the overarching Russian ambition was to establish a dominant position in most of Central and Southern Asia stretching as far as Korea. The British were only too conscious of the vulnerability of the North Indian plain to attack which is why such a priority was given to defending the North West Frontier.

The rivalry with Russia stemmed back as far as the Crimean War and the longstanding British support of Turkey against Russian ambitions of gaining control of Constantinople and with it access to the Mediterranean. Should that have occurred, British sea lanes would have been exposed - a big enough issue in the 1850s but even more so following the opening of the Suez Canal in 1867. Furthermore, as the Russian railway network expanded so did the advantage that the Russians enjoyed by having interior lines of communication. The need to retain good relations with the Muslim world therefore became critical to the British and reinforced the need for friendly links with the Porte in Constantinople.[8] The religious inspiration behind the Mad Mullah and other revolts therefore touched a very raw nerve.

This fear was general and in 1906 the Military Correspondent of The Times, Colonel Repington assessed the Russians as "undoubtedly the most serious problem that has ever been incurred by the British Army." He went on to comment upon the new infrastructure that had been installed at Russian expense in Afghanistan - principally railways and likely supply bases comparing all this very favourably with the meagre British preparations. He went on that Britain should have fifty thousand men ready to take Kabul within six weeks and a further two hundred and fifty thousand in Helmand in eight months increasing to half a million in eighteen months with a further one hundred thousand to guard and manage lines of communication. This should be compared with the fewer than one hundred thousand sent to France as part of the British Expeditionary Force in 1914 as giving an insight into the way in which British priorities were skewed towards the protection of India.[9]

It must also have been poignant for Keyes to be engaged in an expedition against the Afridi tribes in precisely the same area as his father had operated for so many years. It was also something of a homecoming as he had spent his first years on the North West Frontier when his father had been in command of the Punjab Frontier Force. Indeed, the expedition commenced from Kohat which had been Charles Keyes' base for many years.

The 2nd Battalion of the KOSB formed part of the 4th Brigade which also included the Northamptonshire Regiment as well as Gurkha and Sikh regiments. It was during this expedition that he first saw action and recounted how his batman, Anderson, was shot by his side. As he died, Anderson remarked "You'll find your cholera belt in my haversack, in case you're lying out all night sir." This example of what Wodehouse would call "the feudal spirit" clearly made an impression as it features twice in Keyes' recollections. The only other things known of Anderson were that he was about thirty and smoked particularly pungent pipe tobacco.[10]

On 18 October 1897, Keyes was himself wounded at the Battle of Chagru Kotal, a bullet being partially stopped by a pocket book in his breast pocket and his hand was damaged by a shell splinter. As a result of his actions that day, he was mentioned in despatches and recommended for a DSO. However, his commanding officer arranged for him to be awarded a brevet promotion to Lieutenant instead. Following, his injury, Keyes was invalided down to Rawalpindi where, with some difficulty, he and another injured officer made their way to the Expeditionary Force temporary hospital. He records that when he finally made it into bed, it was dirty and damp with wine. He later learned that the reason for this was that a chaplain had died in it a few hours before and the hospital staff had tried without success to revive him with port.

The Tirah expedition was effectively over by April 1898 when terms were agreed with the Afridis whereby they handed over eight hundred breech loading rifles and paid an indemnity of fifty thousand rupees. Tellingly, another term was that they agreed not to reach an agreement with any other power that would result in railway lines or roads being built in the Khyber Pass thereby preventing the spread of Russian influence.

On 11 October 1899, the Second Boer War began and it soon became the principal focus of British and Imperial military effort. Indeed, by the war's end in 1902, approximately five hundred thousand troops had served. It was obviously frustrating for a young and ambitious officer to be stuck on garrison duty and missing out on the main event. Keyes therefore made repeated requests for transfer from the British Indian Army regiment, the 38th Dogra Bengal Infantry to which he had been posted following his time with the KOSB.[11] These were repeatedly blocked by his commanding officer who accused him of showing a lack of patriotism and esprit de corps and reminded him that his father had remained with the same regiment for over thirty years.

There are photographs of Keyes taken in 1900 during his time with the 38th Dogras. He was twenty three at the time and looked much younger than his brother officers. There is nonetheless a degree of detachment present which underpin the impression of this being a not particularly successful and happy time for him. He alone of the officers in the photographs did not remain in the regiment and rise in turn to its command. This sense of not quite fitting in with a wholly military environment, preferring a more solitary even perhaps individualist role is borne out by his subsequent conduct and later career.[12]

In 1900, a famine broke out in Central Provinces and volunteers were sought. Keyes signed up not least because there were generous allowances on offer and he had run up significant debts. He travelled with his groom (*sais*) and water carrier (*bhisti*), the latter being a young boy who had talked his way onto the relief train without Keyes' knowledge. On arrival, he was given responsibility for finding food and work for five thousand locals although later his allotted area was expanded so that he had seventy five thousand people under his care. He made his way to his new headquarters which turned out to be a mud hut without windows or doors in a remote and unhealthy area. Fortunately, Keyes discovered that the local Revenue officers had already established a feeding station.

His first priority was the distribution of clothing to young girls to protect their dignity. This done, he moved on to finding in order work for the men, work for the women and children, food for women with small children and finally feeding the children themselves. He seems to have been a proto-Keynesian as funds were distributed to enable the building of roads and irrigation channels. Food was distributed from communal kitchens one to each village feeding up to four hundred a day each of whom were required to say, as a kind of grace, "Victory, Victory to the great Queen."

It is clear that this was a brutal introduction to the world of civil administration and Keyes also had to deal with peculation by the clerks engaged who were over-recording the numbers of people fed and siphoning off the surplus food. He soon devised a process of naming and shaming those caught to deter others.

He also had to deal with what, he rather tellingly, refers to as the "usual cholera." The frequency of cholera epidemics at a time of primitive sanitation and limited medical resources was inevitable but it also emphasises the contingency of life in India at that time even for a comparatively privileged individual like Keyes. He set about organising the burning of huts to serve as funeral pyres for the dead inside and seeking to maintain standards of cleanliness so far as possible. That he did not spare himself is borne out by the fact that he contracted cholera himself and was only saved by his *bhisti's* care.

On his return to the 38th Dogras in Ferozepur in Punjab, Keyes found that he had missed out on various training courses and that he had, as he put it, "lost caste." There was also a minor faux pas over his role in proposing the Loyal Toast. It is not clear whether this loss of status was that he had sought a secondment or the nature of the secondment itself. However, his military career appears to have floundered at this point. No doubt, having seen active service and also having had a taste of civil administration, garrison duty in a backwater would have seemed dull and unrewarding. Things looked up however when, between December 1900 and autumn 1901, the 38th Dogras were engaged in a largely passive blockade of the area of Waziristan controlled by the Mahsuds. This concluded with a series of raids into Mahsud territories by a number of Dogra columns beginning in November 1901. These were successful in bringing the Mahsuds to heel and negotiations for a settlement were successfully concluded in early 1902.[13]

In 1901, he received news of the death of his brother, Charles Valentine. Charles had sought a posting from the Punjab Frontier Force to the West African Frontier Force primarily it seems, to improve his finances. It may also have been precipitated by the shattering of one of his arms in gunshot accident.[14] Between March and September 1900, Charles took part in the Kumasi Relief Expedition which joyously was also known as the War of the Golden Stool. However, on 21 June 1901, he was murdered "by a gang of French cattle stealers, he was trying to arrest." [15]

Keyes' relations with his siblings remain opaque but it must have been galling for him for his brother to be sent to Eton and then set up in his father's regiment whereas he had to make do with the far less glamorous Dogras. No evidence survives but it is likely that financial constraints played a part in inspiring Charles Keyes to send his sons to such varying schools with, presumably, varying careers in mind.

Chapter 2:

The Indian Political Service

"The job of a Political in Waziristan was as dangerous as that of a Scouts officer. Since he must not seem to fear or distance himself from his tribes, he seldom went about his work with Scouts or military escort. Normally he was escorted only by *Khassadars* (Police in Pashtu) or tribal *badraggas* (escorts) and he could never be certain that they would provoke a blood-feud by defending him against their fellow-tribesmen."[16]

It is not clear precisely when Terence Keyes left the British Indian Army for the Political Service or the reasons behind it. One very obvious one for someone without private means was that the pay in the Political Service was considerably higher than in the military. Furthermore, his experience administering famine relief would have marked him out as having the necessary skills which were flexibility of thought, confidence in decision making and the necessary subtlety to deal with conflicting pressures. It must also have been important for someone whose career was destined to be spent on the North West Frontier that he had a strong grasp of Russian both from his travels and surely also from study.

It is also unclear whether the decision to change course came from Keyes himself or whether others approached him. It does however seem that he was frustrated and unhappy where he was. Nevertheless, deciding to abandon the career which his father had chosen for him must have been difficult. Whether it was the fear of living in his father's shadow and the possibility of unfavourable comparisons being drawn cannot be ascertained but he must have been aware of the possibility.

The role which he was about to undertake was a complicated one and very different from that of an army officer. Political officers were key to the administration of the frontier areas both settled that is British controlled or tribal. They reported to the Deputy Commissioner and supervised both the collection of taxes and the distribution of subsidies. There was a need for a firm grasp of Property and Revenue law as legal adjudications were frequent. They were responsible for the economic development of their particular areas and so would often be involved in, for example, organising irrigation works or road improvements.

Political Officers regularly commanded significant admiration from the tribes who respected men of command who could make decisions on their own authority. Regular direct dealings with tribal leaders were essential in establishing a rapport so that in many cases they were able to rule by personal influence alone. A large part of the role was to prevent local issues festering that could lead to tribal uprisings. This brought them into conflict with the military forces on the ground which, predictably, were more inclined towards a military solution to problems. Political Officers had a degree of authority over their local military counterparts which could and did lead to resentment.

Political Officers along with other British officials were not meant to travel into tribally controlled areas without direct approval. They therefore were reliant upon their Political Agents who were locals who had proved their loyalty to the British and acted as intermediaries and information gatherers. After 1901, Political Officers did not generally attend the bi-annual *"Jirga"* or assembly of all the tribes in the area but sent Political Agents instead. The *Jirga* formed an important part of regional government as it served both as a discussion forum and also the place where allowances were distributed.

The first recourse of a Political Officer if problems arose would be to the Irregulars. These were locally raised units commanded by officers of the British Indian Army on secondment. They had a brief to head off trouble by demonstrations of force but frequently sought to mediate problems. They protected the safety of friendly tribes and confronted ones who were becoming hostile. An irregular enlisted for a fixed period and was given a small pension upon its completion.

Generally, Political Agents (at the direction of Political Officers) would not seek to intervene in tribal matters unless an issue of importance had arisen. The Political Officer would also have to monitor the conduct of the *Khassadars* who received money but not arms or uniforms from the British and were increasingly regarded as a cost efficient method of ensuring control so that by 1924 there were four thousand six hundred *Khassadars* in Waziristan alone.[17]

Keyes' first posting was as Vice Consul to Seistan and Kain in Baluchistan in 1904.[18] This area had been the subject of dispute between Afghanistan and Persia for some time and, following a mission led by General Sir Frederick Goldsmid, a compromise was agreed in 1872. This had left too many issues unresolved and the Second Sistan Boundary Commission sat between 1903-5. It was headed by Colonel Arthur Henry McMahon and confirmed Persia as the ruler of Seistan and Baluchistan. Keyes had many things in common with McMahon. They were both Old Haileyburians for a start but the similarities went deeper; the McMahons were also a British Indian family whose origins lay in Low Church Ulster. It was to be one of the defining relationships of his lifetime.

It seems that Keyes' time in Baluchistan was curtailed by travels into Russian Central Asia during the Russo-Japanese War (February 1904 to September 1905) probably between spring and summer 1905.[19] In his account of the journey, he does not go into detail about what he was doing there and disingenuously refers to himself as "a perfectly innocent traveller."[20] Whatever his motives, it is clear that the Russians did not believe him as they trailed him through Bokhara, Tashkent and Samarkand. It is apparent that this was an officially sponsored mission along the lines of those of Younghusband and other players of the Great Game.[21] Keyes' knowledge of Russian would have stood him in good stead and it was no doubt further burnished by virtue of his travels.

He recorded that, as cover, he let it be put about that he was writing a book on Persian carpets. adding that this would have more credibility if he carried out research with a view to the actual publication of a book. During his travels, he collated material which he stored in a black metal despatch box. This mostly consisted of notes and diagrams and samples of wool. The fruits of his other, more official, research, he committed to memory other than one document which he stored in his toothbrush holder. Upon his return to Persia, the despatch box was stolen whilst baggage was being loaded onto camels. Keyes believed that it ended up in Russian hands and that they would be long occupied trying to work out a connection between the notes for his draft book on carpets and his espionage mission.[22]

His journey started at Seistan and then to Turbat i Haidari both now in Iran but then in the part of Persia that was subject to British influence.[23] He left his servants, horses and tents at Turbat i Haidari and then travelled through Bokhara, Tashkent and Samarkand in what is now Uzbekistan. As he returned to Turbat i Haidari before completing his travels, it is likely that he would have travelled through what is now Turkmenistan both on his way out and return. It is unfortunate that he gives no account of the journey as it must have been fascinating as well as brave to travel through such hostile territories without an armed escort. The destinations which he picked further undermine his assertion of being a "perfectly innocent traveller." These cities, particularly Tashkent, were important centres in (then) Russian Turkestan. Tashkent had only been under direct Russian rule since May 1865 and Bokhara since 1868 and Russian influence was far from universally accepted by the local population. The British therefore were active in espionage and were manoeuvring there in much the same way that the Russians sought to make trouble in British influenced Afghanistan.

Keyes gave a detailed and colourful account of his journey from Turbat i Haidari back to Seistan.[24] This, whilst giving a direct insight into the difficulties of frontier life, sits easily within the tradition of Imperial servants' dealings with indigenous peoples. In this case, Keyes recounts in detail his conversations with Ibrahim who he describes as "an old chief of a Persian-Baluch Nomad tribe." What is of greater interest is his account of coming across a herd of Asiatic Wild Asses or Onagers. It is noteworthy that Keyes called them "Ghur" which is archaic Persian although he might have found this term familiar from seeing Indian Wild Asses which were commonly called Khur.[25] There is some potential confusion here as he also refers to seeing "the flying hooves of Prejevalsky Horses" which are a distinctly different species and had been first brought to the attention of the West in the 1870s.[26] It is not apparent whether it was Onagers or Prejevalsky's Horse that Keyes had shipped to London Zoo. However, it is not in doubt that he was made a Fellow of the Zoological Society in 1907.[27]

Following his return, he remained in Seistan for the rest of the year learning the skills of a Political Officer. He was promoted to Captain in January 1906; whether this is connected with his travels of the previous year is not clear but showed that his ability and skills had been appreciated. Furthermore, in February 1906, he was given the post of Consul of Turbat i Haidari and Karez. This surely was recognition of his abilities and also represented his first independent Consular position.

For the next two years, he was based at Tarbat i Haidari which must have been a lonely posting with few Europeans living there. The town is in the north east of Iran and an obvious gateway to Afghanistan. The climate is that typically found in Central Asian steppes with very cold winters being followed by hot, rainless summers. Keyes spent his time travelling around the area preparing maps where the existing ones were defective (as was frequently the case). When submitted to London, they resulted in him being elected a Fellow of the Royal Geographical Society.

Keyes later wrote of his time in Persia about how he was shadowed on his travels by a spy riding a camel and who was so unsubtle in his tracking that his mission became obvious. Keyes declined a suggestion that the spy be killed as "it was better to be followed by someone so inefficient and obvious than by an expert."[28] On the same trip, Keyes met up with a Persian- Baluch nomad tribe and was made particularly welcome when it became clear that he was the son of Charles Keyes. The head of the tribe was an old man who recounted how, when young, he had been had been entrusted with a large sum of money by his father and sent to India to buy camels. He had lost the entire sum and faced the prospect of returning without beasts or money. Somehow, Charles Keyes had learned of his predicament and had spared his embarrassment by arranging for him to be given a number of camels which exemplified the way in which the British retained influence and control over the nomad tribes. This policy worked as the chief remained grateful and invited Keyes to stay. After a day or two, Keyes noticed that the spy was no longer trailing him. He made enquiries of the chief who confirmed that he had had him killed because "how could I let such an unworthy creature spy upon Your Excellency."[29]

Keyes underwent great physical hardship as well as loneliness in Turbat i Haidari where fresh fruit and vegetables were so scarce that he was reduced to growing mustard and cress on damp trousers. However, in 1908, after two years in post, he was promoted to the staff of the Agent to the Governor General of Baluchistan. This must have come as a welcome relief not least because he would be based in Quetta which was then an important military and civilian base in British India and likely to be far more lively than the backwater of Turbat i Haidari.

Keyes had not been home to England since he arrived in India in 1897. He therefore put in a request for home leave but it was turned down and he was allowed sixty one days' leave which was insufficient to reach England. With the help of his *Babu* (clerk), he managed to extend the period by invoking every possible allowance permitted by regulations. Therefore, by small increments he stretched his entitlement to such an extent that he was able to travel home for several weeks before returning by steamer.[30] What is striking was his decision to travel by post horse towards Bander Shah (now Bandar Torkoman) on the Caspian Sea across Russian dominated Central Asia where he would have stood out as a lone Englishman. It is hard to imagine that many of his military contemporaries would have had the confidence or ability to do this but no doubt, his knowledge of many of the local dialects and indeed Russian would have helped.

Keyes crossed the Caspian Sea by steamer to Baku and joined the Russian railway network, crossing Azerbaijan and Georgia to reach the Black Sea presumably at Batumi. He then picked up steamers to Constantinople and then Brindisi where he caught the train to England. During his leave, he spent three weeks in Ireland, presumably the family property in Croghan, before catching a steamer back to India. As it happened, the boat was delayed by two days in the Suez Canal and the train from Bombay to Lahore took a day longer than it should which meant that he was going to miss his appointment with his new commander, Henry McMahon, then Agent to the Governor General for Baluchistan. Once it became apparent that the reason for his lateness was a failure to obey orders to take local leave, there would inevitably be serious trouble. However, with yet another stroke of good fortune that always seems to have come his way at times of crisis, he ran into McMahon at a race meeting in Lahore and was therefore able to report for duty there and then.

Chapter 3:

Baluchistan

Whilst it must have been a significant change to be back in an area of direct British rule, Baluchistan was on the border between British India, Afghanistan and Persia. In fact the border had only been fixed in 1893 by Sir Mortimer Durand with the eponymous Durand Line running from Chitral in the north near the Chinese border down to the Arabian Sea.

Baluchistan was a remote and under populated area whose significance was essentially geographical and political rather than economic. It formed the logical access point from Persia and Afghanistan to India and control of the passes from the mountains onto the plains was a strategic imperative for the British.[31] Its climate was harsh with cold winters, frequently with snow falling and hot summers with temperatures reaching fifty degrees centigrade. Not surprisingly, it was sparsely populated with most inhabitants living in and around Quetta.

Quetta itself was then expanding fast and was well on the way to warranting its later name of "Little London." It was the largest garrison town in India and had developed from a mud brick fort with three hundred dwellings to having a population of 18,802 in 1891, 24,584 in 1901 to 33,922 in 1911 of whom seven percent were European.[32] It was a far more comfortable and sociable posting for Keyes than the austere existence in Tarbat i Haidari. Photographs of the time show a well established European settlement with substantial churches and municipal buildings as well as the cantonment.

The role of the Political Department was to help in the administration of justice; from 1901, through the Frontier Crimes Regulations which formalised the *Jirga* system for settlement of disputes referred to the Deputy Commissioner. The council of elders was entrusted to report findings to the Deputy Commissioner who would then decide the case. Primarily, however, it was to maintain British authority and influence both politically and administratively in an area where control varied significantly from absolute in and around Quetta to largely notional in the outlying hills that were run by independent or quasi-independent chieftains. The structure was pragmatic and loose and lacked administrative coherence to the extent that contemporaries described it as being "legally, a bit of a muddle."

Baluchistan itself was divided between native states such as Kalat, British Baluchistan and Agency Territories. The latter had been acquired by leases from Kalat or various tribes. There was a further category known as "tribal country" where control or influence was extremely tenuous.

Keyes' role was to assist McMahon with the government of Baluchistan both in those parts that were effectively under British control and the tribal areas. They were guided in this by the Sandeman System after its originator and friend of Charles Keyes, Sir Robert Sandeman, who had devised a method of peaceful intervention into Baluchistan whereby the Khan of Khalat was recognised as the principal ruler and he and subsidiary chieftains received payment of subsidies in return for guarding trade routes and mountain passes and also implementing the decisions of *Jirgas*.[33] It was part of an overarching strategy formulated by the late nineteenth century British Indian administrators known as "the Forward Policy" which promulgated a greater involvement and intervention in the affairs of the North West Frontier.[34]

The policy had been highly successful in Baluchistan and had led to the establishment of relatively stable system of government. In contrast, when attempts were made to apply the same policy to Mahsud area of the North West Frontier - known as the Bruce or Maliki System - it failed entirely, possibly because of the more fissile and fractious nature of the Mahsud tribal area but also because, unlike Sandeman, Bruce lacked the military resources to pacify the area entirely as a preliminary step.[35] The Sandeman System has been criticised for being too dependent upon one man - Sandeman himself - but the results achieved by McMahon and others in Baluchistan speak to the policy's effectiveness. Recently, Sandeman has been the subject of renewed study as governments continue to struggle to find an effective system of governance over the same ground.

It is obvious that Keyes and McMahon worked well together and he became a guide as well as close friend. Indeed, one of the first things that he did was to introduce Keyes to Freemasonry which was to play an important part of his life from that time. He joined McMahon Lodge no 3262 as an apprentice on 19 November 1908, took his Fellowcraft on 10 December 1908 and became a Master Mason on 13 May 1909. He then left the Lodge - possibly because of a posting- but rejoined on 16 June 1910. He again left the McMahon Lodge in 1921 but returned to be Worshipful Master in 1924. It is clear that his Masonic career was successful and extensive.[36]

McMahon's own Masonic connections were significant. Later in 1917, he was elected to the Supreme Council for the Empire and served as Lieutenant Grand Commander of the Supreme Council between 1929-48. He then became Grand Commander of the Supreme Council. He has been described as "the highest ranking freemason of the Empire who was not a member of the Royal Family."[37] He was already a senior and respected Mason in 1906 when he was responsible for persuading Lord Kitchener, then Viceroy and District Grand Master of the Punjab to agree to the initiation of HM Habibullah Khan, Amir of Afghanistan into the three Masonic degrees in one night which apparently was almost unprecedented. This could be regarded as an example of McMahon pursuing the Forward Policy even when he was off duty.

Freemasonry was an important part of the social fabric in British India and facilitated communication and the establishment of good relations between officials, both military and civil as well as in the commercial world. In a highly stratified society, it acted not only as a solvent but also a safety valve as being one of the few places where the various strands of Imperial Rule came together in a social environment. Becoming a Freemason was therefore an important step for Keyes to take and it is obvious from the way in which he progressed through the various degrees that he was enthusiastic and committed Mason.[38]

McMahon, like Keyes, was the son of senior military officer based in what is now Pakistan. His father was Lieutenant General Charles Alexander McMahon, FRS, FGS who had been the former Commissioner of Lahore. This must have created an obvious bond of recognition between them although it is fair to say that this dynastic quality pervaded British India both in military and civil sectors. As has been seen, in Keyes' own case both his parents' antecedents lay in the senior echelons of military India.

In another, far more significant way, McMahon influenced Keyes' life when he introduced him to his sister Edith Beatrice who was staying with him at the Residency in Quetta. Edith who always signed herself off in her letters to her mother as "Edith" was also known (certainly to Keyes himself) as "Betty."[39] There are glimpses of their courtship in her letters home to her mother. Keyes soon becomes a regular part of her social life in Quetta first making an appearance in her letter of 31 January 1909 when she describes him as "most difficult to deal with." Quite how this "difficulty" manifested itself is not clear but it does not seem to have prevented them going on rides together, her horse being called "Johnnie" and his "Bismillah."

Keyes' sister, Phyllis, was also in Quetta at the time and there was a busy and hectic social scene. Edith recounts one particularly spectacular duck shoot which she had watched from a distance. This was an epic affair with most of the British community participating. Many locals were engaged in driving the ducks towards the guns and, in a stark vignette illustrating contemporary British racial attitudes, Edith records that directions were shouted "to the retriever natives already in the water."[40] It is perhaps not the comparison with spaniels which is so remarkable, although as they were almost certainly Muslims, this would have been particularly insulting but that clearly nothing in any way offensive or critical was intended.

Keyes very rapidly made an impression on Edith and by 24 February he had proposed to her and been accepted. She described him to her mother as "just the nicest person in the world and much too good for me."[41] Keyes had suggested that they marry in April but she was keen to defer matters until autumn so that she could travel home and ensure that her mother was happy for the marriage to proceed. Notwithstanding her wishes, Keyes' forced the pace and swept away all objections. Edith clearly felt conflicted between her loyalty to her mother and to Keyes but, either through Keyes' insistence or McMahon's support for an early marriage, she relented. They married on 15 April 1909 with the service being carried out by the Bishop of Lahore. Keyes' best man was Captain Ramsey who, like Keyes, was also to spend the better part of his career in Baluchistan.

They honeymooned in Peshin before resuming duty in Quetta.[42] Edith had great plans for decorating their new quarters wanting their main room to be in the same colours of her family seaside home - white and green. Keyes however had already bought blue. Other than that, married life seems to have been happy for them both and she records domestic details such as Keyes shaving off his moustache and also having "such bad neuralgia." Their first child was born on 6 February 1910. He was Christened Roger McMahon but always known as Rory.[43] This was followed by the birth of a daughter, Rosemary, on 15 September 1911.[44] By that time, however, Edith had returned to England. She did not return to India until 1921.

If British India's dominant preoccupation was the North West Frontier then Britain's influence in India was the dominant foreign policy consideration of the Empire as a whole. It was the protection of trade and supply routes to India that had led to Britain acquiring a position in Malta, Aden, Socotra and indeed Malaya, Burma and Ceylon. Indeed, it could be argued that the British control over Singapore and Hong Kong was a by-product of its commitment to India.

It was concern for India that led to the longstanding British support for Turkey which in turn inflamed relations with Russia as well as leading to Anglo-French tensions over French ambitions in Syria. It also led to a near fatal imbalance in British military resources with far too great a preponderance of military assets being based in India and the Far East and in defending the ports en route to the neglect of domestic protection. In 1903, Lord Curzon had said that "the geographical position of India will push her into the forefront of international politics. She will, more and more become the strategical frontier of the British Empire."[45] Later, in 1906, the former Military Member of Curzon's Viceregal Council wrote: "in all the discussions which have taken place...upon the vital subject of the defence of the Empire, at least three main points stand out, and the fact that the defence of the land frontier of the Empire means the defence of the land frontier of India. It is true enough that the defence of India has been recognised as the essential military problem of our times. It is fortunate that the Prime Minister of the United Kingdom has proclaimed more than once, in clear and unmistakable language that the problem of the British Army is the problem of the defence of Afghanistan - in other words, of the defence of India."[46]

The situation was somewhat ameliorated by the Haldane Reforms of the British Army which took effect between 1906-12 and led ultimately to the formation of an Expeditionary Force with the express intention of being able to intervene in a European conflict. Even with these, the British contribution to holding back the German advances during the summer and autumn of 1914 were barely adequate. Without them, it is likely that the Germans would have achieved the early breakthrough they had planned. Ironically, in that situation, all the steps taken to defend India and other Imperial outposts could have been for naught.

British foreign policy was turned on its head during the first decade of the twentieth century. To begin, Britain finally ended a century of isolation when it entered into an alliance with Japan in 1902. The treaty recognised Japan's rapidly growing power - particularly at sea - and whilst purely defensive in nature, it significantly reduced Britain's commitment in the Pacific. It also recognised that following the Russo-Japanese War, Russian resources had to be concentrated on its eastern seaboard rather than in Afghanistan and Persia. The alliance gave Britain greater ability to focus upon the naval arms race with Germany which was to become an increasingly influential factor in foreign policy. This Dreadnought Race which ran from 1898 until it was finally called off in 1912 when the German Chancellor, Bethmann-Hollweg sought improvements to Anglo-German relations as he was concerned about Germany's increasing isolation.[47] It is noteworthy that neither side paid much attention to the development of submarine warfare concentrating instead upon building battleships which played a relatively minor role in the coming conflict. One person who did was Keyes' brother Roger who was then Commodore with responsibility for undersea warfare.

Following Russia's humiliating defeat by Japan, its previous expansionism was brought to a halt and it was not in a position to pose a threat to British interests either in Afghanistan or Persia. At the same time, it was convulsed by the 1905 Revolution and its aftermath which dominated its political life for the next few years. Thus, whilst Russian intrigues continued in Central Asia, the tempo had abated.

Gradually, over the next two years, Anglo-Russian relations improved as it was in both sides' interest to work towards this goal. The Russians were keen to reduce their military commitment to Central Asia which would be possible if the perceived threat of a British invasion was removed. There is no evidence that the British ever intended an invasion of Russian controlled territory but the Russians believed that they did. That both sides regarded their own motives as defensive is, of course, a continuing theme throughout the twentieth century. The British wished to preserve a neutral but friendly Afghanistan to protect the North West Frontier but were particularly sensitive about Persia. This was not only because of the threat to Baluchistan but also because of the likely presence of considerable oil reserves in Persia. This was of vital concern to Britain since the new Dreadnoughts were driven by oil fired turbines rather than coal and therefore acquiring a secure supply of oil was a strategic imperative. Ensuring that Persia remained compliant was therefore a priority and that meant reaching an accord with Russia to prevent mutual campaigns of destabilisation.

On 31 August 1907 at St Petersburg, the Anglo-Russian Convention was concluded. The key component parts were, first, the division of Persia into three parts - a Russian zone of influence in the North, a British one in the South East and a neutral zone with its heart in the capital of Tehran. Secondly, lines were drawn delimiting the areas of British and Russian influence with both sides recognising that they had no rights beyond those areas and thirdly, that Afghanistan was recognised as being a British Protectorate and that Russian interference there would cease.

The effect of the Convention was to neutralise Anglo-Russian tensions in Central Asia but its real purpose was as an attempt to restore the European balance of power which was threatened by the Dual Alliance between Germany and Austria-Hungary. This was summarised by Eyre Crowe, then Senior Clerk in the Western Department but later Permanent Under Secretary at the Foreign Office as:

"Germany is defiantly aiming at a general political hegemony and maritime ascendency, threatening the independence of her neighbours and ultimately the existence of England."[48]

The conclusion of the Anglo-Russian Convention headed off somewhat erratic attempts by the Kaiser to entice Russia into joining the Dual Alliance and also underscored the strength of the Anglo-French Entente. However, as a corollary it reinforced German fears of isolation and led to increased German involvement in the Middle East. As will appear, these were greatly facilitated by the effect of the Convention on Anglo-Turkish relations.

Whilst Britain and Russia were competing, an Anglo-Turkish friendship made sense and Britain had traditionally supported

Turkey against Russia. This fitted with British strategy which was to deny Russian ready access to the Mediterranean as well as ensuring that the boundary between Russia and southern Asia was distinct and properly defended. It is also important to note that, by virtue of its Indian possessions and interest in Egypt, not to mention various points in between such as Aden and Socotra, Britain was ruler of a large part of the Muslim world and therefore needed to keep a careful watch upon the loyalties of its subjects who could easily resent being governed by an overtly Christian power. Friendship with Turkey assisted considerably in this regard by virtue of the Sultan's role as Caliph.

All of this was turned upon its head by the Anglo-Russian Convention and Britain almost immediately lost its influence in Constantinople. The problem was exacerbated by the assumption of power by the Young Turks in 1908 who not only were profoundly anti-Russian but were also - and very dangerously for Britain - pro-German. Therefore, in solving the problem of the North West Frontier, the British created another, namely an increasingly hostile Ottoman Empire. In some ways, this was a worse problem since Turkey, with German assistance was far better placed to threaten Britain's sea routes to India than Russia had been whilst it was bottled up in the Black Sea. Furthermore, Ottoman territory adjoined or even surrounded British territory in Egypt, Aden and the Persian Gulf.

The new threat was made all the greater by the building of the Berlin to Baghdad railway. Whilst this was still far from complete by 1914, it was perceived as a major threat to the security of India. The German intention was that after Baghdad, the railway would continue to the Persian Gulf where a major port was to be developed. This would not only threaten British dominance of maritime trade but would also give Germany ready access to sources of oil. As the railway progressed and by 1914 there was still a gap of three hundred miles, concern mounted and its role as a putative cause of World War One is still a subject of considerable debate.

It is at least arguable that the focus upon India and the perceived Russian threat was a symptom of the lack of balance in British foreign policy and that retaining good relations with Turkey would have paid dividends in 1914 when the Allies sought to dissuade Turkey from joining the Central Powers. A quiescent Ottoman Empire would have meant that the British were spared from the expenditure of men and materiel in Mesopotamia, Palestine and indeed Gallipoli during the forthcoming war.[49]

It is this complicated and rapidly changing environment that Political Officers like Keyes had to keep in mind in the performance of their duties. Muslim discontent was an increasing factor following on from the Anglo-Russian Convention; tribes on the North West Frontier then, as now, were religiously conservative and also held the Sultan-Caliph in high regard. They, like many Muslims, were painfully aware of the increasing number of countries that were falling under Christian control - Libya had been lost to unprovoked Italian aggression and Persia had effectively been dismembered by Russia and Britain even before Turkey was virtually ejected from Europe as a result of the two Balkan Wars of 1912-13.

With all these challenges, Keyes remained in Baluchistan in the same post and since 1910 on his own again. He wrote regularly to Edith informing her of his activities both professional and social. The letters were generally composed over the days or sometimes weeks leading up to a postal collection and give an impression of his daily life both when in Quetta and when on his travels around Baluchistan. This was explicitly set out in his letter of 5 January 1913 when he summarised his usual routine when on what was a typical expedition.

Whilst other trips must have been very challenging, this one was less Spartan so that he and the other Europeans rose at 6.30 and then rode their camels a distance of between seven and fifteen miles to where the servants had set up camp the night before. They then had a bath and breakfast after which he wrote until 1pm. The bathing arrangements alone must have required considerable organisation in a barren country both in terms of finding water and then heating it for it would certainly have been cold in January. They then struck camp and rode a similar distance before having dinner at 6.30 and bed at 8.30. They slept in the open so that the baggage train could go on ahead and set up camp for the following morning. The diet would have been monotonous although they "shot any patches of purple we go through and so keep the pot full."

The letters also reveal Keyes' concern for Edith and his young family as well as trying to exercise some control over what were clearly very limited financial resources. Money worries feature regularly throughout the correspondence. On 8 January 1913, he urges her to "take a furnished flat not in the Isle of Wight but in a cheaper place within hail of London."[50] This suggestion cannot have been welcome news to Edith for whom the Isle of Wight was the nearest place she had to home and nothing came of it. He could not look to his family for help for in the same letter, he told her that "mother wants Eva [Roger Keyes' wife] to present her [at Court] as she is too old and poor." This was certainly true because by then she was sixty five and had been living in a grace and favour apartment in Hampton Court for eleven years.

Keyes, like many others in his position, struggled to keep financially afloat in a world which demanded running two households, one in India and another in England, as well as maintaining the standard of living necessary for social position. This was a continual theme in his life and had blighted his military career from its outset when he was unable to join his father's former regiment and had to settle for the far less glamorous 38th Dogras. As has been noted, it had also indirectly contributed to his brother Valentine's death because he had had to leave the Frontier Force and join the West African Frontier Force in an attempt to patch up his finances.

The problem of meagre pay and allowances was exacerbated by the Keyes' family's relative indigence. Both his parents came from long standing British Indian families but neither had the private wealth that enabled many brother officers to live in greater comfort.

His brother, Roger's position was greatly assisted by the fact that he was on board ship for much of the time but mostly because of his wife, Eva's, private means.

Keyes remained in Baluchistan until the end of his tour of duty in 1913 when he finally returned to England on leave. He remained there until April 1914 when he was posted to a Bahrain as British Resident. Edith and his family did not accompany him on what was then a tough posting and remained in England. Keyes therefore missed the birth of his daughter, Lavender on 15 May 1914 on the Isle of Wight.

Chapter 4:

Bahrain

On 8 February 1914, not long before Keyes' arrival in Bahrain, the political world of the Gulf had been shocked by the seemingly accidental death of John Gordon Lorimer, the British Resident at Bushire. He had shot himself in the stomach and died shortly afterwards. His death was marked by the lowering of flags and Major Arthur Prescott Trevor (who Keyes was shortly to replace as Resident) wrote in his diary that "the sudden and tragic news shocked everyone."

The death of a Resident at the relatively young age of forty three in such circumstances was bound to cause something of a stir and it was widely reported as being a tragic accident; the Spectator describing it as a "gun accident." This is questionable and Keyes reflecting a no doubt widespread view in a letter to Edith of 29 April 1914, describes Lorimer as having "shot himself." There may well have been a wish to cover up what was then seen as a shameful and criminal act. What was also not reported was that Lorimer was the author of *"The Gazetteer of the Persian Gulf, Oman and Central Arabia"*, the most encyclopaedic (and then secret) guide to the area and one that certainly would have been consulted by Keyes in the performance of his new role.[51]

The posting to Bahrain represented a significant promotion for Keyes - he was, for the first time, the most senior officer in a state albeit a small and then not particularly rich one. The downside of such an appointment was that Bahrain was a backwater in comparison with Quetta and certainly far more uncomfortable. The climate itself must have been extremely punishing but it must also have been lonely with only a small European community with whom he could socialise. This would contrast with Quetta which had a lively and relatively large British contingent. It is probably for these reasons that Edith and his children remained in England.

The posting to Bahrain was logical bearing in mind Keyes' previous roles in Persia and Baluchistan. There was a clear nexus between the Indian Political Service and the Gulf and a large number of Residents were IPS officers. This meant that Keyes would have known his neighbouring Residents by reputation if not personally. It was also true that many of the British officers in the gulf were also Freemasons and Keyes together with Robert Hamilton (Lord Belhaven) and Frederick Johnstone were amongst the most senior. There is some debate as to whether Freemasonry led to conservative or radical impulses. Both seem to be true in differing circumstances; the Young Turks were closely associated with Freemasonry in their revolution in 1908 but in the case of Keyes and his many Masonic contemporaries in the IPS, it appears to have encouraged already conservative impulses. In an example of Masonic humour, Keyes himself was described as "an Arch Mason and an arch conservative."[52]

Correspondence with Edith started even before Keyes embarked from Dover for Bahrain in April 1914. Once on board, he wrote "curs[ing] myself for my horrible, critical and unsympathetic treatment of you" adding that he had been so unhappy and confused that "for the last year, I have hardly been able to pray at all" which showed the depth of his misery because Keyes' religious faith otherwise always comes across as committed and unyielding. Later that month, he wrote "I do want you to know clearly that I've got no bitterness....and really feel as if we've made a fresh start. I wish there was some good old name symbolical of reconciliation which we could call Lavender" and adds that "Betty, you must start a habit of happiness and make a second nature of it before I come back"

It is therefore obvious that having been apart for three years, their first time together in England was fraught and that Keyes caused Edith much heartache and she him. For Keyes' part, he was worried by her ongoing battle with what sounds very like depression and it must have been very difficult to leave her with a baby almost due, a toddler and unsettled living arrangements. As far as the latter are concerned, Edith had her way and they remained on the Isle of Wight probably living at Farringford which was Lord Tennyson's former home together with "ten babies and nannies." Later, on 20 July 1914, Lavender was christened at Bembridge.

As well as regretting their mutual unhappiness, Keyes also regularly brought Edith up to date on gossip. On 29 April, he told her about litigation that was proposed by a Colonel Whyte against Keyes' best man, Colonel Ramsay "for turning him out of Baluchistan." Bearing in mind, the close-knit nature of relations amongst the political and military in Baluchistan, this must have been a major talking point although not unprecedented since Keyes also reports that Whyte has consulted the same solicitors as another disaffected British officer. On what he regarded as a more cheerful note, Keyes reports that he is spoken of as resembling the Foreign Secretary, Sir Edward Grey.[53]

Keyes' principal role was to ensure that British interests were maintained. Bahrain was a British protectorate and was then nominally ruled by the Al Khalifa family but in very definite consultation with the British.[54] Bahrain had been in the British sphere of influence since the 1820s and had developed strong mercantile links with India. Traditionally, it was dependent upon pearl fishing but trade was increasingly important during the late nineteenth and early twentieth centuries, leading Bahrain to become regarded as the most cosmopolitan of the gulf states. Oil did not then form part of the Bahraini economy as it was not discovered there until 1932.

Before he could have properly settled in to his new role, Keyes' position was greatly complicated by the declaration of war in the summer of 1914 and, even more, once Turkey openly joined the Central Powers by firing on Russian Black Sea ports in October 1914. What is now Saudi Arabia, Iraq, Syria and Israel were at least notionally part of the Ottoman Empire although in reality, Ottoman rule was fitful and limited in many cases to the principal towns of the area. Further, the Turkish navy was concentrated in the Mediterranean and Black Sea and was not in a position to challenge British dominance in the Persian Gulf.

Bahrain did not play a significant part in the forthcoming war but control of southern Iraq, particularly the Shatt al Arab and Basra, was critical and led the British into the Mesopotamian campaign. The British were not only concerned about the threats to trade and shipping posed by a Turkish presence in Iraq but were also keen to limit any threat to the oil supply critical for the Navy.

Keyes describes some aspects of his life in Bahrain in detail.[55] One of the most telling is an account of a death threat he received in August 1914. This indicated that he would have his "throat cut with a sharp sword" at 3 pm on the following day. It is testament to his linguistic facility that he is able to correct his clerk's Arabic. The story is an exercise in English sang froid with Keyes at the centre. Nonetheless, it must have been alarming to be threatened by "a hundred faithful *Khalifa*" when he had only nineteen sepoys to defend him.

The cause of the threat was an announcement that he had been instructed by Delhi to issue criticising the Turkish government's decision to join the Central Powers. That this had come to the attention of the Government of India which had issued it within days of the Turco-German alliance is evidence of an efficient intelligence service. Nonetheless, it would have been a cause of serious concern to Keyes as the nearest meaningful reinforcements were very far away in India. Setting to with a will, he fortified the Residency and laid in provisions for a siege before deciding to put on a show and took his horse through the bazaar pausing only to buy a watch so that he would be on time for his 3pm deadline. Fortunately, everything passed off without incident.

What is particularly compelling about this account is the detail that Keyes puts in about Bahraini life at the time. His description of the workaday products on sale in the bazaar are contrasted with the colour and vibrancy of their Indian equivalents. It is clear that the local diet would have been dull and monotonous as fruit and vegetables would rot in the heat. He gives the impression of an entire society subsisting on mutton and whatever fish could be caught. He also describes the ancient trade routes by camel from the Mediterranean and then by dhow from Basra to India which were then still functioning more or less as they had always done.

In fact, the reality of the situation was more mundane, if still alarming for the death threat was addressed not to Keyes himself but to the entire English colony. It is also untrue that his Arabic would have been better than his clerk's or even that it was more than rudimentary as, over a year later, he was to write to his mother that "I have started working at Arabic which I loathe. It's hard enough taking up a new language at my age." Later in 1914, he reported on the incident that "*Jehad* has been preached in a Mosque near my gates and my escort consists of herring gutted Hindus from the 25th ...but I need not have worried as there isn't a kick in a town full of these bastard Arabs" which implies rather less concern for the situation he faced than he later related. A greater worry was the threatened attack on Bahrain by the *Emden*, a German commerce raider which achieved great notoriety in the early months of the war and even shelled Madras. Fortunately, this proved a false alarm and the *Emden* was eventually tracked down to the Cocos Islands and captured by *HMAS Sydney* on 9 November 1914.[56]

Following the decision to protect shipping in the Gulf an expeditionary force was assembled with a view to taking control of the head of the Persian Gulf and Basra in particular. This was led by Brigadier General W S Delamain and arrived in Bahrain on 23 October 1914. The presence of troop ships was unpopular with the local population and Keyes reported back to Stuart Knox, the Resident in Bushire and therefore his superior that he felt "some uneasiness" not least because the Persian population of Bahrain was known to be pro-Turkish.[57] Keyes was confronted with a difficult situation and was probably rather less sanguine about his position than he appears in his stories.

His main task was to assemble supplies for the expeditionary force and to prevent the troops landing bearing in mind the hostile attitude of the local population. He was later to report that "we have hardly a sympathiser in these islands ... they are all pro-Turk." He attributed this to the anti-British nature of the large Persian population in Bahrain for whom he had reciprocal dislike writing, "the Persian with his quick wit, shallow ideas and hatred of Russia has done our cause great harm."

Keyes also wrote about another facet of his duties as Resident which was to sit as a judge in civil and criminal cases involving foreigners.[58] This, in itself, gives some idea of the breadth of skills required by Residents; Keyes' legal training would have been scanty to say the least and he must have been sitting as a quasi-stipendiary magistrate rather than a qualified judge and, as such, been heavily dependent upon the interpreter Clerk of the Court referred to in his first Bahraini story.[59] Keyes himself reported, not long after his arrival in Bahrain, that his judicial workload was very heavy and that there had been 1484 civil cases and 382 criminal ones. He broke down by nationality the 1284 civil cases which he had heard sitting without a *Majlis* or local:

Persian   1083
Turkish   526
British   469
Independent Arabs   121
Muscati   48
Manumitted slaves   46
Somalis   21
French   4
Italian   2
German   1

Even allowing for the fact that the category "British" included British Indians, this is a clear indication of British involvement in Bahraini trade. Most of the disputes turned upon the pearl trade.

Keyes had a dismissive view of the native Bahrainis describing the local economy of Bahrain as operating in a way that "the labour of the fishing falls on the slaves and slave descended divers, the Bahraini who takes the first profit, never does a hand's turn, his business is the tongue and a more persistent and poisonous gossip is not to be found in the East." This dependence upon foreign labour to perform the tasks essential to the economy has survived the replacement of pearls by oil as the dominant industry in the region.

Keyes gives a colourful account of his handling of a case brought against one Mahbruk, a pearl diver, who had incurred substantial debts by extravagant living. It sits well within the traditional trope of a bewildered official struggling to understand eccentric natives.[60] Behind this, however, are insights into both British and Arab concepts of race and religion. Mahbruk himself is described as a "gigantic negro" which presumably meant of Somali slave origin. As a pearl diver, his life would have been physically risky and highly contingent upon luck. His choice of bride, "a merry little negress", makes clear that both of them were towards the bottom of Bahraini society.

Mahbruk having struck lucky in a spectacularly successful catch resulting in an interim share of twelve hundred Rupees blew the lot during Ramadan on a series of festivities celebrating his temporary marriage. This was "an enormous sum" for one who would normally expect to earn fifteen Rupees a month. Ultimately, Keyes organised a composition with all creditors and Mahbruk and his wife joyously concluded their binge by invoking the relaxed laws on divorce during the holy month. It is quite clear that the normal societal proprieties are not expected from such as Mahbruk. It is inconceivable that respectable Bahraini society would act in this way but that notwithstanding, all present in Court - mostly merchants owed monies by Mahbruk - are greatly amused by his extravagances. There are also hints of financial naiveté with Mahbruk paying more than Keyes himself for mutton - presumably unthinkable in such a society. The language used by Keyes whilst uncomfortable to modern readers is characteristic of the time; there is an implied acceptance of a racial hierarchy that renders people low down the social order either invisible or, as in the case of Mahbruk, colourful buffoons.

What also emerges from the account is the sheer lack of comfort in Keyes' life. The Courtroom, without fans and damp seeping from the sea must have been extraordinarily hot even before it was packed with litigants, Court officials and spectators and the stench appalling – "the walls streamed; the witnesses sweated; the smell of decayed seaweed drifted in from the shore."[61] As was made clear in his first Bahraini story, fruit and vegetables were more or less unknown and mutton expensive as it had to be shipped in. Keyes' diet would have been monotonous and unexciting - no wonder he wistfully referred twice to the "many tins of luscious Californian peaches" which Mahbruk had acquired whilst on his spree.

Keyes' third Bahraini story follows directly on from the second and relates an account of a court case concerning some of the pearls collected by Mahbruk alongside an account of a sepoy going mad in the heat. This shows Keyes' style evolving and improving as he manages to interweave the two threads with details of the layout of the Residency and, as an aside, further details of his duties, particularly, that of being part time meteorologist for it seems that he was required to report temperatures to the Government of India on a regular basis.

As far as the Residency was concerned, Keyes presents something that whilst strange to modern eyes would have been far from uncommon at the time as the Residency complex incorporated elements of Courtroom, offices, barracks and fort as well as forming Keyes' domestic accommodation. It must have been noisy and bustling with a mix of official visitors, litigants and soldiery all going about their business under a sullen tropic sun. What comes across is the compactness of it all; it seems to have been not much more than twenty yards from one side to another even including the courtyard. As the Residency was home not only to Keyes and his servants but also nineteen sepoys, there cannot have been much room to spare.[62]

What is also apparent is the squalor of the neighbouring seashore in a town without sanitation and an insignificant tide.[63]

Keyes' legal abilities are taken in a new direction as he has to decide a dispute between two Arab merchants over the sale of pearls with a value of £20,000.[64] He is called upon to assess the value of the pearls mercifully not because he was expected to act as expert as well as judge but so that he could learn about Bahrain's most valuable export. Once again, to modern eyes, the informality and amateurishness is remarkable but it must surely be a concomitant of slow and limited communications. Certainly, the much greater autonomy enjoyed by Keyes and his contemporaries carried with it an inherent risk of inconsistency but the process seems to have been conducted with a promptness and expedition that puts contemporary administration of justice to shame.

Again in a way that appears incredible to modern readers, Keyes is called from his deliberations to deal with a sepoy who had lost his mind. He immediately calls for his pistol lamenting that it was a Colt automatic and therefore heavier than a revolver and, together with the Court Usher, goes to investigate. Quite why he called upon the aged usher rather than any of the eighteen presumably still sane sepoys remains a mystery.[65] He recounts how he had witnessed a Muslim soldier "go *ghazi*" once before who had invoked "God the Merciful and Compassionate" whilst in a murderous frenzy and "snarling like a wolf" and was then bayoneted by his comrades.[66] In contrast, this Hindu sepoy appeared to be listless and complaining of being friendless. Keyes with the usher made a dash towards him whilst the sepoy fumbled with his rifle in an ultimately successful attempt to blow his own head off. Keyes is left covered with gore but soon changes and returns to finish hearing his case. Keyes concludes that it was the temperature that caused the sepoy's derangement whilst he, in an early prefiguring of Noel Coward, went out in the midday sun.

After the departure of Delamain's expeditionary force to Basra, Keyes remained busy ensuring that British interests in Bahrain were protected. He also had to assist the Sheikh in handling the collapse of the pearl trade following the declaration of war as the market for such luxury items had unsurprisingly disappeared. This, in turn, led to the return home of many of the foreign merchants particularly the Persians and Indians and with them the falling off of his judicial duties. One judicial duty he did participate in was the arrest of a Herr Harling who whilst ostensibly the manager of a German company in Bahrain was actually a political agent who had been plotting to prevent the landing of Delamain's forces. Harling was well known to Keyes and they had met and got on well together before the commencement of hostilities.

One of Keyes' most important roles was to do what he could to foster pro-British feeling in Bahrain but this was an uphill struggle. He believed that the chief reason for this was Britain's alliance with Russia which was seen as being both anti-Turkish and anti-Muslim. It is ironic that having spent much of the early part of his career actively scheming against the Russians whilst enjoying relatively benign relations with Turkey, he should find himself with the roles being completely reversed. His main problem in this regard was the avowedly anti-Russian attitudes of the Persians in the area.

It is obvious Keyes found his posting irksome and wanted to contribute to the allied war effort in a more active and martial way. He wrote to Edith on 5 October that he would "rather command a company of Terriers [Territorials] than be Resident in the Gulf."[67] Indeed later, on returning to Bahrain from Basra, he wrote to his mother that he "was on [his] way back to another term of penal servitude."[68] This comparative inaction must have rankled particularly given not only his military training but also that so many of his friends and associates were in action and, in many cases being wounded or killed. Keyes regularly mentions news of casualties in his correspondence and scanned the newspapers however out of date for news. Like many long-standing officers, he had a wide circle of acquaintanceships in both the Indian and British Armies as there had been a regular turnover of regiments sent to India in peacetime and, in a racially segregated world, they would have regularly socialised even if they had not worked together professionally. Unsurprisingly, Keyes was particularly upset by the death of his sister Dorothy's husband Brig Gen Sir John Gough in February 1915. Gough was a very well known soldier who had won the Victoria Cross in 1903 and was thought of being a potential head of the army. He was on the staff of Douglas Haig's First Corps and was regarded as Haig's sounding board. He was killed by a sniper on a rare visit to the front. Keyes' letters to his mother reveal not only his concern for his sister but also his pain at the loss of a military paladin.

Although the Indian Army was never intended to serve outside India and the Far East, an Indian Expeditionary Force consisting of two cavalry and two infantry divisions was sent to France in August 1914. The Indian Army was equipped for frontier service which required limited artillery support. It did not perform as well as expected but this was in large part owing to the inadequacies of its equipment as well as problems with the climate and morale. There was also soon a paucity of officers with the necessary language skills and eventually, in October 1915, the infantry divisions were withdrawn to Egypt. Keyes understandably followed its actions closely and was very perturbed by its reported underperformance. His analysis was harsh remarking to his mother on 24 February 1915 that "half the Indian Army ought to be disbanded and there is no good denying the fact that most of them are mere mercenaries [although] the two Punjabi regiments with good officers are better than British regiments for Indian frontier work."[69] This was unfair as the Indian regiments are now regarded as having done as well as could be expected in trying conditions and certainly performed better later when engaged in a style of warfare that was more familiar to them such as in Mesopotamia and Palestine.

From his exile in Bahrain, Keyes continually pushed to be allowed to travel to Basra where there would be more action and whilst he was only able to manage visits in between the performance of his

normal duties, what happened to him there is what featured most
prominently in his correspondence and reports

Chapter 5:

Mesopotamia

The fighting between 1914-18 in what is now Iraq has always been referred to as the Mesopotamian Campaign. This was the name given to the area by the British which in fact consisted of three Ottoman *vilayets* or provinces; namely, Basra, Baghdad and Mosul. These were then backwaters of the Ottoman Empire and there was persistent tension between the Turkish authorities and the indigenous Arabs.

The deterioration of British relations with Turkey and the subsequent Turco-German alliance of August 1914 meant that the British were faced with an enemy on the borders of Egypt and its various interests in Aden and the Persian Gulf. Whilst the Turkish military presence was initially weak so were the British forces and so steps were immediately taken to protect the vital link to India and the Suez Canal in particular but the position in Mesopotamia was of equal strategic concern.

The British had been involved in the Persian Gulf and Mesopotamia since the seventeenth century both for the purposes of trade but also to protect the sea routes to India. The Tigris and Euphrates had been since ancient times one of the trade routes between Europe and Asia and access to them remained important. By the nineteenth century, Britain had established naval control of the gulf and had stopped the endemic piracy and also the slave trade. It had also, to a great extent, brought an end to the historic internecine fighting of the surrounding Arab chieftains. In time, treaties of friendship had been reached with most of the chieftains allowing Britain various rights in the governance of their territories and in some cases the right to land troops. It is by virtue of one of these treaties that Keyes was in Bahrain in 1914.

Control of the Gulf in turn led the British to seek and obtain navigation rights up the Shatt al Arab, the confluence of the Tigris and Euphrates which runs from Al Qurnah to Al Faw. Later still, Britain took over responsibility for piloting and buoying. The river formed a boundary between Ottoman Mesopotamia and Persia.

The importance of the area was increased by the discovery of oil in southern Persia in 1908 by George Bernard Reynolds and the establishment of the Anglo Persian Oil Company ("APOC") in 1909. One of the company's primary tasks was to construct a one hundred and forty mile pipeline to Abadan on the Shatt al Arab which soon became the world's largest oil terminal. British control of the oil industry changed from being a commercial to a military imperative following the decision in 1911 by Winston Churchill when First Lord of the Admiralty to create a new fleet of oil powered battleships. Use of oil as a power source instead of coal increased the speed and range of ships as well as enabling heavier guns to be fitted. As a result, the recognition of the importance of oil deposits in the Middle East, led to international interest and the creation of a rival to APOC in 1912, the Turkish Petroleum Company ("TPC"). This was founded by British, Dutch and German interests and looked to obtain concessions in Ottoman territories, principally what is now Iraq. At a governmental level, the British also sought to retain control of the nascent oil industry and between 1911 and 1913, negotiations with the Turkish government led to the Anglo-Turkish Convention. This addressed the issue of the extent of Turkish suzerainty over Bahrain, Qatar and Kuwait as well as the proposed final destination of the Baghdad railway (Basra rather than Kuwait which would have created a much more direct threat to British control of the Gulf). In 1913, TPC merged with APOC and in the days leading up to the declaration of war, the British Government acquired a fifty one percent stake in APOC thereby fusing the commercial and military interests. APOC ultimately became known as BP.[70]

Control of the oil supply was particularly important to Britain as, in the case of a war, normal supplies which were then largely from Russia would have been cut off. In peacetime however, it was recognised that the cost of shipping oil from the Persian Gulf westwards was uneconomic and that the principal market would be India. All the European powers were coming to recognise the importance of oil as the fuel of the future and that it was in large part the motivation behind the Anglo-Turkish Convention. Although not formally acknowledged, gaining access and control of the Middle Eastern oilfields played a significant part in British thinking during the Mesopotamian Campaign.

It was also recognised during the negotiations between Britain and France which culminated in the Sykes-Picot agreement in 1916. It is no coincidence that the British Mandate included most of the oil producing areas. France's determination to obtain the Kirkuk oilfields within its mandated territory reflects French own economic imperatives, British agreement to this was an attempt to sweeten the pill. It also, in large part contributed to the artificial boundaries carving up the old Ottoman *vilayets* with consequences that resonate to this day.

Against this background, it is perhaps surprising that that Britain had taken practically no steps to defend its interests in the area although this can also be seen as another example of imperial overstretch. The declaration of war with Germany therefore precipitated an immediate rethink. Initially, Turkey declared itself a neutral but in fact had already entered into a secret treaty of armed cooperation with Germany as early as 2 August 1914. As mentioned in Chapter 3, traditionally Britain had enjoyed good relations with Turkey. However, with the accession to political power of the Young Turks, German influence had increased. In particular, the Turkish decision to accept German financing of the Baghdad Railway was a clear indicator of the way in which its foreign policy was evolving.

Anglo-Turkish relations were irreparably damaged by the Anglo-Russian Convention of 1907 as it was inevitable that Britain would not be able to maintain good relations with Turkey whilst allied to Russia and indeed, it was drawn into agreeing to Russian dominion over Constantinople as a war aim. Nevertheless, Turkey probably had little to gain and much to lose by entering into the war and clearly did so with some reluctance. Two things helped rally Turkish public opinion behind an alliance with Germany. The first was the decision by Britain to seize the dreadnoughts, *Reshadiye* and *Sultan Osman* from the Armstrong-Whitworth shipyard even though they were in the process of being handed over to Turkey. Britain was well within her rights to do this and indeed offered full compensation but the ships not only were a symbol of Turkish pride but also had been funded at least in part by public subscription. This caused enormous public outcry against Britain. The ships were renamed *HMS Agincourt* and *HMS Erin* and both were present at the Battle of Jutland as part of the Grand Fleet.[71]

Secondly, in August 1914, the German battle cruiser, *Goeben* and its supporting cruiser, *Breslau*, managed to escape from pursuit by the Mediterranean Fleet and sailed into Turkish waters and were promptly purchased by Turkey, the German crews exchanging their naval caps for fezzes. Within days, the British naval mission had been dismissed from Constantinople. Nevertheless, negotiations between the various parties continued over the next two months with the Entente powers offering to defend Turkish independence if it maintained "scrupulous neutrality." However, Enver Pasha (Minister of War) and the other Young Turks did not want neutrality particularly since the Germans had offered to assist them in the recapture of Egypt and so in late October, the Turkish navy including *Goeben* and *Hamidieh* led an assault on Russian ports including Sebastopol. By this act, without a formal declaration of war, Turkey became a full combatant.

In Mesopotamia, the Turks concentrated upon blockading Abadan. Their forces in the area were weak and those around Abadan amounted to a single gunboat and a small number of troops on the west bank of the Shatt al Arab. Turkey, at that time, saw Mesopotamia as a recruiting base rather than a battle zone and its attentions were focussed upon its borders with Russia and the proposed invasion of

Egypt. There was scant ability to meet a British threat and indeed three regular divisions had been redeployed to the Egyptian front.

On 25 August 1914, the Admiralty requested that troops be sent to protect Abadan. As the Persian Gulf fell within the purview of the India Office, the ultimate person responsible was the Secretary of State for India (the Marquess of Crewe) and the Viceroy, (Viscount Hardinge.) They fully recognised the potential threat to the Government of India of leaving Abadan and the head of the Gulf undefended. As Sir Arthur Hirtzel, Political Secretary to the India Office put it "the political effect in the Persian Gulf and in India of leaving the head of the gulf derelict will be disastrous and we cannot afford politically to acquiesce in such a thing for an indefinite period."[72] However, events in France took precedence and there was also concern not to give the Turks, who after all were then still neutral, the opportunity to denounce British aggression and call for a jihad.[73]

The only potential force available was the Indian Army which then consisted of seventy six thousand British and one hundred and fifty nine thousand Indian troops. They were all volunteers and their primary purpose was to defend India against internal and external threat. Until the exigencies of 1914, there had been no question of the Indian Army being used other than in Indian or adjoining territories and it had been equipped with this in mind.

In 1903, Lord Kitchener had commenced a series of reforms of the Indian Army abolishing the old Presidency Armies and forming a unified force. Nine divisional areas were created with a heavy emphasis upon the North West Frontier. This in turn led to the abandonment of well-established garrisons and the creation of new bases all of which was expensive and remained incomplete in 1914. In any event, the improvement of Anglo-Russian relations following the 1907 convention took the pressure off the Government of India and in turn led to cuts in equipment and materiel. This meant that an Indian Army Division had far less support in terms of engineering, artillery, communications mechanical transport and medical staffing and equipment than its British Army equivalent.

In September 1914, Major General Barrow, the Military Secretary at the India Office warned that the Turks were fomenting trouble with the Arab population and would then "proclaim a *Jehad* and endeavour to raise Afghanistan and the Frontier Tribes against us."[74] Barrow was concerned to prevent this happening at all costs and concluded that the best way to do so would be to establish a military presence immediately even though the Turks remained formally neutral. He was fortunate in that the defeat of the Germans on the Marne had taken some of the immediate pressure off the Government of India to send as many troops as possible to France. Therefore, on 26 September, the Brigade group led by Brigadier WS Delamain was instructed to make its way to the Persian Gulf. Originally, its destination was Abadan but it was later decided that this would give the Turks a casus belli so it was dispatched to Bahrain.

The brigade consisted of one British battalion, the 2nd Dorsets and three Indian ones, 20th Punjabis, 104th Rifles and 117th Mahrattas. Together with support detachments including engineers, artillery and medical and logistic staff, the force totalled over five thousand troops and a little under thirteen hundred horses and mules. It left India on 15 October arriving in Bahrain on 23 October. This was the force that caused Keyes "some concern." Keyes' worries would have been allayed a few days later as, following the Turkish assault on the Black Sea ports, Delamain received an order to "clear the Turks out of the Shatt."[75]

The first step was to clear the Turkish fort at Al Faw which sits on the mouth of the Shatt al Arab and this was soon done. The force then moved upstream to clear Turkish troops opposite Abadan before landing at Sanniya where Delamain turned back an attack by three hundred Turks. Later, Delamain was joined by a force led by his divisional commander, Lieutenant General Arthur Barrett. Together, they then marched on to take Basra on 20 November 1914. This decision by the military forces on the ground to exceed their political instructions that were essentially defensive has been criticised as taking the concept of "active defence" too far. This was regrettably to become a common theme during the first part of the Mesopotamian campaign.

The problem that the British faced was that whilst there was a clear-cut initial objective in protecting Abadan and the Shatt al Arab, there was no obvious next stage. One of the initial objectives had been to impress the Arabs and prevent them from joining forces with the Turks. This had, to a large extent had been achieved and there was a need to keep on impressing them which could only be done by annexations of territory and further victories. Logic pointed to continuing the advance up the River Tigris to Baghdad but that was to commit to long lines of communications with an army that was essentially un-mechanised.

It is likely nonetheless that an early assault up river might well have succeeded, as Turkish forces were then weak. However, there was limited initial appetite to do so. When, later in 1915 an attempt was made, it was against a reinforced Turkish army and led ultimately to the British being besieged and defeated at Kut al Amara. It took substantial reinforcements and expenditure including the construction of railway from Basra to facilitate supplies before the campaign would succeed.

Keyes remained British Resident in Bahrain until he was replaced by Hugh Steward in March 1916. During the previous year, he was not only promoted to Major but also participated in the Mesopotamian campaign when, in the winter of 1915, he took part in a raid carried out on a potential Turkish sympathiser, Sheikh Hassan al Jarriah somewhere near Basra.[76] It is not clear how this came about as his official role remained in Bahrain but Keyes was clearly in command of the raiding party which consisted of a two platoons of "a famous West Country Regiment." It is also not obvious why, writing many years later, he was so coy about its identity bearing in mind that it could only have been the 2nd Battalion of the Dorsetshire Regiment.

He gives a clear account of the botched journey to the Sheikh's village during which the party regularly became lost amongst the palm groves that used to grow on both sides of the Shatt al Arab. At that time, there would have been up to eighteen million trees which no doubt explains the number of times that they went off route.[77]

The account of the raid is in line with the tone of Keyes' other accounts of his adventures with himself at the centre. The Sheikh is portrayed as a heroically Rousseauesque figure in comparison with his half brother who had "seemed to have acquired all the vices of the West without having learned any of its virtues." Keyes, at his most Low Church, bonds with the devout Sheikh in their shared distaste at the younger brother's collection of erotic postcards which come across as being even more of a crime than possession of firearms and collusion with the Turks. Indeed, even the firearm is a "nasty, cheap, German automatic."[78] To add to the series of stock characters, there is also an "immense negro, the whites of whose eyes roll in astonishment", an over keen subaltern and a cheery but disappointingly non-cockney sergeant.

The more interesting sections are often the small details and asides. For example, Keyes gives a detailed account of the layout and contents of the Sheikh's house, the way that it is configured so that there is no chance of the women being seen from the street, the colourfulness of the clothes which would be worn in the house as opposed to the black and indigo burkas worn when strangers were present. It is also worth noting that Keyes struggles with the women's domestic Arabic as he would normally only have spoken to men.

Once again, where it is possible to crosscheck Keyes' story, discrepancies emerge. In a letter to his mother of 24 February 1915, Keyes describes what is plainly the same raid. This time however, there is no mention of a dissolute half-brother and the hidden revolver plainly belongs to the Sheikh. Doubt must also be cast upon Keyes' ability to speak Arabic to the standard implied in his story bearing in mind his letter to her of several months later when he indicated that he had only just started to learn the language.[79]

Keyes managed to reach Basra for a short visit in late December 1914 or early January 1915 returning in February to stand in for the Commissioner of Police, a Mr Gregory, whilst he travelled back to Karachi for "a few days."[80] He recounts that he becomes involved in a planned raid on anti-British conspirators but this proves to be "a fizzle out." However, Keyes does manage to capture a wanted man on his own initiative. In spite of the excitement of being closer to the heart of the action, Keyes did not enjoy police work at this level as he still hankered after a more martial role.

He was interested in Basra which was far more bustling and cosmopolitan than Bahrain and he reported on the composition of its population with "a tremendous number of Christians and Jews." Basra then was regarded as a lively and civilised posting with a considerable European population very different from the Shia enclave that exists now. His training was such that he would inevitably seek to familiarise himself with local political issues and his views upon the future of Mesopotamia became increasingly trenchant over the next year.

During the summer of 1915, he participated in operations in the Persian Gulf. On 23 August, he was responsible for persuading Sheikh Abdullah to demand the surrender of a hostile fort at Doha. This was largely done by the judicious payment of five thousand Rupees to the Sheikh on condition of a successful outcome. Within a few days, he joined a small squadron chasing hostile dhows in and around Dilwar (now Delvar). This was part of a naval operation to curtail a rebellion by Tangistanis or, as Keyes refers to them, Tangsiris. They had been encouraged to rebel by a German agent, a Wilhelm Wassmus, the former Consul to Bushire who later became known as "Wassmus of Persia." He was a significant participant in the long-standing campaign of destabilisation which the Germans mounted in Persia throughout the war but particularly in 1915-16. Like the Kaiser, he too was supposed to have converted to Islam. Although ultimately unsuccessful, Wassmus caused great alarm and also managed to evade capture by the British. However, he left behind his baggage which included the German diplomatic code book. This assisted British Intelligence to decrypt German telegrams quickly - one of them being the infamous Zimmerman telegram whose leaking was instrumental in bringing the United States into the war.

Keyes continued chasing Tangsiri dhows and on 1 September 1915 he came under fire at Dilwar from "twenty to thirty well concealed men." In response, Keyes and the Naval detachment he was with shelled some Tangsiri boats and killed some of the attackers. Later in September, Keyes recommended a raid up the Mand River with "a hundred men" to destroy Tangsiri Dhows which were hiding safe from the British ships whose draft was too deep to pursue them. The Tangsiri raids and the Navy's involvement with them has been described as "a very small affair" and in comparison with what was going on at Kut, let alone the Western Front, it all seems very remote and insignificant.[81] However, at a time when Britain aimed to adopt a "Monroe Doctrine in the [Persian] Gulf" threats to shipping were treated very seriously, as was anything that might challenge the sea routes to and from India.[82] In some ways, this was a foretaste of his mission to Mekran in Persia in the following year which, as will be seen aimed to head off trouble fomented by German agents.

By 19 September, Keyes was back in Bahrain and writing to an unnamed friend or colleague. He mentioned that he has had discussions with Sir Mark Sykes who was the War Office expert on Arab issues and sat on the de Bunsen Committee which advised the cabinet on Middle Eastern issues. Sykes, of course, achieved later fame when he led the negotiations that led to the Sykes-Picot Agreement in 1916. Sykes was also in part responsible for renaming the former Ottoman provinces by reference to their classical names which led to modern Syria, Iraq, Palestine and indeed Mesopotamia.

Following his discussions with Sykes, Keyes shared his outlook for the future of the Middle East and Mesopotamia in particular. He was of the view that the British policy of attacking the Turks in Mesopotamia as well as destabilising the Ottoman Empire in Saudi

Arabia "made annexation inevitable even if were not for the pot valiant speech of Old Squiffy's at the Guildhall."[83] This referred to a speech made by Herbert Asquith on 9 November 1914 in which he raised the issue of a potential disposal of Ottoman territories outside of the Turkish homeland of Anatolia at the successful end of the war. Old Squiffy was one of the less endearing nicknames for Asquith and obviously referred to his notorious bibulousness. Keyes' lifelong conservatism led him to have highly sceptical views of many leading Liberal politicians and, as will be seen, he later developed a visceral loathing of Lloyd George

The problem of what to do with Turkey was an inevitable concomitant of the Anglo-Russian Convention since Russia had clear and obvious designs on ready access to the Mediterranean. Asquith's opinion was that Britain should not seek to profit from the dismemberment of the Ottoman Empire. However, this was not a view shared by many in his Cabinet and, to some extent, the position developed once it became clear that other countries were not so scrupulous. Lord Kitchener believed that as partition was inevitable, it was important that Britain secured control over Mesopotamia to protect its interests in the Persian Gulf as well as the sea lanes to India. Unsurprisingly, the Admiralty supported this view. Separate from this, there was concern to ensure that British interests in Egypt were not threatened by the emergence of Russia as a Mediterranean power and France exerting control over Syria and Lebanon. This, ultimately and fatefully, led to British ambitions upon Palestine to protect Egypt's flank. Lloyd George also supported a move on Palestine "owing to prestige involved in its occupation."[84]

To add further complication, Asquith's speech of 9 November 1914 was also viewed by Zionists and their supporters - not least the Home Secretary, Herbert Samuel - as opening up the possibility of a Jewish homeland. Interestingly, this does not appear to have made much impression upon Keyes whose thoughts were entirely imperialistic in conception. Having said that, he might have been expected to support the transfer of a conquered Mesopotamia to the Government of India as he was, after all, very much a British Indian. However, he opposed this on the basis - probably correctly - that the Indian Government "would treat it merely as another outlying province of India such as Burma." This perhaps reflects the frustrations he encountered in obtaining clear instructions whilst Resident in Bahrain.

Keyes' proposed solution was the creation of a Near Eastern department of the Foreign Office to which men from the Indian, Egyptian and Levant services were seconded adding that "if there is any difficulty in providing for Kitchener after the war, why not make him Dictator of Egypt and our share of Turkey." This is revealing not only of the way in which the old imperialist way of thinking persisted and with it the prospect of further expanding the empire but also the scant regard paid to notions of self-government by the indigenous population who would simply swap one imperial master for another. It is also implicit from Keyes' comments that he perhaps saw a place for himself in a newly created department.

This oversimplification does not do Keyes credit. His entire professional career had been spent operating at the margins of empire and he, more than many others, would have appreciated the need to balance British imperial ambitions with the limited resources available to achieve them. It also ignores his role not only in combating attempts to destabilise British influence - such as the raids against the Tangsiris and later in the Mekran and indeed Russia - but also in promoting destabilisation against the Turks. Notwithstanding that, Keyes is clearly typical of his time in being unashamedly determined to promote British interests. This is borne out by the description of him by his friend Lt Gen H G Martin "He loved books as well as he loved field sports. Yet there was something Cromwellian about him. He carried a bible with him and read it daily. He could be quite ruthless. His methods of bringing to justice murdering ruffians on the [North West] Frontier were as unorthodox as they were effective. To the greater glory of God or the British Empire, he would have hewn Agag to pieces unhesitatingly."[85] It is indisputable that Keyes regarded British rule - particularly in India - as being wholly beneficial in imposing order and the rule of law on what would otherwise be chaos. He had no doubt about a British mission to govern and yet also had a similarly clear vision of a mission to serve. This seems to have been sufficient to square the circle of his political and religious motivations.

Personally, Keyes continued to find Bahrain lonely. There had been a move for Edith to join him there earlier in 1915 but this had come to nothing and he evidently disliked being so far from the centre of events. There were however some compensations, one of which was tennis but this was not always available. He wrote to his mother on 8 October 1915 that the "weather is very nice now but I can't get a decent game of tennis as the Roumanian has got blood poisoning and then septicaemia and can't put up a fight."[86]

In amongst the performance of his normal duties, Keyes had extensive dealings with Ibn Saud, later the first king of Saudi Arabia who was one of the leaders competing for British support at the time. Ibn Saud was the leader of the House of Saud and was engaged in a long running dispute with the Rashidi clan. He had formed a strong relationship with Captain William Shakespear who was British Resident in Kuwait and Keyes' contemporary in the Indian Political Service and also his subordinate. In one of the many what ifs of the war, Shakespear had persuaded Ibn Saud to support the British against the pro-Ottoman Rashidis and was likely to have ensured that he received significant British support in return. Shakespear accompanied Ibn Saud when he fought the Rashidis at the Battle of Jarab in January 1915 and, declining a suggestion that he take cover, was killed. The Rashidis then cut off his head and hung his solar topee on the gates of Medina. Thereafter, relations between Ibn Saud and the British deteriorated with British support being concentrated upon Hussain Bin Ali, Sharif of Mecca who ultimately was the loser to Ibn Saud in a power struggle over control of the Arabian peninsular.

Keyes describes his impressions of Ibn Saud in a letter to Sir Mark Sykes of 10 January 1916. Keyes pointed out how in 1914 Ibn Saud had "sat on the fence until Shakespear pulled him down on our side but he behaved very badly when Shakespear was killed." Keyes met Ibn Saud at a meeting in Qatif in December 1915 and "shared the same dish as him."[87] This led Keyes to change his view of Ibn Saud who "hates Turks" and he suggested that Sykes review British policy and increase support for him. Bearing in mind later events, this was prescient and long term British interests would have been better served if Keyes' views had prevailed.

As well as being impressed by Ibn Saud politically, Keyes was also very much taken by his domestic arrangements informing Sykes that "though no more than thirty five he told me [he had been] married sixty five times and *Inshallah* will take unto him two hundred more wives. He has the most attractive smile and I am sure is very nice to them whilst it lasts. Three days, he says, is the usual time." He had told much the same story to his mother on 2 January 1916 explaining that Ibn Saud was "an ardent admirer of Solomon in his matrimonial ventures."[88]

In early 1916, Keyes prepared to leave Bahrain for his new posting leading the political element of an expedition in southern Persia. Before he left however, he almost certainly would have met the Arab explorer, Gertrude Bell.[89] He finally left Bahrain, no doubt with considerable relief in March 1916.

Chapter 6:

The Mekran Mission

The political position of Persia had long been of strategic importance because of its geographical position lying as it did at the junctions of the Russian and Ottoman empires as well as forming the western boundary of British India. The division of Persia into Russian and British spheres of influence with the Persians having autonomy only in the central part of the country around Tehran had been one of the most important outcomes of the Anglo-Russian Convention of 1907. Whilst this gave stability to one of the most fraught areas in dispute between Russia and Britain by protecting the vulnerable western border provinces of India, it opened up yet another area of potential conflict between Britain and Turkey.

Until 1914, the defence of India had been the dominant consideration in British foreign policy and, in many ways, of greater concern than the growing threat of Germany. The Empire's military strength was focussed upon India and the supply routes to the East. There was a powerful Indian lobby mostly in the India Office but also in large parts of the military. This is reflected in the disproportionate weighting of military resources around the Empire to the detriment of Britain's home defences. Although the focus shifted as the First World War progressed, Indian defence remained a vital component of British foreign policy right through to the Second World War.

The perceived benefit of the Anglo-Russian convention was that it appeared to achieve both British objectives; it strengthened the alliance against the Central Powers whilst protecting India's borders. The collateral problems caused as a result only became apparent as German links with Turkey grew ever stronger and ultimately the position in Persia became wholly confused following the Bolshevik Revolution.

Following the outbreak of the First World War, Turkey and Germany sought to encourage Islamic insurrections in Persia, Afghanistan and India. The Sultan, as Caliph, was greatly respected by the culturally conservative tribes who, in any event, resented British (and therefore non-Muslim) interference in the region's politics. The British as rulers of one of the largest Muslim populations in the world were only too conscious of that threat and took pains to retain good relations with Muslims and their rulers. However, the fact that the Sultan had declared a jihad against the British was bound to lead to considerable difficulties and there were repeated attempts by German agents to incite rebellion both in Persian and Afghanistan as well as encouraging Indian nationalists to mutiny. These threats were real but also had a slightly eccentric quality so that rumours were put about that the Kaiser had converted to Islam. Whether or not this was a deliberate echo of Napoleon's alleged conversion whilst campaigning in Egypt is unclear. Equally unclear is the extent to which such rumours were believed. It is hard to accept that anyone would be so credulous but then Napoleon's conversion was accepted at least in part so it is hard to tell. Whichever is correct, the fears of such conspiracies were fully justified and considerable resources were devoted to subverting them.[90]

The position in Persia in the beginning of 1916 was chaotic. There were a number of competing interests involved and divisions between allies so that there was considerable mistrust as between the British and Russians as well as between Germany and Turkey. The Persian government vacillated between them all. At this time, the country was nominally governed by the last member of the Qajar Dynasty, Ahmed Shah Qajar, aided by a cabinet of advisers and a *Majlis* or Council. In fact, cabinets were regularly replaced reflecting the political orientation of the moment - chiefly whether pro-Allied or Pro-Central Powers - but also reflecting each individual participating nation. The country was practically bankrupt and authority outside Tehran and its environs was tenuous and there had been an attempted coup by a pro-German faction in November 1915.

In December 1915, a new government was formed headed by Farman Farma who was pro-British. He made a serious attempt to restore the government's authority outside Tehran and over the tribal chieftains. More specifically, he dismissed a number of the senior officers of the pro-German Swedish Gendarmerie. This organisation had been formed in 1910 as part of an ongoing attempt to create a modern European military and police. It had a primary responsibility for ensuring that the highways and trade routes were kept safe. The Swedes were chosen to run it as a neutral choice between the British and Russians.

The chief concern of the British was to prevent the Russians from straying outside their sphere of influence in North Western Persia as well as preserving their own influence in South Eastern Persia. The British were also highly sensitive to any threat to the oil concessions in South Persia. The Russians on the other hand were actively engaged in fighting the Turks in North West Persia and also had ambitions to increase their influence in Persia and potentially of achieving the long term objective of reaching the Persian Gulf.[91]

As far as the Central Powers were concerned, Germany wanted to establish a pro-German but independent Persia which would form part of German backed Islamic Federation with direct access to Afghanistan and thereafter India. Germany also had ambitions on seizing the British oil concessions. Whilst control of these would have been of limited practical use to the Germans in wartime as they lacked the means to transport oil until either the Berlin to Baghdad railway was completed or the British blockade lifted, denial of an oil supply to the British would have caused serious logistical problems for the Navy east of Suez.

In contrast, Turkish ambitions were more directly acquisitive. This caused friction with the German mission which was only kept under control by the respect which the Turks held for Freiherr Colmar von der Goltz, the German Field Marshal who acted as military aide to the Sultan. Following von der Goltz's death in March 1916, relations between Turkey and Germany sharply deteriorated in Mesopotamia and Persia.[92]

The key issue dominating Persian politics during early 1916 was the ongoing siege at Kut al Amara in Mesopotamia where an Anglo-Indian force led by General Charles Townshend were trapped. There were various attempts to raise the siege all of which were unsuccessful and Townshend surrendered together with approximately thirteen thousand troops on 29 April 1916. The surrender marked the lowest point in the Mesopotamian campaign and most of the captured British and Indian troops died in captivity. The siege had a direct impact upon Persia since it meant that a large part of the available Turkish troops were tied down. This gave great impetus to a Russian offensive led by General Baratov. Indeed, Baratov was marching towards Kut when news came of its surrender. Subsequently, the Turks were able to release forces for a counterattack.

Relations between Germany and Turkey deteriorated when Turkey insisted on mounting a campaign in western Persia against German military advice. This was initially so successful that an alarmed Commander in Chief in India pressed for another advance up the Tigris by the Mesopotamian Expeditionary Force to put pressure on the Turks to divert troops away from Persia. The reason for his concern was the potential for disruption in Afghanistan and thence India. Whilst the request was turned down, it is yet another indicator of the British sensitivity about the defence of India's borders.

In August 1916, the Persians were pressurised into entering into a disadvantageous treaty which, in return for an annual subsidy of two hundred thousand Tomans (about £65,000) and the beginnings of a unified paramilitary force under joint British and Russian supervision, they agreed to control of the national finances by an Allied commission. During the autumn of 1916, the Turks began to advance into Eastern Persia. In October, a column of Turco-German Bakhtiaris were defeated near Isfahan by a combination of Russian troops led by General Baratov and the South Persia Rifles which was led by Sir Percy Sykes and consisted of about four hundred and fifty Bakhtiaris under British command. Sykes then declined to join the Russian forces preferring to remain at Isfahan so as to ensure that the British oil fields were protected.[93]

The Turks renewed their advance in late October but failed to make much progress against Baratov's forces probably because of supply difficulties and with the onset of winter, both sides regrouped. So, 1916 resulted in no decisive change either politically or militarily in Persia; the Persian government had been pressured into agreeing to a disadvantageous treaty that favoured the British and Russians, the British and Russians had just about held off the Turkish assault and had protected the oil fields, they had also managed to disrupt many of the German inspired missions to eastern Persia and Afghanistan. The conflicting policies towards Persia had placed stress upon Turco-German relations as well as depleting Turkish forces in Mesopotamia, something of which General Maude was to take advantage in capturing Baghdad in 1917.

The Mekran Mission formed part of the overall policy of preventing the spread of Turco-German influence in Afghanistan through the porous borders of Baluchistan and Afghanistan. As Sir Charles Monro, the Commander in Chief in India wrote "the inability or indifference of the Persian Government gave scope here for the penetration of enemy agents into Afghanistan."[94] In many ways, it can be viewed as the East Persian equivalent of Sir Percy Sykes' activities in South West Persia.

In late 1915, the Niedermeyer-Hentig expedition had successfully reached Afghanistan. This was organised by the Germans but ostensibly led by an exiled Indian prince, Raja Mahendra Pratap. Its aim was to encourage Afghanistan to declare independence from the British and then join the Central Powers and attack India. It was a cause of serious concern and unsuccessful attempts were made to cut it off before it reached Afghanistan. Upon reaching Kabul, protracted diplomatic and political intrigues took place including personal interventions with the Emir, Habibullah Khan, by Viscount Hardinge, Viceroy of India and indeed George V. It may have been these or the appreciation by the Afghans that joining the Central Powers would leave them vulnerable to attack by the substantial forces of the Indian army in circumstances where they could expect no practical assistance from either Germany or Turkey that ultimately led to them remaining neutral.

At the same time, German agents were active in South East Persia chiefly in and around Kerman, a city close to the Baluchistan border. They were led by Lieutenants Zugmeyer and Griesinger the former of whom had been an academic who had spent months in Mekran prior to the war conducting research on local fishes and reptiles. At the same time, he had cultivated good relations with local tribal leaders. He returned to Mekran in 1915 to stir up anti-British feelings and encourage rebellion. It was in fulfilment of this role that he and Griesinger linked up with one of the feints sent out by Niedermeyer and Hentig whilst en route to Afghanistan.

By January 1916, Zugmeyer and Griesinger had established themselves at Kerman. Their arrival is described by Edmund Candler in *The Long Road to Baghdad* as:

"The townspeople flocked to meet the Germans, Zugmeyer and Griesinger, sacrificed a sheep and a cow in their honour; and in spite of the Governor-General, who protested, the German and Turkish flags were hoisted on a house outside the city. Later the tireless Zugmeyer incited the people to crowd into the mosque and declare a Jehad and kill all English and Russians. The British subject Farrukh Shah was murdered, and the murderer, as at Isfahan, took refuge with the Germans.

The Persians have a conveniently medieval system of bast, or inviolate sanctuary, which exactly fits in with the Hunnish renascence of the era of assassination. "A small party of Englishmen," wrote Zugmeyer to a certain chief, "have come to Dehaneh Baghi. It will be very easy to crush them. Proceed at once, kill them and take possession of all their property, arms and ammunition, and send me one rifle of each kind possessed by them as a specimen." There is something medieval in this direct appeal. It is murder become routine."[95]

The Germans managed to persuade the local governor to expel the British Consul and then send out parties to incite the local tribes to rebel. The Germans had particular success with the Damanis who were a Baluch tribe who lived both in Baluchistan and South East Persia including Kerman. The Damanis were either convinced by German claims that the Kaiser had converted to Islam following a secret visit to Mecca and had the blessing of the Sultan of Turkey as Caliph or, more likely, had been persuaded by German subsidies.

In response to the raiding of supply lines in Baluchistan, Brigadier Reginald Dyer who later became infamous as the officer in command during the Amritsar Massacre in April 1919, moved against the Damanis in July 1916 with what became known as the Seistan Force.[96] Previously, he had adopted a more directly confrontational approach and sought to split the two elements of the Damanis (the Yarmahomedzais and the Gamshadzais) by occupying the strategically important village of Khwash in May 1916. In a series of operations between 12 and 29 July 1916, he inflicted significant defeats on the Yarmahomedzais and captured most of their flocks - in a semi-nomadic society, their lifeblood. During August, he continued to traverse Damani territory returning to his temporary base at Khwash on 24 August. Dyer returned to India on grounds of ill health in October 1916 and was replaced by Brigadier General C O Tanner. Ultimately, an agreement was reached with the Damanis whereby they paid fines and agreed to refrain from future hostilities.[97] Tanner also managed to obtain agreement from the Damani chiefs to pay a fine and to cease raiding. He continued to police the area and local forces were engaged in sporadic melees with gunrunners but not at a significant level.

Following his posting from Bahrain, Keyes relished being back in Baluchistan and in particular Quetta where he had spent much of the previous twenty years. He was, however frustrated by his brief which was to work alongside Dyer with the intention of defusing tensions and persuading the local tribes to stay loyal or at least not be swayed into joining the German backed insurrection. Whilst in Quetta, Keyes had great difficulty in assembling a viable force having been allocated a fraction of the two hundred infantry, fifty cavalry and two guns that he had requested. He set about improving matters by the judicious manipulation of a system which he had come to understand completely since the occasion when he had had to be helped by his clerk to extend his period of leave back in 1908. He found six men of an Indian mountain regiment who were willing to be bribed to put in for a discharge and to accompany him. He also managed to find an artillery unit who would train his men to use the two obsolete mountain guns he had been allocated. He also established good relations with his junior officers who included Captain John Hotson who had previously worked exclusively in civil administration in Bombay and had volunteered for military service. Hotson was to remain in Baluchistan, latterly, as Consul in Shiraz in Persia, until 1920 and he and Keyes became close friends and colleagues. Like many British Indians, Hotson was more than just an administrator and soldier; he was also a keen amateur naturalist and used his time in the Mekran and Persia to identify new flora and fauna including Hotson's Jerboa and Hotson's mouse-like hamster.

The mission started from Gwadur, a port on the coast of Baluchistan in April 1916. By May, it had reached Mand and began to encounter more hostility. Two British officers of the Mekran Levy Corps, Lieutenants Hughes and Horst were murdered either by their own troops who had been radicalised which was what Keyes believed or by a Rind (a tribe in Persian Baluchistan) which had been bribed by the Germans which is what Sir Percy Sykes thought.[98] Either way, it was an atrocity that reverberated around Baluchistan. Keyes wrote of it that "there is a distinctly widespread though not very deep [religious] revival" adding "*Ghaza* was then being preached in three of four centres in one - Het near Rask- by a man who is believed to have taken German money." However, by then, he was confident that the worst of the German threat had been seen off and that this was acknowledged by the locals - "the people know that the German bubble is burst and I don't think that we will have a revival but you never know with these light headed swine."

This calls into question Keyes' attitude to race. He had been born in Abbottabad which was then in the Punjab but later became part of North West Frontier Province and had spent the best part of his career in Baluchistan. He spent more time in this section of India than anywhere else in his life and clearly had a deep knowledge and fondness for it. Equally, it is plain from his stories that he had affection and respect for its people. Nonetheless, it is also plain that he retained an innate belief in his own superiority as an Englishman and that this view was prevalent amongst most of the British Indians. Having said that, as a Political Officer, his dealings with local people - whether Indian, Baluch or Arab - were more nuanced than many others in British India who would be most unlikely ever even to speak to an Indian in a non-servile capacity. Keyes would therefore be well aware that describing Muslims in general and Bahram Khan in particular as "swine" would be extremely offensive. Against that, he also plainly had a greater respect for Muslims than he had for "herring gutted Hindus."[99] The fairest way to describe him is as being a product of his time and class. He was very far from being alone in believing in the racial superiority of the Anglo-Saxon world; it is prevalent in contemporary literature and politics. Therefore, however, surprising his language might be to a modern reader, it should not colour the overall judgment of the man.

The principal threat with which Keyes had to deal was from Mir Bahram Khan who was the leader of a Baluch tribal confederation, de facto ruler of part of Persian Baluchistan and had established the short-lived Barakzai dynasty. He not only had significant military force - up to ten thousand rifles - but also allied himself with a religious leader, Khalaifa Khair Mohammed of Karawan. Bahram Khan was in close contact with German agents and was in receipt of financial and political support from them. In 1915, he had raided the Kech valley to the consternation of the British.

The position was therefore confused with overlapping jurisdictions. Political authority for the long border between Persian Kerman and Baluchistan rested with Keyes' best man, Lieutenant General Sir John Ramsey who was the Agent to the Governor General and was based in Quetta. He had appointed Major W G Hutchinson to act as Political Agent for Chagai who, in turn, was to advise Dyer although Dyer frequently chose to bypass him and rely upon his own sources for political advice. Colonel A B Dew was Political Agent at Kalat (capital of Baluchistan) and was Keyes' superior. For much of the relevant time, Dew was out of touch dealing with a German inspired rebellion in Jahlawan, Baluchistan. Finally, there was, of course, Sir Percy Sykes' mission in South Persia.[100]

As far as Dyer and Keyes were concerned, there were two entirely separate methods of approach at work; Dyer's orthodox military one and Keyes' more subtle political one. This is, in many ways, a continuation of the traditionally differing approaches adopted in Baluchistan as opposed to the North West Frontier Province and the Afghan borders with Keyes following the model laid down by Sir Robert Sandeman which was considered in Chapter 3. Inevitably, it was likely to lead to tension between its proponents and Keyes found Dyer's conduct infinitely frustrating.

Keyes' concern was that Dyer wanted a military solution that would make the Damanis British subjects. Keyes was against this as it would disrupt relations with other tribes in the area and "might bring the Baranzais in which was a bigger thing that the government wants. So, I am afraid that it was pure devilry him saying this to my *Sardars* [local tribal leaders]. I am afraid that he means to bring the Baranzais in and to conquer them."

Keyes was therefore concerned that Dyer's ambitions would lead to a far more complicated situation arising and there is also a hint that Dyer was motivated by personal ambition as Keyes informed Dew that Dyer "is a very gallant sportsman and very easy to get along with personally but I am afraid is determined to make a big thing of this and is not particular about the means." This also fits in with Keyes believing that Dyer was deliberately avoiding him to the extent that he "slipped away in the night" before Keyes could speak to him. Later, Keyes was more explicit stating that Dyer "was determined to add another province to the Empire."

On 8 August 1916, Keyes wrote to Dew from Gusht where he had become increasingly disenchanted with Dyer's attitude pointing out that "he is not playing the game at all." This comment was precipitated by Dyer's intention to attack Bampur using the recently defeated Damanis as allies. Keyes complained that with Dyer acting as he did, "how can I persuade the Baranzais to believe anything I say." As if that was not bad enough, Keyes was furious that Dyer was "determined to keep me in the dark and doesn't confine himself to the truth in order to do so."[101]

Indeed, Keyes' letter played a significant part in alerting the Foreign and Political Department of the Government of India to the danger posed by Dyer's actions since a meeting was called on 2 September to discuss East Persia. It was attended by General Fitzpatrick, the Chief of the Indian General Staff and two representatives of the Foreign and Political Department alongside others with specialist knowledge of East Persia. The meeting discussed the best approach to the Damanis and reached a conclusion along the lines suggested by Keyes. Although not minuted, it is likely that Dyer's future role was discussed as, not long afterwards, his earlier request for temporary leave on grounds of ill health was accepted and Brig Gen Tanner appointed on a permanent basis.[102] Dyer was far from pleased with being replaced and it shows the respect in which Keyes was increasingly held by his superiors.

Dyer continued with his career unchecked notwithstanding this setback and in the light of the controversy surrounding his later actions in Amritsar in 1919, it is difficult not to form the view that the lack of judgment demonstrated here perhaps should have been picked up on by his superiors before he caused real and permanent damage.

On 21 August 1916, Keyes again reported to Dew about the progress that had been made in confronting the German inspired rebellion in Mekran. He expressed his concern about extremism writing "the thing that I disliked the most was all the religious feeling." He added with relief that had the German agent, Zugmeyer pressed on earlier with his attempt to raise the Baranzais, matters would have been much worse. As it was, he had been partially responsible for persuading Bahram Khan, who was regarded as the most potent threat faced by the British, to change side. This was following a very fraught meeting, which on the British side was attended by Keyes, Captain Hotson and another officer, Captain, C H G H Harvey-Kelly of the Baluch Light Infantry, who was in charge of the escort which consisted of one platoon of Gurkhas, one company of Baluch Light Infantry and a section from the Indian Field Ambulance – approximately one hundred and fifty men in all.

Bahram Khan brought with him five hundred men some of whom kept their rifles trained on the three British officers throughout the meeting.[103] Bahram Khan also demonstrated his contempt for them by keeping "his hands covered with a silk handkerchief" which would signify to his followers that he believed the British to be unclean. However, probably because Bahram Khan realised that the Germans were unable to sustain a viable rebellion and that British reprisals would inevitably follow if peace were not reached, he changed sides. Indeed, soon after, he turned a party of raiders away from Bampur.

On his return to Charbar in February 1917, Keyes wrote a report suggesting the establishment of a Persian authority with British assistance and "for a time under our aegis."[104] It was only by strengthening the Persian government that the tribesmen of East Persia could be controlled in their home territories and Keyes believed that British assistance would enable taxes to be collected as well as order maintained. It was, to a great extent, the logical next step in increasing the political reality of the sphere of influence agreed with the Russians back in 1907.

Keyes' views were favourably received and a letter was sent to Lt Col Sir John Ramsey stating that the "Government of India fully endorse [his] good opinion of the work undertaken by Major Keyes and of the interesting report which he has submitted. They consider that Major Keyes has carried out a difficult task with tact, firmness and judgment."[105] Keyes was appointed a Companion of the Order of the Indian Empire in June 1917.[106]

Chapter 7:

Romania 1917

Keyes' involvement with Russia dated back to his travels there after leaving Haileybury in 1895. His career on the North West Frontier involved journeys around Russian controlled Southern Asia. He was a fluent Russian speaker and was regarded as a Russian expert by the Indian Political Service. As such, although all his prior experience had been in India, Persia and the Arabian Gulf, it is not altogether surprising that he was attached to the Russian Army in 1917. Initially, he was posted to Romania and acted as a liaison officer as well as carrying out an intelligence role. One of his principal responsibilities was to design a propaganda campaign to encourage the Russians to continue to support Romania against the Central Powers.

Romania's decision to join the Allies in 1916 had a long gestation. The country had been ruled by Hohenzollerns since 1866 and they were predictably pro-Central Powers to such an extent that King Carol I had persuaded his then Prime Minister, Ion Bratianu, to indicate Romania's secret support for the Triple Alliance between Germany, Austria-Hungary and Italy which was concluded in 1882. However, by 1914, Romanian public and political opinion favoured the Allies so there was a lack of political support for declaring war in support of the Central Powers. Romania was able to avoid its treaty obligations because it was only required to declare war if a Triple Alliance country was attacked and it was able to claim that Austria-Hungary had been a belligerent.

Romania's position was a precarious one. It was faced with the much larger Austro-Hungarian Empire to its west and north and Russia to the east. It also had a traditional antipathy towards Bulgaria to its south. The Romanians were ethnically distinct from the Germans and Magyars of Austria-Hungary and the Slavs of Russia and Bulgaria. To make matters worse, there were bones of contention on all sides. The Romanians had ambitions on Transylvania which had a substantial Romanian population alongside many Hungarians and Germans which was a ground for dispute with Austria-Hungary whereas to the east, a similar situation obtained in relation to Russian Bessarabia.

Strategically, Romania was important as it controlled the final stages of the Danube and in particular its access to the Black Sea. This was vital to the Central Powers as it formed the only maritime route whereby predominantly German armaments and supplies could be transported to Turkey. This, in turn, was crucial to Turkey's continuing ability to fight since almost all its arms and equipment were German and it lacked the capacity to manufacture or repair weaponry domestically. The importance of this route increased as the Allies' blockade on other trade routes to Germany tightened so that by 1916, it represented one of Germany's few access routes to the outside world.

Further, Romania was a substantial exporter of grain as well as having the only major European oil wells at Ploesti. This, perhaps more than anything else, underpins the logic behind both Allied and Central Powers' strategy in Eastern Europe with the Germans and Austro-Hungarians clamouring for access to raw materials and foodstuffs and the Allies doing all they could to deny them. As will become apparent, this fundamentally underpinned Allied actions in Russia in 1917-18.

Romania was therefore an important ally for both sides. The Germans seem to have accepted that the best that could be hoped for was continuing neutrality as this would fundamentally give them what they needed whereas for the Allies, a belligerent Romania could not only add a considerable addition in terms of manpower (the Romanian Army was estimated at approximately six hundred thousand) but also in denying the Central Powers' access to the Black Sea as well as Romanian resources. Romania was also strategically well placed to support Russian moves against Austro-Hungary as it could form a southern wing of any offensive thereby threatening the Austro-Hungarian flank.

The advantages to Romania of becoming a belligerent were less clear-cut. Romania would immediately be threatened both by the Austro-Hungarians in the west and north but also by the Bulgarians in the south. Equally, Romania was understandably concerned about long term Russian ambitions to be the dominant Slav power which posed an obvious threat. In hindsight there is much to be said for continuing Romanian neutrality but that must be weighed against the potential advantages that Romania perceived both in obtaining control of Transylvania and increasing its power in South Eastern Europe at the expense of its neighbours. It is important as well to take into account the close cultural and economic ties that existed between Romania and France dating back to Napoleon III's aid in putting Carol I onto the Romanian throne in 1866.

In 1915, Lord Kitchener sent Lieutenant Colonel Christopher Thomson as Military Attaché to Romania. He reported that Romania would be more of a liability than an asset as an ally. He took the view that Romania was vulnerable to attack from Austro-Hungary, Bulgaria and Turkey and that its military forces although numerous were ill prepared and poorly equipped. As a result, he predicted that Romania could become yet another drain on Allied resources as it would need to be supplied with weapons and military advisers. His views although prescient were not accepted and he was instructed to negotiate an alliance with Romania.[107] On 17 August 1916, the Allies and Romania concluded the Treaty of Bucharest which committed Romania to entering the war on the Allied side. The key terms were that in return for declaring war on the Central Powers, Romania would be entitled to territory from Austria-Hungary including Transylvania, Bukovina and the Banat. The former two areas had a majority Romanian population but this could not be said for the Banat which was ethnically even more mixed. Ultimately, Romania received much of its promised territory at the Treaty of Trianon in 1920 and with it a substantial non-Romanian population most of whom were Hungarian and unhappy about the transfer. This unhappiness has not entirely dissipated over the passage of time and it is noteworthy that it was Timisoara with its substantial ethnic Hungarian population which led the revolution against Ceausescu in 1989.

The military articles of the Treaty of Bucharest provided that Russia was to send two infantry and one cavalry divisions to support the Romanians in Dobruja which runs south along the Black Sea coast from Russian held Bessarabia. By doing this, it was hoped that the Bulgarians would be deterred. Equally, the British and French agreed to mount an expedition from their base at Salonika which would serve to tie down Central Powers' (particularly Bulgarian) forces. The Allies also committed to provide military support and expertise together with thirty tons of supplies daily.

Romania declared war on Austria-Hungary on 27 August 1916 and Germany responded by declaring war on Romania on the following day with Bulgaria and Turkey following suit over the next few days. The proposed attack from Salonika under the French General Serrail had been delayed by a spoiling attack by the largely Bulgarian forces in Macedonia. However, it gradually gathered pace and by the time that it fizzled out in October 1916 had advanced approximately twenty five miles and caused the Central Powers to suffer casualties of sixty thousand men although at a cost to the Allies of fifty thousand.

The Romanian army was large for a country of its size but with many vulnerabilities. During the summer of 1916, 813,758 men were called up together with 19,843 officers. Romania also had reserve forces totalling 420,870.[108] It advanced into Transylvania initially meeting with little resistance which was what had been hoped for as the Allies believed that all available German or Austro-Hungarian reserves were committed either to the Western Front where the Somme Offensive had been started in July 1916 together with the ongoing attritional battle at Verdun or, in the east, to fending off the Brusilov Offensive. Unfortunately, this proved to be overly optimistic and Field Marshal August von Mackensen led a multi-national force attacking Dobruja from Bulgaria. Commencing on 1 September, he met with scant resistance and advanced swiftly into Southern Romania.

The Romanians therefore called off their Transylvanian offensive and turned to meet the threat posed by Mackensen and later Falkenhayn. The Romanians were roundly defeated in a series of battles over the coming months and Mackensen took the major port of Constanza on 22 October and Bucharest on 6 December. By 1917, the Romanians had been pushed back to Moldavia on the border with Bessarabia. This left the Central Powers in control of most of Romania and in particular its natural resources. Lieutenant Colonel Thomson had taken responsibility for the destruction of most of the oil assets so denying the Germans their use for many months.

The Romanian government and King Ferdinand was re-established at Jassy in Moldavia. Rather than submit to German demands for an unfavourable armistice, the Romanian government continued its resistance and obtained considerable support from the British and in particular the French. This took the form not only of the supply of weapons and military supplies but also military missions of which the largest was led by the French General, Henri Berthelot, with sixteen hundred men. During 1917, there was a considerable amount of retraining and re-equipping of the Romanian forces by the Allied military missions. This included the proper establishment of a Romanian Air Force with a mixture of French and British aircraft.

The Romanians were able to support the Russians in the doomed Kerensky Offensive and were also able to maintain their control over the rump of the country against extensive German counter offensives led by Mackensen. However, with the collapse of Russian military capabilities following the Bolshevik revolution in November 1917, Romania was isolated not only physically but also from any possible military support. Consequently, it effectively had to surrender to the Central Powers and agree to the Focsani Armistice in December

1917. This coincided with the Bolshevik armistice and effectively brought to an end active hostilities on the Eastern Front. Later, on 7 May 1918, Romania was forced to conclude the Treaty of Bucharest which contained such punitive terms that King Ferdinand refused to sign it. By the Treaty, Romania was required to cede Southern Dobruja and part of North Dobruja to the Bulgarians as well as control of the Carpathian passes to Austria-Hungary. The Central Powers thereby continued to administer part of the country including Bucharest and Constanza. The Romanians also had to grant the Germans a ninety year lease of its oil production centres. By the conclusion of the war, the Germans had repaired the oil facilities and supplied up to one million tons of oil to Germany along with two million tons of grain. These had been critical in keeping the German war effort going during the last months of the war.

It can therefore be seen just how complicated and ultimately fruitless a role Keyes had to perform upon his arrival in Romania in 1917. His principal task of liaising with the Russian forces and producing propaganda to keep them actively contributing towards the allied war effort was almost certainly doomed to failure given the political state in Russia following the February Revolution and completely hopeless once the Kerensky Offensive had ignominiously collapsed. Nonetheless, his efforts were clearly appreciated as he was later made a Knight of the Order of the Star of Romania with Swords by the King of Romania.[109]

The account which Keyes gives of his time in Romania is brief and again more reflective of Keyes than the ostensible subject matter which is the memories invoked by scent. He begins by giving an account of an evening in Donegal where he and his father tried out a horse but then moves on to his first battle and his dying batman's concern for his wellbeing as well as fondness for a particular brand of pipe tobacco.[110] He then proceeds to describe how the scent of raspberry leaves evokes time spent in the Carpathians.

In his account, Keyes, in his role as liaison officer with the Russians, went between the lines prior to the commencement of a Russian offensive. This must have been part of the Kerensky Offensive of June 1917 which swiftly broke down and led to a counterattack by the Germans and Austro-Hungarians that advanced one hundred and fifty miles beyond the Russian start line.[111] This failure and the fact that much of the Russian army refused to fight with many desertions marked the turning point in the Provisional Government's fortunes. Thereafter, it lurched into the crisis of the July Days which it only barely survived and then limped along to the sad conclusion of the Bolshevik takeover of power in November 1917.

Bearing in mind Keyes' attachment to the Russian forces in Romania and that the story takes place in the Carpathians, it is likely that he was at the very southern edge of the offensive.

He recounts how, alongside a Russian Colonel, he crept forward into no-man's-land and they found themselves looking down on an Austrian trench. He was in the position of firing the opening shot in of the offensive but when faced with a cheerful and tuneful Austrian carrying a cooking vessel, deliberately misses. In case that there should be any doubt about his marksmanship, he makes clear that he hit the kettle which the Austrian was carrying "fair in the middle." He adds that he was prouder of that shot that when he "bagged the record Ovis Erskini in a snowstorm on the Kopet Dagh" or shot his first tiger "through the heart" both of which are likely to have required shooting skills of the highest order.[112] This is particularly remarkable given that Keyes was extremely short sighted.[113]

There are many reasons to doubt the veracity of Keyes' account not least that it is extraordinary to think that a Colonel on the Russian staff and a senior British liaison officer would have been permitted to put themselves at risk of injury but more to the point capture bearing in mind the sensitive information to which they would have been party. Normally, they would have been kept busy with staff work at the Russian headquarters some distance away and not allowed to go anywhere near the frontline let alone eighty yards beyond it as Keyes relates. Even at that distance for Keyes to be able to pick out the details of the Austrian soldier and then hit the kettle which he was carrying defies belief.

Keyes then recounted how he and the Colonel remained hidden amongst the wild raspberries for several hours before returning to the Russian lines. Whilst they were there, the Austrians put down a barrage between the Russian lines and their reserves which, despite their inept fusing, caused many Russian casualties. On their return, Keyes had to dissuade the by then disconsolate Colonel from committing suicide. The story is also illustrative of the attitudes and mores of that time. Keyes places himself at the centre of events and clearly amongst Russian panic and despair is the only one with any grip. The Russian soldiers mostly run away and the only officer identified wishes to commit suicide. As for the Austrian, he is something of a stereotype down to the fair hair, big belly and cheerful song. Nevertheless, he fares better than his imagined wife, "a broad bosomed cow-like woman with the motherhood of the world in her eyes."[114] Notwithstanding all that is going on around him, Keyes alone remained calm and in control. In reality, it must have been extraordinarily difficult for him to deal with bearing in mind all his previous experience and would certainly have made his task of persuading the Russians attached to Romanian forces to keep fighting even though their homeland was convulsed with revolution and economic chaos almost impossible.

Prior to going to Romania, Keyes had been very briefly posted to the British Embassy in Petrograd "nominally running military propaganda, I was really doing political intelligence for the Ambassador."[115] He had left Petrograd in late June or early July 1917. The clearest evidence available about Keyes' time in Romania comes from a letter to his brother Roger dated 31 July 1917. Like Keyes' other letters, it goes into some detail about his actions and also his view of the political situation. Presumably, it was sent by diplomatic bag as its contents would have definitely been of interest to the Russian intelligence service and he must have been confident that it would not have been intercepted.[116]

In it, Keyes gives a description of the July Days - the political and economic dislocation caused by the rioting against the Provisional Government led by Alexander Kerensky. This was a precursor of the later Bolshevik coup in October 1917 and caused embarrassment to Lenin and Trotsky when details of the funding which the Bolsheviks had received from Germany became public. What emerges from Keyes' letter is that the Russian army was in a state of collapse with "thousands of soldiers...travelling on each train - like swarms of bees on the roofs and footboards."

On arrival at the Romanian Headquarters in Jassy, he learned of the failure of the Kerensky Offensive and that any advance that had been made was down to "our armoured cars, a Brigade of Austrian prisoners and by a few Russian regiments, whose first wave consisted almost entirely of officers." The reference to "our" armoured cars was to the Armoured Car Expeditionary Force led by the extraordinary freebooter, Oliver Locker Lampson, which fought on various sections of the Eastern Front including Galicia. Locker Lampson seems to have paid scant attention to orders and operated more or less as an independent agent. This account is consistent with other sources and is likely to be true. It also throws Keyes' account of witnessing the commencement of the Offensive into doubt.

Keyes deplored the proliferation of soldiers' committees which had sprung up and which crippled any concept of military discipline and which must have been entirely alien to him. He attributed the poor discipline and morale of the Russian infantry to the influence of agitators as well as the formation of "death battalions" which had taken all the elite and committed troops leaving the remaining ones vulnerable to politicisation. Keyes placed the source of revolutionary activity as being the cities, principally, Kiev and Odessa - the latter being "full of pro-German Jews and spies." He also identified the source of radical thought as coming from the middle classes who were militating for a general peace with no indemnities or reparations - "all the lawyers who heckled me said that all powers were equally guilty and all must subscribe for the restoration of Belgium and

Servia. One could generally convince them in the end but they are such an unstable lot that all the good that is done is probably undone the next day."[117]

Keyes' willingness to engage in political discussions in such a fractious and combustible environment is extraordinary although equally remarkable is the respect which he received from local Russian and Ukrainians. This is probably as a result of the Anglophilia which spread throughout Russia in the run up to the revolutions of 1917; the principal cause being increased British supplies of armaments and other materiel as well as direct military assistance such as Locker Lampson's armoured cars.

The power of the army committees is emphasised by Keyes who explained how the one in the Russian IX Army worked. This consisted of one hundred and twenty men including some officers who controlled military transport, "enquiries [in respect of] deserters, press, library etc. and one for the propagation of revolutionary ideas among the Romanians" so that "when the Queen [of Romania] came out to open a hospital the other day Russian soldiers tried to persuade Romanian soldiers to arrest her. This committee is subsidised by the Army Staff!."

In contrast to his pessimistic view of the Russian forces, Keyes was impressed by the largely French trained Romanians who had been badly let down by the Russian forces in Galicia and so had had to call off their own offensive and were concerned that they would be abandoned to the Germans by a Russian retreat as indeed later took place. Keyes foresaw trouble in this area and accurately predicted of the Russians that "unless there is a miraculous change in their spirit I am afraid that they won't stick it after November." He was later to complain bitterly about the way in which the French had been willing to incite the Romanians and later the Ukrainians to fight the Germans when they faced inevitable defeat. He very plausibly was of the opinion that the French realised what they were asking their allies to do but believed it justified because of the temporary alleviation of pressure on them on the Western Front.

Keyes speculated about the best way forward for Russia and summed up the whole problem of the British position namely that Russia was in the process of collapse and the only hope for its salvation lay in "a dictator" but that there were too many competing factors "the country is so enormous, the different races so opposed to each other, the people so ignorant and so easily swayed by the countless half educated but plausible agitators who are some of them genuine but many in German pay." However, with all of this going on, British policy was still to keep Russia in the war which was in direct contradiction to the position on the ground.

For all his hatred of Bolshevism and instinctive conservative and imperialist views, Keyes was astute enough to identify the structural problems that the old regime (and those who wished to return to it) faced. He recounts a Russian General saying that "it was impossible to force men to face death in front unless they had the fear of death in the rear" and that "all the other generals agreed with him…. I am afraid to say that this is how the Russian officer still looks on his men and they have no idea of initiating a new discipline, or getting in touch with their men except by the reintroduction of all the old abuses." There is a note of sheer hopelessness in Keyes' account of his time in Romania which continued during his time in Russia.

It is not clear quite how many other British officers were working alongside Keyes at the time. The party certainly included Major J K L Fitzwilliams who following long service on the Western Front had been posted to act as propaganda officer to the Russian troops in Romanian-Hungarian frontier. Fitzwilliams, like Keyes, was also involved in intelligence issues and was later required to carry £40,000 in cash with the promise of more to Ukrainians and Cossacks to persuade them to continue to oppose the Germans.[118] Unlike Keyes, however, he was primarily a soldier and returned to active service before being killed in France on 30 August 1918.

Keyes' role in Romania brought him into contact with the Romanian Royal Family and he recounted how on the day of his return to Petrograd which was probably sometime in late September or early October 1917, he was summoned to a meeting with both the King and Queen. The King clearly impressed him and he described him as a "gallant gentleman, certainly the first gentleman in Romania" and, although he was a Hohenzollern and his Court originally "Boschophil" he had "stuck to the Allies like a hero." He was equally impressed by the Queen, Marie who was a granddaughter of Queen Victoria and had been brought up in part in England. Keyes described her as "an extraordinarily beautiful and attractive woman [although] her voice is not quite so attractive as the rest of her." It is testament to the level of trust that Keyes had inspired that she gave him "one rather delicate mission to perform in Petrograd and asked me to try to get a letter through to her sister, the Grand Duchess Kiril who is in Finland."[119] His assistance was appreciated and remembered and he was made an Officer of the Order of the Crown of Romania in January 1920.

Chapter 8:

Russia - Background to Revolution

It is difficult at this point in time to see Russia in the way that it must have appeared prior to the First World War; namely, as a leading exporting nation blessed with bounteous natural resources and a rapidly growing population. In other ways, arguably little has changed; Russia remains essentially an autocracy and has an underdeveloped professional middle class made worse by a dysfunctional legal and administrative system. Overall, the difference is one of world perception; in 1900, Russia was regarded as the future whereas now it is regarded as the burnt out rump of a failed political experiment that slaughtered its own people and wrecked its economy. Then, it was then perceived as a future world leader in manufacturing and agriculture which was reflected in phenomenal growth in urban areas whereas now it is overly dependent upon natural resources and struggling with decaying infrastructure and a declining population.

In the early part of the twentieth century, Russia was an economic powerhouse racing to catch up with the leading western economies. Between 1850 and 1905, Russia increased its railway system from eight hundred and fifty miles to almost forty thousand, its oil industry rivalled that of the United States and it was the fifth largest industrial power in the world. The pace of growth had quickened in the years leading up to 1914 so that between 1900 and 1905, the gross output of Russian industry had increased by forty five percent and, even allowing for the economic slump following on from the Russo-Japanese war, it continued to increase. Using 1900 as a base line, output had grown by over two hundred percent by 1913. The rate of growth in industrial capital stock during the same period was three times higher than the United States.[120]

The changes came about largely through foreign capital investment so that France - which had lost many of its coalfields when Alsace-Lorraine was annexed by the Germans in 1870 - became a controlling force in the Russian coal and iron industries in the Donetz basin and on the Don. Over half of all French overseas investments went to Russia in 1902 and the trend continued in the period leading up to 1914. All of this investment was effectively written off as a result of the revolution. The severe impact upon the French economy of such a loss was masked by the economic devastation caused by the dislocation and near bankruptcy caused by the First World War.

The French also had political reasons to invest in Russia following the Franco-Russian Alliance of 1892 which formed the main plank in French diplomatic efforts against Germany. French loans were made on favourable terms to enable Russia to modernise its military capabilities and also to improve its railway connections with its western borders. The Franco-Russian Alliance provided for each country to mobilise and indeed declare war on the Triple Alliance of Germany, Austro-Hungary and Italy should any of those nations mobilise or declare war on France or Russia. Accordingly, it was imperative for France that Russia could compete in the race to mobilise. This investment may ultimately have actually paid off as Russian mobilisation in 1914 was far swifter than anticipated by the Germans and led to the drawing away of troops from the west to meet it. It is likely that it was this weakening of the German forces that prevented a German victory in France in August and September 1914.

Britain's relationship with Russia was less clear-cut and was in many ways contradictory. Britain saw Russia as a disruptive force in Southern Asia and increasing Russian military capacity was the cause of great alarm. Equally, Britain had marked and longstanding objections to Russian ambitions to gain unfettered access to the Mediterranean. Against that, Britain's role as the dominant financial power inevitably meant that it would be drawn to what was then the world's leading investment target. Accordingly, Britain had invested heavily in the oil industry in the Caucasus and the copper and platinum extraction industries in the Urals and Caucasus were controlled by British and American consortia. Britain also played a major part in the development of the Russian cotton industry with a Lancastrian diaspora helping establish and operate Russian mills. Robert Bruce Lockhart, as a junior Consul in Moscow would regularly turn out for Harry Charnok's Morozovtsy football club "the best team in Russia" and which mostly consisted of expatriate mill workers.[121]

Other countries had also invested heavily so that Russian trams in the main towns were operated by Belgian companies and approximately seventy percent of Russian electrical companies were ultimately under German control. The financial investment in Russia funded its growth and the gradual modernisation of its industry. It also enabled the opening up of Siberia which was seen in much the same way as the American West had been in the previous century. This led to a threefold increase in the amount of Siberian land under cultivation as well as the doubling of its population between 1905-14. Overall, Russian agricultural exports, chiefly grain, rose tenfold and by 1912, Russian grain exports mostly shipped from South Russia and Odessa in particular exceeded those of the United States, Canada and Argentina combined. The relative insignificance of the present day Russian grain trade is testimony to what was lost.

There are many parallels to be drawn between pre-war Russian and the present day emerging economies; both attracted substantial inward investment and increased foreign influence if not absolute control over substantial sections of the economy. The foreign control was far from popular and, in the short term, meant that the Russian economy was vulnerable. This was to become painfully clear when the global financial markets were fundamentally disrupted by the First World War.

Another parallel is that both in the pre-revolutionary boom and currently, the political structures lagged far behind economic developments. Tsarist Russia had a population of one hundred and thirty million in 1897 of whom eighty percent were peasants and one and half percent nobility the remaining eighteen and a half percent were spread between various recognised grades of society such as priests, townsmen and merchants. The fastest growing group was the urban working class who primarily worked in the newly prospering manufacturing concerns. By 1900, there were almost two million of them - about the same number as there were nobility. Most of them were peasants or the children of peasants who had made their way to the cities attracted by the possibility of higher wages. However, they found that the civic infrastructure lagged far behind so that accommodation was scarce and expensive with the result that some workers ended up sleeping underneath their workbench. Town planning was rudimentary which led to factories being built in residential areas and a wholesale failure to meet the increased need for sanitation. By 1870, St Petersburg had the highest mortality rate of any of the major cities in Europe and typhus and cholera epidemics were a regular occurrence

In many ways the industrial working class in Russia resembled the black population in the United States. They had both been legally emancipated from servitude at the same time - 1861 in Russia and 1862 in the Federal controlled part of the United States. Both had found that emancipation was more of a legal concept than anything tangible so that the conditions of those who remained on the land remained broadly the same. Those that moved to the cities found themselves vulnerable to exploitation by their employers as there were no protective employment legislation and they were also prey to slum landlords in an environment where the available housing stock was failing to keep pace with the ever burgeoning urban population. Poverty was endemic and in many cities there were no-go areas where crime and prostitution was rife. Such people were ready for revolution as they had no viable stake in the society in which they lived.

The peasants who remained on the land found only modest changes to their living standards and their world continued to revolve around the *mir* or village. The more enlightened members of the government recognised the need for change and Pyotr Stolypin, when he was prime minister (1906-11), began to implement land reforms that created a new landowning peasant class who became known as Kulaks. He established the Peasant Land Bank which would purchase land from private owners and then sell it on to Kulaks. He also cancelled Redemption Payments which bound the peasants to the land by saddling them with crippling repayments to the state to recompense it for paying off the landowners for agreeing to emancipation. By doing this, Stolypin broke the power of the village commune and permitted private as opposed to family or communal ownership. His reforms were only partially successful so that although up to fifteen percent of peasants became Kulaks, there was resentment from the remainder and the changes were unpopular with some nobility who were pressurised to offload their family land. Others, however, were happy to take advantage of the rising land price and were willing sellers.

The reforms also fuelled the move to the towns as peasants disposed of their interests in land and sought new lives in the burgeoning factories. Stolypin's rule was controversial and he was unpopular in many sectors of Russian society and this led to his dismissal in 1911. However, it is telling that when he was assassinated in September of the same year, the Tsar begged for forgiveness whereas the far more reactionary Tsarina said "he is gone, let us hear no more of him."

The Russian nobility had traditionally maintained order in the countryside where local government was rudimentary. Their grasp weakened in the years leading up to 1914 but remained powerful. Those nobles who remained were isolated in a sea of increasingly disaffected peasantry which would in time led to the chaos of 1917 when all the landed estates were swept away frequently with much bloodshed and destruction of property. By then however, many noble families had sold or reduced their agricultural landholdings and reinvested the proceeds in property and stocks and bonds. The nobility were not only landowners and rentiers but also traditionally the official class that dominated administration, the military and the professions. They together with the urban middle class essentially constituted what amounted to the intellectual life of Russia; it is no accident that a sizeable number of the revolutionaries - including Lenin, Dzerzhinsky who founded the Cheka and Kerensky were of noble origin.

Russian expansionism in the nineteenth century had increased the size of the empire but then failed to assimilate the varying non-Russian peoples who had been conquered. Russian rule - particularly in the Caucasus and Central Asia - effectively amounted to occupation and the policy of Russification introduced in an attempt to bind the empire together merely stoked up resentment and national movements. This was particularly the case in the west where the Poles Balts and Finns all had vibrant national movements in the early twentieth century which not only expressed themselves politically but also culturally.

The lack of sophistication of Russian political structures contributed towards the inability needed to manage a fast growing economy and rapidly increasing population. Increasingly, the state bureaucracy proved to be leaden footed and inept in dealing with demands for change and the autocratic nature of government meant that only the smallest proportion of the population had any stake in society so that even noble families were increasingly alienated by Tsarist rule. In many ways, it was the worst of both worlds, the bureaucracy acted as a brake on change whilst failing to administer effectively. In such a society grievances were rarely addressed and pressure for change came from all sections of society.

Russia's involvement in the First World War put all the tensions inherent in society under extreme pressure. The administration successfully managed to call up enormous armies but then failed to supply them adequately with food and clothing let alone weapons. By the time these defects were addressed, too many defeats had been suffered and too much territory lost. Russia also suffered greatly not only from state interference in the economy but also the loss of much of its export market with the closure of access to the Mediterranean in 1914. Trade continued particularly from Vladivostok in the east and the northern ports of Murmansk and Archangel but at a much reduced level. Similarly, although the British and French had the potential to supply many of the weapons which the Russian army needed, difficulties of supply were great. It was not until late 1916 that these logistical problems were overcome and by then the Russian war effort had been hollowed out.

Russia's antiquated bureaucracy was notoriously incompetent and corrupt and this was dangerously exposed in wartime. Many of the difficulties with obtaining munitions can be attributed to the failure to coordinate purchasing policies which would have ensured that a large amount of a limited range of weapons or other materiel were acquired. Instead, there was a multiplicity of types and occasions where Russian purchasing agents from different departments ended up bidding against each other with foreign suppliers. The situation was not helped by the endemic corruption in Russian life both in terms of the administration and business where a culture of kickbacks and nepotism undermined the conduct of trade and in particular the supply of goods to the government.

Russian contribution to the war effort was critical to Allied strategy as it was only by forcing the Central Powers to divide their forces that the Allies believed that they had a chance of victory. This was not only for military reasons as peace with Russia would allow Germany to build up a preponderant force in the west but it was also because it would break the Allied blockade and allow the Central Powers access to food and raw materials denied to them largely by the British Navy. It was therefore imperative that Russia remained a combatant if at all possible failing which that it continued to deny Germany and Austria-Hungary access to its natural resources. The impact of the blockade on German and Austro-Hungarian industrial output increased as the war went on and the British were able to close off loopholes with neutral countries particularly Holland and Norway; German imports from Sweden were never entirely blocked and there remained a large pro-German lobby in Sweden throughout the first (and indeed second) world war.

The British had originally envisaged that their role in any war would largely be limited to enforcing an effective blockade and providing financial and military support to Russia and France both of which, with their large conscript armies would do the bulk of the actual land fighting. The British believed that their military commitment would be limited to the relatively small expeditionary force with the remainder of the army engaged on imperial garrison duty. This role was effectively a re-run of British policy in the Napoleonic wars and, certainly, Britain had invested very heavily in its navy so that it could fulfil this part of its bargain. Whilst the value of an effective blockade remained a vital part of overall Allied policy, the illusion of a limited military commitment was soon dispelled. Gradually too, Allied hopes of the Russian steamroller achieving victory in the east faded and with increasing realism dawned the need to prop up the Russian war effort so that it could at least continue to tie down a large part of the Central Powers' forces not only in Eastern Europe but also in the Caucasus and Eastern Anatolia. It was this pressing need to supply Russia that gave impetus to the Gallipoli campaign and the later landing in Salonika.

Chapter 9:

British Presence in Russia

Until 1914, the British maintained a relatively small diplomatic presence centred upon the Embassy in St Petersburg. There was the larger but less well regarded Consular Service in cities throughout the country that concentrated more upon visa and trade issues. The Consular Service was however an important source of information for the Ambassador whose staff only rarely left the capital.

Before the war, there were relatively few Embassy staff but they were often socially very well connected not least because all new entrants to the Diplomatic Service were required to have a private income of at least £400 per annum and to receive a personal endorsement from the Foreign Secretary.[122] This, of course limited the class and type of entrants particularly since junior officials were not paid at all for the first two years of their service. The situation did not much improve thereafter as pay levels only rose to a reasonable level for senior ranks notwithstanding the expectation that all staff would participate in local society. Unlike the Consular staff, members of the Diplomatic Service were barred from supplementing their earnings by journalism which made maintaining a reasonable standard of living even harder for those without substantial private means particularly in St Petersburg where accommodation was limited and therefore expensive.

Embassy and Consular staff performed roles that had long been set out for them. Robert Bruce Lockhart describes his first visit as a Consular official to the Embassy in Petrograd in 1915. Notwithstanding the growth in the size and scope of the work carried out in the Embassy following the declaration of war - not all of it directly at the behest of the Ambassador - he was struck by the fact that typing and ciphering was being carried out by Old Etonian junior officers rather than clerks.[123] This did change in the light of wartime demands but the whiff of amateurism remained and the Diplomatic Corps came in for much criticism not least for failing to head off the rush to war in 1914. This seems unfair since, although many members of the Diplomatic Service gave an impression of insouciance, there was also much hard work done. As for criticism by politicians, this too could be seen as self-serving; the Government could and did when it had to, increase the resources available to the Diplomatic Service which, in turn, enabled it to attract talent from a wider spectrum of society. In any event, the principal decisions which led to the declaration of war in 1914 were ultimately taken by professional politicians rather than diplomats.

The British Ambassador to St Petersburg between 1910 and January 1918 was Sir George Buchanan who was a career diplomat and who fought to maintain the traditional role of Diplomatic Service at a time when it was under increasing pressure to permit large scale espionage operations to be conducted from the Embassy building. Although Buchanan never mastered Russian, this was less of a handicap at a time when most of the people he dealt with would habitually speak French or English. He also came to have the ear of the Tsar although his advice was generally not acted upon because of the hostility of the Tsarina.

Buchanan was initially of the view that the Bolshevik coup in November 1917 would eventually break down through lack of support and that Lenin would have to form a new coalition with some of the socialist parties resulting in a reversion to the instability that had become normal during the existence of the Provisional Government. Like many others, he was not prepared for the brutality that the Bolsheviks would employ to remain in power. On 16 November 1917, he informed London that the Bolsheviks would "discredit themselves before many weeks are over" but he soon became increasingly pessimistic and on 16 January reported that "Bolshevists are masters in the North and... are regaining the upper hand in Moscow." In the next two months, whilst he continued to be strongly anti-Bolshevik, Buchanan increasingly was of the view that

Britain should give de facto recognition to the Bolsheviks as being the established government since this would protect the relatively large British contingent resident in Russia and assist with their evacuation. He had also recommended that Russia be released from its treaty obligations to continue the war as he believed that it was pointless to "force an exhausted nation to fight against its will."

These two views were in direct contradiction of the more aggressive approach favoured by most of the military representatives in Russia who, with some reason, regarded the Bolsheviks as being in German pay and were already manoeuvring towards active intervention in Russian politics with a view to securing a new government. In very general terms, there was to emerge a tension between the Foreign Office and War Office over the best approach to handle the Bolshevik issue which was never entirely resolved and contributed towards the contradictory nature of British policy over the coming years.

Although, in some ways a typical diplomat - his father had been an Ambassador as well and he was said to have an austere and distant manner - Buchanan took pains to ensure that information obtained was accurate and thoughtful and he clearly was regarded as having the utmost integrity. Bruce Lockhart described him as having "remarkable powers of intuition and an abundant supply of common sense. To Russian cleverness he opposed complete honesty and sincerity tempered with caution." He was also in many ways almost a caricature of a career diplomat and "was worshipped by his staff. When he took his daily walk to the Russian Foreign Office, his hat cocked on one side, his tall, lean figure slightly drooping under his many cares, every Englishman felt that here as much as the diplomatic precincts of the Embassy itself was a piece of the soil of England."[124]

Bruce Lockhart's views have to be treated with some caution as he was an avid self-promoter who, as will be seen, endeavoured to establish close personal relations with the Bolsheviks - particularly Karl Radek, George Chicherin and most of all, Leon Trotsky. It is more likely than not that whilst he was claiming to have established a position of influence over them, they took advantage of his ambitions to play a significant political role to their own ends. His memoirs were written almost fifteen years' after the Revolution and paint a very different picture from what appears from the records. It suited his narrative to praise Buchanan, who was one of his few locally based supporters. His real influence lay in the respect that his dispatches commanded in London particularly from Lloyd George who had a well-established aversion to career diplomats and saw in Bruce Lockhart another Celtic chancer striving for recognition.[125] Buchanan was assisted from summer 1915 by Francis Lindley who was appointed Acting Counsellor and became Chargé d'Affaires when Buchanan left Russia in January 1918, broken in health and spirit.

The British Embassy's traditional policy of being detached from local politics was increasingly compromised as the war progressed and following the Bolshevik takeover, interference was more or less overt. This had led to an ambiguous and sometimes contradictory approach being taken even before 1917 with steps being taken not only to gather intelligence but also to influence government policy. As a consequence, Buchanan had to have painful interviews with the Tsar in which he unsuccessfully urged him to institute reforms. The position was further complicated by the rapid growth of the British Military Mission following the declaration of war. This was led by General Sir John Hanbury-Williams but he spent most of his time at the Russian military headquarters or *Stavka* and the principal work carried out in Petrograd was done by the experienced Alfred Knox who was Military Attaché.

A further complication was the establishment of the British Intelligence Mission which, as its name implied, was principally concerned with information gathering and increasingly espionage. As the war progressed, the size of the Intelligence Mission increased, as did its involvement in espionage as well as domestic politics. There was therefore a bureaucratic turf war with Buchanan and the Foreign Office insisting that the Embassy should be the principal source of information on Russian affairs as opposed to the Intelligence Mission which reported to the War Office. This tension was never entirely resolved and also contributed to the ambiguity in British policy which became increasingly apparent as the Bolsheviks gained overall control.

During the course of the war there were a number of missions to Russia from various government departments including the Treasury but, inevitably, most of them were of a military nature. As mentioned in Chapter 7, one of the most colourful was Locker Lampson's squadron of armoured cars which, although part of the Royal Naval Air Service, appears to have gone more or less where its commander wished. As well as playing a part in the Kerensky Offensive in July 1917 where his activities were favourably noted by Keyes, Locker Lampson later played a small and rather questionable role in the attempted coup led by General Kornilov in July 1917 when he intended that his squadron would support Kornilov. It is telling that although Locker Lampson was meant to report to Buchanan, he deliberately chose not to inform him of his intriguing with Kornilov. He did however report to General Sir Charles Barter who had replaced Hanbury-Williams as British representative at *Stavka*. Astonishingly, Barter in reporting to the War Office requested that "this information be kept entirely secret, especially from our Ambassador in Petrograd", no doubt because he feared that Buchanan would actively seek to prevent this reckless scheme from taking place.[126]

One of the most relevant actions by the British was the creation of the Russia Supply Committee (which became known as Rusplycom) by Lord Milner and Sir Henry Wilson in January 1917 with the aim of ensuring that British military supplies were properly distributed and did not fall prey to the corruption and inefficiencies of the Russian logistics system. Lord Milner was a colonial administrator who had played an important role in the Boer War and, as someone with experience of efficient administration, had been brought in by Lloyd George when he became Prime Minister in December 1916 even though he was both an imperialist and Tory. General Sir Henry Wilson had been instrumental in establishing close relations with the French military and Brigadier Foch (as he then was) in particular and it is largely down to his efforts that the British Expeditionary Force reached France as quickly as it did in 1914. He was a military politician who was not altogether trusted. Asquith, who never forgave him for encouraging the Curragh Mutiny against Home Rule in 1914, described him as that "poisonous tho' clever ruffian."[127]

The urgent need to ensure the efficient supply of munitions and other materiel to the Russian military was readily apparent from increasing evidence of Russian military and political collapse and, on a practical basis, was assisted by the creation of a rail link to the ice free port of Murmansk which would enable the rapid transportation of British supplies to the Russian military. Milner and Wilson appointed Brig Gen F C Poole to ensure that supplies were efficiently dispatched. Poole had retired from the Army with the rank of Major before re-joining on the commencement of the war. He was well known to Wilson having been on his staff in France. He was successful in overcoming many practical difficulties and British equipment became more widely available as a result. Rusplycom's mission was transformed by the Bolshevik takeover and the commencement of peace negotiations with the Germans that eventually led to the Treaty of Brest-Litovsk. Once it became clear that the Bolsheviks had little intention of actively fighting the Germans, Poole's chief objective was to prevent not only British supplies but also other commodities including foodstuffs and raw materials falling into German hands.

Keyes was appointed to Poole's staff in late 1917 to handle political matters but he himself describes his role as "doing political intelligence work for the Ambassador." This ambiguity perhaps underscores the clandestine nature of Keyes' role which clearly included close links with the British Secret Service.[128] It is likely that officially his role was kept deliberately vague. Keyes was at all times an ardent interventionist and invariably took the more aggressive

War Office line rather than the more conciliatory one held by the Foreign Office.

The problems that those on the ground faced was that British strategy not only changed during the course of the war but, at many times, was confused and often contradictory. The one overarching aim was to keep the Russians fighting and holding down as many Central Powers' troops as possible. The main strategic advantage that the Allies had was that both Germany and Austria-Hungary had to fight on two fronts and this not only was costly in terms of military commitment but Russia also forced Germany in particular into providing military and financial support to its much weaker allies, Austria-Hungary and Bulgaria. The existence of an Eastern Front also completed Germany and Austro-Hungary's economic encirclement. The importance of the blockade became increasingly apparent as the war progressed and Germany failed to find adequate alternatives to its dwindling domestic supply of foodstuffs and industrial raw materials. A neutral Russia that renewed its trading relationship with Germany could undo all the damage that was being caused to the German economy by virtue of this blockade. Accordingly, all steps possible were taken to keep Russia engaged as an active participant. This led to Allied pressure on the Provisional Government to mount the Kerensky Offensive in July 1917 which ultimately proved to be counter-productive as it destroyed the Russian military as an effective force. After that, Allied attentions were concentrated upon doing all possible to keep Russia as a belligerent albeit a quiescent one.

At the same time, considerable efforts were expended in trying to prevent the Germans from enjoying the fruits of their conquests by denying them access to Russian markets and raw materials. This is what informed the volte face in General Poole's mission whereby his primary objective switched from supplying the Russian military to buying up goods and raw materials so that the Germans would not be able to obtain them. Poole was also understandably very concerned about protecting the extensive supply depots which had been built up in Vladivostok, Archangel and Murmansk particularly the latter bearing in mind its geographic proximity to newly independent and pro-German Finland.

Equally, the Naval Attaché, Captain Francis Cromie, spent much of his time pursuing schemes to ensure that Russian naval assets did not fall into the hands of the Germans. It is not clear to what extent these bore fruit but it is certainly the case that a large part of the Russian fleet at Novorossiysk was scuttled in June 1918 although on this occasion British and Bolshevik aims had coalesced. Cromie was also implicated in extensive espionage activities and played a part in what became known as the Lockhart coup attempt in August 1918, a rather mysterious move to overthrow the Bolsheviks and replace them with a more tractable government. As will be seen in Chapter 17, it is unclear to what extent this plot was engineered from its outset by the Bolshevik secret police, the Cheka but it had certainly been compromised. In the aftermath, the Bolsheviks with some justification decided that the Embassy or what was still left of it in Petrograd was a hotbed of spies and launched a raid in the course of which Cromie was shot and killed.

The Bolshevik takeover caused a major rethink in British policy but the dominant desire to keep Russia from making peace with Germany and, if it did, from gaining access to Russian resources and foodstuffs remained in place. The immediate commencement of peace negotiations with Germany by the Bolsheviks caused great concern and led to a divergence in British thinking even up to Cabinet level, some, like Buchanan and later Lindley and even more vociferously, Bruce Lockhart advocating de facto recognition and even military support, others particularly, those with a military background such as Poole and Cromie, believing that the primary objective had to be the overthrow of the Bolsheviks. In reality, no firm decision on this was ever reached and the British continued with contradictory policies which rendered both approaches nugatory. So, for example, Bruce Lockhart spent much time trying to convince Trotsky, with whom he had particularly close relations, that British support would be forthcoming should the Bolsheviks decide to break off negotiations with the Germans whilst, at the same time, different parts of the British presence were giving support to any number of counter-revolutionary schemes. Trotsky was well aware of this from Cheka sources and anyway is likely to have been playing Bruce Lockhart along the whole time. He accurately informed Bruce Lockhart that British "policy towards Russia right from the beginning has been indecisive and vacillating.[129]

From a German perspective, things were not much clearer. If the overarching principle behind British policy was to keep the Russians in the war, the opposite was plainly true for them. The whole of German pre-war thinking had been to prevent the long-term continuation of a war on two fronts but with the failure of the German offensive in the west, this had become inevitable. The Germans knew by 1915 that they could never win the war militarily by conventional means and this is what led Falkenhayn, the Commander in Chief of the German Army, to resort to measures which had previously been considered unlawful. These included the use of poison gas which was used for the first time on the Eastern Front at Bolimow on 31 January 1915, unrestricted submarine warfare and also the use of Zeppelins to bomb London which also began in January 1915.

The Germans also actively embarked upon a campaign of political destabilisation against the Allies with a view to creating internal dissent and possible change of government. Prominent amongst these were the campaigns against the British in Persia and India. The German main effort however was against Russia which was rightly seen as being particularly vulnerable because of the dislocation between the autocracy and many of its educated subjects. The Germans therefore made contact with a range of potential opponents of the Tsar ranging from liberals such as the Cadets to more revolutionary parties. The idea of fomenting socialist revolution even in an enemy country was not something that would have been countenanced prior to 1915. As well as being thought unacceptable, it also carried with it the risk of backfiring with revolutionary contagion spreading back to

Germany itself. This indeed proved to be the case and by 1918, the German army in the east was increasingly politically infected with the revolutionary virus. This spread to forces on the Western Front when Germany was finally able to transfer men west following the Treaty of Brest-Litovsk.

The extent of German links to the Bolsheviks remains unresolved. There is no doubt about their role in permitting Lenin to travel from Switzerland to Russia in April 1917 on what became known as the Sealed Train. However, the connection between the German Foreign Office and Secret Service and the Bolsheviks remains murky. One of the key figures is Alexander Helphand, also known as Parvus, a professional revolutionary who had been brought up in Odessa. He also spent much time in Germany and Turkey and probably was recruited by the German Secret Service some time after the 1905 revolution. By 1915, Helphand was in touch with the German High Command and presented a plan for the revolutionary destabilisation of Russia called "Germany and the Revolution in Russia." Helphand met Lenin briefly in 1915 but thereafter Lenin was at pains to avoid further contact. Whether this was because Lenin saw through him or because he perceived a need to remain distant from a relationship that might prove dangerous is not certain. What is certain is that over the coming years, the Germans indirectly provided considerable funds to the Bolsheviks and that these were largely used in spreading anti-Tsar and anti-war propaganda in Russia.

Understandably, the Bolsheviks were at great pains to deny the extent to which they were in German pay and the discovery of damning evidence of such contact led to Lenin's flight to Finland during the July Days. Typically, the Provisional Government failed to push the matter with sufficient vigour - it would certainly have justified the death penalty against Lenin and Zinoviev - and allowed the issue to become bogged down in an official investigation which had failed to make much progress by the time of the October Revolution. The Bolsheviks' paranoia about being exposed as being recipients of German funds, is shown by the case of one NM Weinberg who was the Petrograd agent for a Berlin based bank, Mendelsohn & Co. Weinberg was adamant that he had paid Bolsheviks twelve million Roubles on behalf of the German Government in January 1918. These payments had been against receipts allegedly signed by Lenin, Trotsky and Dzerzhinsky, the head of the Cheka.[130] In November 1918, Weinberg was arrested and interrogated by Dzerzhinsky personally who required the return of the original receipts. When Weinberg failed to hand them over because they had already been sent back to Berlin, he was tortured and then shot.

The fact that the Bolsheviks received German money and were understandably sensitive about it does not mean that they were German agents. Even though the British were in no doubt that they were, there is scant evidence of the Bolsheviks acting on German instructions following the October Revolution. Having said that, the terms agreed by the Bolsheviks at Brest-Litovsk were punitive and Russia lost eighteen provinces and thirty percent of its pre-war population which might hint a degree of payback for German support but equally it reflected the hopelessness of the Bolsheviks' bargaining position. Either way, the Germans ultimately gained dominance over much of the Ukraine with its agricultural resources as well as the iron and steel and mining industries. It is noteworthy that the final stages of the negotiations with the Germans were carried out by Lenin personally; whether or not his decision to accede to all German demands was practical politics or the result of clandestine links is unclear.

Keyes' transfer to Petrograd therefore was played out against a backdrop of a number of tensions with the British desperate to keep Russia involved in the war ideally as a belligerent not only to prevent the Germans gaining access to Russian resources but also to tie down as many troops as possible to prevent them being transferred to the Western Front where major German offensives were anticipated.

Chapter 10:

November 1917

Up until 1917, Keyes had baulked at being at what he saw as the sidelines of the war. He had disliked being in Bahrain between 1914-16 and would happily have swapped his role as Resident for fighting on the Western Front.[131] It is unclear whether he saw his subsequent posting to Mekran in 1916 in the same light for, whilst it at least involved action, he remained very much of the edges of the conflict that convulsed Europe and in which so many of his family and friends were engaged. It must have been frustrating for someone who clearly wished to play a significant role in world affairs to be stuck mediating peace treaties with tribesmen who he plainly regarded as being untrustworthy primitives and he could not fail to view his career in sharp contradistinction with others, not least his Naval brother Roger whose role in the Dardanelles and then commanding the Dover Patrol was at the heart of wartime action.

After his brief posting in Romania, Keyes returned to Petrograd in autumn 1917 and found himself at the epicentre of world affairs and would soon be taking part in events which would define his career and overshadow the remainder of his life. They would not only colour his political outlook; for the remainder of his life he would be an outspoken anti-Bolshevik but also his career as, for the first time, he became implicated in the failure of British policies. It also damaged his health since, by 1920, there is evidence that he was in practical terms burned out and close to a breakdown. The consequences of his actions in Russia continued to plague him for the rest of his career and, in particular, right up until the 1930s, he was regularly called upon to give evidence in litigation arising from British plans to gain control of certain Russian banks ("the Bank Schemes").[132]

The events leading up to the Bolshevik takeover have been covered in great detail over the years with numerous versions of events being put forward. It was, in many ways, the founding myth of the Russian Communist Party that the workers spontaneously rose en masse to overthrow bourgeois tyranny. This was advanced as early as 1919 by John Reed in *"10 Days That Shook the World"* where he describes how "on every corner immense crowds were massed around a core of hot discussion." It is fair to say that Reed could not be regarded as an impartial observer to such an extent that Lenin himself wrote the introduction to one edition of the book. Reed was also for some time Soviet Consul in New York before returning to Russia where, in1920, he died and was buried with considerable ceremony in the Kremlin.

This validation of what was in effect a political putsch has been roundly rejected in more recent histories. Orlando Figes cites Trotsky as saying that between twenty five and thirty thousand at most were involved. Figes believes that "there were probably something in the region of ten to fifteen thousand people milling around the Palace Square; but not all of them were actually involved in the "storming of the palace although many more would later claim that they had taken part."[133] Keyes' account, which has never previously been published, confirms this more considered analysis and emphasises the sheer amateurishness both of what remained of the Kerensky government and the Bolshevik forces.

Keyes' description is contained in a letter which he wrote to Edith in the days immediately following the Bolshevik takeover.[134] Like many of his letters, it is a detailed account of his activities but written in an impersonal style. It is clear that Keyes sent more or less identical versions of his letters to a range of correspondents with limited personalisation so that his letters to his brother, Roger and, whilst she was still alive, his mother were practically the same as the ones which he sent to Edith. This is unsurprising as correspondence was the only way in which he could stay in touch with friends and family who he had not seen since his departure for Bahrain in April

1914. It is a great shame that only one side of the correspondence survives and that, in particular, none of Edith's letters are available.

Keyes outlines the background to the coup making it plain that, even then, he held no brief for the Bolsheviks who were "dirty beast[s] and most of the leaders are openly in German pay." However, his views were more nuanced than that as he plainly recognised that their right wing opponents failed to distinguish between the various left wing parties and "call all on the left Bolsheviks and tar them all with the same brush." This failure was to dog every attempt to form an effective opposition to Bolshevik rule and all opposition forces were prone to splits between right and left. The main reason for this was that Tsarist autocracy had stunted the growth of any political consciousness so that moderate views were squeezed out. This was later exacerbated during the civil war where the former Tsarist officer class predominated in the counter-revolutionary movement. Their views were in general profoundly reactionary and they were indeed inclined to view all left wing parties as being essentially the same. This led to an inability to gain meaningful support from the peasants and workers, many of whom were unhappy with Bolshevik rule and meant that there was never a genuinely popular movement for change.

Keyes was dismissive of the Provisional Government's ability to control the situation so that the Minister of War, Verkhovsky was a "dirty dog" for going over to the Bolsheviks and Kerensky a "vapouring ass." In fact, Verkhovsky may have been doing no more than recognising that the total collapse of Russia's ability to continue with the war was inevitable and that peace was essential. He was roundly condemned for this view and one paper described him as having "jumped on the footboard of Comrade Trotsky's chariot."[135] This contempt for the Provisional Government and bewilderment at its failure to assert control was not confined to Keyes and there is repeated evidence of its leaders, particularly Kerensky's lack of realism so that opportunities to crush the Bolsheviks such as during the July Days were missed. The internal tensions were exacerbated by Kornilov's attempted coup so that by November the Government had lost the ability to command the loyalty of sufficient numbers of troops to oppose the Bolsheviks even though it was by then clear that a coup was inevitable.

On 7 November, the Astoria Hotel, which was where many members of the British Embassy staff as well as other foreign representatives stayed, was taken over by troops loyal to the Military Revolutionary Committee. Although they were unfailingly polite to Keyes and the other residents, they disarmed any Russian officers present. Keyes then became aware that "large pickets of sailors, guards, Reserve Regiments and Red Guards or armed civilians were at every corner and patrols down every street [but that] everything was orderly and only the Winter Palace and Staff and Government Offices were held for the Provisional Government by Yunkers or cadets of the Military Schools and women of the Women's Battalions." It is illustrative of the regime's failure of will that, with a coup attempt imminent, the Provisional Government was unable to command the loyalty of any of any other units of the Russian army.

Later that evening, Keyes along with other Embassy officials, was ordered to move from the Astoria to the British Club which was close to the Embassy in case of trouble. In fact, he was still dining there when the hotel was taken over by Bolshevik sailors led by a Midshipman. Keyes therefore requested that he be escorted to the British Club which was approximately a mile distant and, somewhat surprisingly, the Midshipman agreed. Their first attempt failed as they came under fire from government forces in the Winter Palace and surrounding buildings and Keyes had to prevent the Midshipman from fleeing. They then worked their way up Morskaya Street towards the Palace Square ducking from one basement door to the next. Meanwhile, the Winter Palace was shelled from the St Peter and Paul Fortress and the cruiser, Aurora but the shells burst high. Keyes' escort then insisted on him returning to the Astoria where he initially decided to leave his belongings and to try to make his way alone. Instead, he ended up being escorted, this time not only by the Midshipman but also a staff officer who also produced a plentiful supply of sweets.

On their return journey, they came across "an English photographer and an Armoured Car Lt. Commander." It is likely that the latter was Commander Oliver Locker-Lampson who, as mentioned in Chapter 9, was in command of a squadron of armoured cars in the Petrograd area at the time. If so, it meant that Locker Lampson was an eyewitness to both the February and November Revolutions. Locker Lampson had stayed at the Astoria when the February Revolution commenced. The hotel was taken over by revolutionaries and Locker Lampson was later annoyed to find them "smoking what I recognised as my cigars."[136] There then took place one of those extraordinary scenes which were common to most contemporary accounts of the Revolution whereby, in the midst of an artillery duel and much firing of machine guns, a political debate took place between the assembled soldiery and, in this case, Keyes himself. The discussion centred upon what was the best way to govern Russia and most of those present indicated that "they were neither for Lenin or Kerensky but that they wanted order, land and the certainty that they would not be exploited by 'bourjui' again." Equally extraordinary was that Keyes participated fully with the discussions pointing out to the participants that "education was very expensive and that you could not borrow money abroad for it and that it must be paid for by economic development, but that they needed foreign capital and help for development which would certainly not be forthcoming if they had a Bolshevik government." The parallels between this analysis of Russia's predicament then and a century later are striking although Keyes was wrong in thinking that the capitalist world would not invest at all in a revolutionary Russia; Armand Hammer for example was later to make his first fortune in supplying goods to Russia in return for Imperial era treasures but ultimately the inability to fund capital projects sapped the will of the Communist regime and contributed to its collapse.

Keyes' opinion of the standard of debate expressed here and in other correspondence is robust; Russians "have the crudest ideas and are easily defeated in an argument." This echoes his views expressed in an earlier letter to his brother Roger in which he describes how "'meeting' has become one of the commonest words in the Russian language - discussing socialism and world politics with the utmost good humour, but generally with the wildest ignorance."[137]

Keyes eventually managed to reach the British Club but on the way witnessed shooting from the beleaguered troops in the Winter Palace but that it "all sounded high and I saw no one hit out of the hundred or more sailors and soldiers who were running away. I have never seen anything like the astounding cowardice of these people…I felt sure that they would never get in and that there was really no fear for the women [regiments in the Winter Palace] and it really did seem a howling farce." Leaving to one side his observations upon their valour, what is noteworthy is the really very small number of people present.

On the following morning, he went to inspect the damage which was much less than it might have been chiefly because almost all the artillery whether it was from the Aurora, the St Peter and Paul Fortress or field guns had failed to hit their targets even at short range and, when they had, the shells had proved to be duds. Keyes "pulled their legs pretty badly about their glorious victory over the women [which in many ways surprisingly] they took…pretty well." This again contrasts with the traditional account of a mass rising with decisive assistance being given by the Aurora's guns. Equally, the myth of a mass uprising which was immediately promulgated by the newspapers reporting that "there had been a thousand casualties on either side" was scotched by Keyes who accounts that he did not "see a spot of blood anywhere and all the time [he] was on the street only saw one man hit and that by a '*rico* [a type of carriage] down a side street" adding that he was "certainly the only foreigner who saw much of the show."

Having said that, the bloodthirsty nature of the new government soon became apparent over the coming days. Keyes recounts how the "poor little Yunkers were rounded up and many killed...isolated officers were murdered and those in our hotel either disappeared in plain clothes or lay very low." The Bolsheviks were clearly justified in their fear of a counter-coup as became apparent on Sunday 11 November when "Kerenski was reported to be in the ascendant and rumours were started that sailors had arrested Lenin, who, open German Agent though he was, was Minister President." As a result, the officers in the Astoria disarmed the guard "who were only too willing and began to wander aimlessly about the place carrying their rifles, talking, talking talking, but doing nothing to organise a defence." The Yunkers, who after all were only cadets, seem to have shown much greater decisiveness and took over the telephone exchange and various other buildings and commenced an intermittent exchange of fire with the Bolsheviks. However, by lunchtime, it was clear that Kerensky was not on his way and the rising fizzled out with the officers having "tamely given up their arms."[138]

As well as the immediacy of Keyes' account, what impresses is his perception of the overall political situation so that, for example, he is in no doubt whatsoever that Lenin was in German pay. The extent of German penetration of the Bolshevik movement has long been contentious but it is becoming clearer that it was far greater than previously believed and that the party's pressing needs for funds overcame any scruples it might have had. As mentioned in Chapter 9, Lenin himself took pains to keep some distance from Alexander Helphand who acted as middleman but must have been fully aware of the connection and the structures that were put in place to channel German funds to Russia during wartime.[139] As has been seen, the Bolsheviks were painfully sensitive that the extent of this connection with the ultra reactionaries of the German Foreign Office should not come out and took pains to cover up all evidence of it even to the extent of murdering those with knowledge.[140] It is uncertain whether Keyes' knowledge stemmed from his role at the Embassy or whether he was merely reflecting public opinion.

Less surprisingly, what stands out is the way in which the opposing forces divided on class grounds with the officer class and cadet Yunkers representing the only effective opposition to the revolutionary forces. The bulk of public opinion however seems to have remained undecided sometimes supporting the Bolsheviks and at others their overthrow. This reflects the fundamentally fragile nature of Bolshevik rule for many months and led to perception amongst many observers and indeed in British strategic thinking that they could not and would not last. What this failed to appreciate was the Bolsheviks' will to power that would lead in time to the brutal suppression of all opposition and the wholesale dismantling of the Russian economy. It also did not take into account the fissiparous nature of the opposition to the Bolsheviks which could never unite to mount a coordinated assault on the Bolshevik regime. This was perhaps inevitable taking into account the way in which the Tsarist regime had stifled mature political debate so that the gulf between the military classes which largely wished for a restoration of the status quo ante and moderate liberalism of the Kadets let alone the moderate socialism of some of the other parties was inevitably unbridgeable.

Later, during the afternoon of 11 November, Keyes had a more threatening brush with the Bolsheviks when he accompanied a RNAS serviceman in delivering provisions to Hugh Sinclair, then Director of Naval Intelligence in Petrograd.[141] En route, they were intercepted by a hostile force of sailors who, "incited by a well-dressed Jew who said he was a Government Commissary tried to arrest me." They managed to talk their way out of this and Keyes then teamed up with another officer called Donohoe and sought to make his way back to the Astoria. On their way they came across a "gang of sailors and Red Guards snarling around three corpses - an officer and two Yunkers - like pi dogs. It was a beastly sight, they had been literally pulled to pieces. They were very nasty, and I must say their long rusty bayonets made me feel rather uncomfortable and was glad that Donohoe could not understand what they were saying." Having made their way past, they then returned upon hearing that a British officer might have been killed. They ascertained from three French officers who were standing guard "to see honour done to the brave dead" that the victims were not British and so continued on their way.

Keyes later gave a more detailed account of this encounter in which he stated that the day in question was 17 and not 11 November and went on to explain that his mission was to deliver a case of whisky from the Embassy to the Naval mission at the Astoria. In this account, he was accompanied by a Captain Desmond of the Intelligence Service who presumably was the same man as "Donohoe" referred to in his letter in the letter as well as the RNAS officer.[142] The account is considerably dramatised so that the three corpses in the letter become "what had looked like a long heap of shovelled earth was really a collection of bodies, laid out in a long line; like a photograph of a big shoot with the sportsmen standing proudly behind their bag." Further, the nurse - or kitchen maid - features in his encounter with the commissar and not with the gang of sailors. In his letter to Edith, written at the time, the nurse, along with a sailor are merely described as having "stood up for [him]" and there is none of the detail in the later story. Bearing in mind the details which are included in his letter to Edith, it is hard to believe that he would not have told her the full story about the nurse/kitchen maid in all its picaresque detail. As with his previous accounts, he was at the centre of events outwitting the commissar by remarking upon his bourgeois appearance saying "Why! - The *Burjui* has got on a silk collar - and it's <u>clean.</u>" This brings the soldiers or sailors (he uses both terms) onto his side and "completed [the commissar's] discomfiture."

In a similar way, he gave a more colourful account of avoiding machine gun bullets by hiding in the entrances to basement shops. He was accompanied by Captain Desmond and the shooting more frightening - "the tat tat tat of machine guns is damnable enough at any time - but when it is accompanied by the screeching of ricochets off the pave and the thudding of bullets into the walls, it is perfect hell." Desmond played a semi-comic role so that his paunch protruded beyond the "massive outcrop of stucco work" and thus exposing himself to fire. Keyes told him to "tuck in [his] tummy" and was then further alarmed when Desmond leant out onto the street to retrieve his cap which had been knocked off by a burst of fire. Keyes recounted how he was then alarmed to find that Desmond's comb-over was brushing against his shoulder as Desmond was otherwise "bald as coot."[143]

It is, of course entirely likely that Keyes would have downplayed the danger he was in and the risks he ran in letters to Edith but he would surely have relished telling her the comic aspects of his life. Further, the events described took place a week later in his story than they do in his more or less contemporary letter to Edith. Accordingly, as with his previous stories, it is hard to resist the conclusion that his later account is not to be relied upon as being accurate and has to approached with some caution.

Keyes also wrote to Edith about the night assault by the Bolsheviks on the Yunkers in the telephone exchange and how Keyes and the other British and French officers in the Astoria took responsibility for looking after the women in the hotel "if the Bolsheviks should lose their heads." To avoid the shooting at the telephone exchange, they "had a cheery little dinner" in the bathroom of the hotel "with a charming Russian lady who had taken asylum with us." He later recounted how the "pretty young wife of a captain...asked if [she and her companion, the wife of a General] might come and sleep in [Keyes'] room if they were frightened." The Captain's wife later went into hiding and Keyes related how he lived "in terror of Mrs General descending on me some night." Although plainly innocent, it is unclear quite how Edith would have taken to this news. They had not met for over three years and presumably the bonds between them were strained by the absence. Once again, it is regrettable that only one side of the correspondence has survived.

Although Keyes had an undisturbed night, the same cannot be said of the Yunkers who, on running out of ammunition surrendered to the Bolsheviks. It did them no good since the "dirty pi dogs scuppered the lot of them." He spent the next night on guard at the British Club as there were rumours that the British Embassy was about to be attacked; something Keyes regarded as inherently unlikely as the Embassy "was the last place, next to the German trenches, that the dirty dogs would attack."

During the following days, Keyes continued his investigations into the storming of the Winter Palace and interviewed an official who confirmed that there were one hundred and forty members of the Women's Battalion of Death present but that "their share of the defence... was not very heroic." In fact, they had become hysterical and had had to be locked in the basement. After the surrender, they were passed between three Russian guards regiments - the Preobrazhensky, the Pavlovski and the Grenadiers - and variously ill treated before General Knox (the British Military Attaché) managed to persuade the Bolsheviks to allow them to return to their battalion.[144]

Of the male troops defending the Palace, only "three Yunkers were wounded.... but some were murdered afterwards." Keyes attributed this to the fact that "the Palace was never rushed but treacherously surrendered", the defending troops taking the view that they had little prospects of mounting a long term resistance and handing themselves over to the Bolshevik, Vladimir Antonov Ovseenko who later became the Commissar for Military Affairs. Of the attackers, Keyes recorded that "only six were killed and few wounded, mostly by the wild fire of their own machine guns."[145]

Keyes concluded with a withering summary of the political situation which essentially reflected his despair at what he was witnessing. This must have been all the more shocking because of the way in which his Victorian certainties were being shattered not only by the war itself but the destruction both physical and intellectual of a country which had a few years previously been an emerging superpower. As an analysis, it is worth quoting at length because it not only reflects Keyes' own political views but in large part, those around him and, in turn, the British Government. It can also be regarded as a more realistic assessment than many of the politically motivated accounts that were to follow. He wrote that;

"If ridicule could kill, Kerensky's wretched Government would die a hundred deaths. Amiable Anarchists trying to run an Empire by talk and compromise, and sheltering themselves in a Palace behind women and boys, while their slightly more anarchichal and less amiable comrades miss the Palace with guns at short range and kill more of their own side than of the defenders by wild firing in the streets in the intervals of running away and talking socialism. My God! This is mighty Russia, the steam roller that was to flatten out Germany. The Frenchman who a generation ago said that Russia was rotten before she was ripe, said a wise thing.

The wretched intelligentsia, including the Officers are hopeless. All but a very few threw up the sponge long ago. As a class they were mere parasites and hadn't the nous or courage to lift a finger to improve or save the only system under which they can exist.

This afternoon there is a strong rumour that a mixed Socialist Government with 40% Bolsheviks is to be formed. Unless it gets to work pretty quick Petrograd will starve in darkness in a very few days.

…One of the men in the Club asked a Tommy orderly if there was enough dinner for the extra officers who might be coming in. "Dinner" said he; "it seems to me more like the last supper."[146]

Chapter 11:

December 1917

Whilst the Bolshevik coup had been anticipated by many foreign observers, very little consideration had been given to how best to respond should it succeed. The British were not alone in believing that it would not last and that a period of anarchy was inevitable before a new coalition not unlike the Provisional Government was formed. Sir George Buchanan informed the Foreign Office that the Bolshevik Government would "not be of long duration and would, before long, provoke counter revolution."[147] This was a logical viewpoint bearing in mind the relatively small number of Bolsheviks involved together with the fact that they then only had power in Petrograd alone. However, by the end of November, the Bolsheviks had extended their control over the heart of the country and, in particular, Moscow and other leading provincial cities. The principal reason for their success was less to do with Bolshevik strength in numbers and more to do with a strength of purpose - from Lenin downwards there was a clear strategy about seizing control of the government machine as well as manipulating the support of the Soviets.

The Bolsheviks' prospects of success were greatly enhanced by Trotsky's decision in early 1917 to join the party. Prior to that he had been regarded as a Menshevik although politically he was closer to the Bolsheviks. He was a compelling public speaker and was in many ways the external face of the party with a higher profile than Lenin. It also became apparent that even though he had no previous relevant experience - he had been a professional revolutionary for all his adult life - he was a formidable political organiser and was able to weld together sufficient military resources at short notice to defeat whatever counter revolutionary forces were assembled against the regime. He had been appointed as President of the Petrograd Soviet and in that capacity had largely organised the destabilisation of the military forces in Petrograd and, once the Provisional Government had been overthrown, he moved swiftly to consolidate Bolshevik rule. Later, following the Demobilisation Conference in December 1917, he became the Commissar of War for the Red Army of Workers and Peasants. Simultaneously, he was also Commissar for Foreign Affairs and so became directly responsible for the new regime's dealings with foreign powers.

The British alongside other Allied powers found themselves confused about how to react to the Bolshevik takeover so that whilst Buchanan recommended de facto recognition, others, particularly in the military missions, took the view that "strong and resolute handling" would be necessary to ensure their swift overthrow. As General Poole put it, only by doing this could Britain "save something out of the wreck...to try and increase British popularity and to get a place in the sun for our trade out here after the war."[148] However, the position was a good deal more nuanced than Poole put it. The chief aim of British policy was to keep Russia in the war as a combatant and failing that as a benign neutral which would decline to trade with Germany thereby preserving the naval blockade which was increasingly hampering the German war effort.

The British recognised that the Bolsheviks had financial ties with Germany and also that they were determined to negotiate a peace treaty with the Germans to bring hostilities to an end. The quandary was whether by supporting counter revolutionary schemes, the British would drive the Bolsheviks into the German camp or whether sponsoring a counter coup was the only way in which to keep Russia in the war. Once peace negotiations between the Russians and Germans began, it was in British interests that these should be drawn out as long as possible and also that limited territory and supplies were handed over to German control. In respect of the latter, Poole and others became swiftly engaged in a race with the Germans to buy up foodstuffs and other supplies from their Russian owners and then to remove them out of range of a possible German advance.

Similarly, the Bolsheviks knew that the German peace terms would be harsh and would inevitably require the surrender of much of Western Russia and its industry and agriculture. At that point the Allied blockade would be breached and the Allies would have no hesitation supporting any forces that would seek a Bolshevik overthrow. The Bolsheviks, principally Trotsky, therefore began an elaborate balancing act whereby the Germans were persuaded to continue peace negotiations and not renew their advance (which the Bolsheviks were powerless to resist) whilst, at the same time, seeking Allied recognition of their rule.

The British policy was therefore contradictory with some, such as Bruce Lockhart actively seeking an accord with the Bolsheviks whilst the others - chiefly Poole and the military missions agitating for support to be given to counter revolutionary forces and ultimately for an Allied military intervention. This ambivalence was reflected in a memorandum prepared by the British Foreign Secretary, Arthur Balfour which was prepared in early December 1917. This recommended that Britain "should avoid as long as possible an open break with this crazy system" concluding that "if this be drifting then I am a drifter by deliberate policy."[149] This policy of drift might have made sense during the period immediately following the Bolshevik takeover particularly bearing in mind the strategic imperative of denying the Germans access to Russian resources but it became progressively more confused as time went on.

Further, once the Russians had finally agreed to the terms imposed by the Germans at Brest-Litovsk, much of the Russian economy ceased to be under Russian control anyway. To put this in context, by the terms of the Treaty, Russia gave up most of its European territories including Poland, Finland and the Baltic States all of which were given independence subject to German tutelage. The Bolsheviks agreed to withdraw from Ukraine which was to become independent although again under close German supervision. As well as territorial losses, it is calculated that Russia lost thirty four percent of its population, thirty two percent of its agricultural land, fifty four percent of its industrial capacity and eighty nine percent of its coalfields. The harshness of the terms imposed by Germany backfired as it is estimated that it had to station approximately one million troops and other service personnel to keep control of its new eastern empire and these could have tipped the balance during the Ludendorff offensives on the Western Front in summer 1918. Further, for a variety of reasons including sabotage sponsored by the Allies, only limited Russian resources had been shipped to Germany by the time of the Armistice. The draconian nature of the Treaty also impacted upon the way in which the Allies later treated the Germans at Versailles.

In the meantime, the policy of drift exacerbated the confusing ambiguity in aims on the ground with some parts of the British presence in Russia actively seeking a Bolshevik overthrow whilst others were seeking to maintain good relations. Buchanan's own position was fraught in that he had promised that the Embassy would not participate in activities aimed at destabilising the new regime which was only to be expected from the representatives of an allied power, whilst at the same time, schemes to achieve precisely that end were taking place in the Embassy and other British controlled buildings in Petrograd. In fact, Buchanan was exhausted and increasingly out of his depth in dealing with the changed realities of Russian political life. He almost certainly was in the throes of a nervous breakdown and left Petrograd for good in January 1918. His replacement, Francis (often known as Frank) Lindley, had been at the Embassy since 1915 as acting Counsellor. Lindley was younger and fitter and also took a more realistic view of the situation and continued to push for de facto recognition being granted to the Bolsheviks.

Keyes continued to formulate his own views of the political situation which he would have had no compunction about sharing with Buchanan and Lindley. These were summarised in a letter to

Edith of 23 December 1917 which began by explaining the way in which the Bolsheviks had circumvented and then neutralised the Constituent Assembly which was due to decide the new form of government.[150] Keyes was in no doubt that the Bolsheviks were doing the Germans' bidding but also that the Germans had, as reinsurance, also funded the Monarchists who wanted a Romanov restoration. The parties in the middle were broadly anti-German although not all of them in favour of continuing the war. The biggest party was the Socialist Revolutionary Party which had split in 1904 when the Bolsheviks were formed. By 1917, it had two wings; the Right and Left SRs. Keyes summarised the right wing as being "amiable academic land reformers" whereas the left were "wild creatures", Marxist and "theoretically first for industrial control thinking that, having secured this, they will drag the peasants in with a new land programme. Their war cries were 'wipe out the bourgeoisie, capitalist and Imperialist' and the 'will of the people'. They promised bread, peace and freedom."

He went on to explain in more detail how the Social Democrats had split into Bolsheviks and Mensheviks and how their difference was primarily one of approach with the Bolsheviks favouring violent revolution and vanguardism and the Mensheviks wishing to proceed "by education and evolutionary methods." Keyes clearly had only slightly more time for the Mensheviks than the Bolsheviks and described how they "cooed peace messages into the ears of both sides" and also included "small groups of Internationalists, some genuine, some German agents."[151]

He had certainly formed a firm and, with hindsight, convincing view on Lenin and his letter may include one of the first uses of the term "Leninism." He described Lenin as a "genuine Bolshevik and Internationalist, in fact, Bolshevism is so misused a term that I prefer Leninism. Having a sense of humour it amuses him to take German money to smash the Russian bourgeoisie, meaning all the while to bring down with it German Imperialism and the German bourgeoisie too and eventually the owning and exploiting classes of all Europe. Being a strong calculating machine with no passion or scruples as to means, he has turned the 'Government of Peoples' Commissaries' whose foundation was Freedom into an autocracy such as no Tzar ever enjoyed"

This represented a remarkably early and clear sighted view of Lenin's approach to government at a time when many others were still seduced by the idealistic rhetoric of a spontaneous people's uprising. Keyes also recognised the sophisticated and determined way in which the Bolsheviks rapidly established a plausible simulacrum of government and "played their cards admirably." He attributed this to the fact that they had "courage and talent - Jewish mostly - and German money and advice."[152] A number of commentators at the time remarked upon the proportion of revolutionaries who were Jewish and there is a subliminal (and sometimes overt) whiff of anti-Semitism in many passages. It is true that many of the leading revolutionaries including Trotsky, Zinoviev, Kamenev, Radek and Peters (one of the founders of the Cheka) were Jewish in origin but bearing in mind the centuries of being confined to the Pale of Settlement culminating in the Tsarist pogroms, this can hardly be surprising. The Tsarist regime's failure to command any respect or loyalty with the Jewish community was to cost the Whites dearly in the Civil War.

As for the German connection, Keyes had no doubt about the influence of German agents and, more importantly, German funds in establishing the Bolsheviks as the obvious challenger to the Provisional Government and later in forming a viable government. What he failed to appreciate was that the Bolsheviks may have been funded by German money but they had not been bought and that the differences and enmities implicit in a mésalliance between German reaction and Russian revolution would soon come to the fore. The Germans themselves were fully aware of this; they realised that in fomenting revolution in Russia there was the prospect that revolution would in turn be re-imported back to Germany. This was fully apparent by the Summer of 1918 when German troops transferred from the Eastern to the Western Fronts brought with them Bolshevik ideas. More to the point it was revolutionary activities in Germany itself - for example, the Kiel Mutiny of November 1918 - that ultimately brought about the German collapse.

The party Keyes clearly felt most affinity with were the Kadets who had been significant participants in the old Tsarist Duma. They were liberal constitutionalists who had initially been in power following the February Revolution but had been superceded by the Social Revolutionaries. Keyes describes them as "a party of professors and *chinovniks* [ie office holders and administrators]" and it is correct that their appeal was broadly to the middle classes which is probably why they ultimately became irrelevant.[153] Keyes acknowledged that they were "now discredited and divided" but believed that "from their ranks will eventually spring a Liberal Federal Party which will save Russia." His sympathy for the Kadets is understandable as, of all the Russian parties, they most closely resembled a parliamentary liberal party. It is possible that had the Tsarist autocracy acted sooner to institute purposeful reform then the Kadets might have had a viable future as a party of government but by 1917, their moderate constitutionalism and support for continuing the war had no traction with the peasants and industrial workers who sought a far more radical solution. Whilst regarded as a party of the middle class by the Left, the Kadets were also despised by the Right which was hostile to their republicanism and opposition to autocracy.

Keyes may have expressed enthusiasm for the Kadets and felt an affinity with their supporters but he had a clear eye for their failings describing the *chinovniks* as "a parasite class, as greedy as the *babu* for Government service and damnably corrupt, lazy and incompetent."[154] In fact, the administrative class demonstrated a remarkable instinct for survival and the system with all its faults has survived broadly intact to this day.

Having witnessed events at first hand, Keyes recognised that the Bolsheviks had been obliged to make promises which assisted them in consolidating power but which they would struggle to keep. As a result, "freedom has gone. All papers protesting are suppressed and all active opponents arrested. Bread is no easier to get. The last of their promises - peace - seems nearer but at a price that even the Bolshevik will hesitate to pay." There is a sense from this that Keyes, like the other foreign observers was shocked by the ruthless way in which the Bolsheviks kept power establishing a regime that was far more oppressive than that of the Tsar. He describes how "their Commissary for Foreign Affairs, Trotzki, alias Braunstein, has at his disposal four papers, the most unscrupulous that have ever disgraced journalism. The opposition papers are closed so often, and are so fainthearted that it is impossible to counter the attack."[155]

This ruthlessness stood in stark contrast to the anarchic freedoms of the Provisional Government which had allowed a free press to flourish and had failed to act against the Bolsheviks and Lenin during the July Days even though it had "found enough evidence to hang him for a traitor a hundred times over."[156] It would also enable Lenin to force through acceptance of the harsh terms of the Treaty of Brest-Litovsk even though it dismembered Russia and also split his party.

Keyes' knowledge of events outside Petrograd was more restricted but he described how "Finland, the Ukraine, the Crimea, Siberia, the Kirghiz and the South East Coalition of Cossacks and Caucasians [had] declared themselves autonomous." The latter is important, as Keyes himself was about to become much more closely involved in their affairs. It was an unhappy marriage between the Don Cossacks led by Kaledin and the Party of Collection which was run by Alexeyev, the former Chief of Staff of the Tsarist Army and Kornilov who alongside Brusilov was one of its most successful generals.[157]

Within Russia, all was chaos and Keyes writes of "peasants looting and burning in the country and Red Guards and sailors carrying out a reign of terror in the towns."[158] The assault on the countryside largely came about when peasants took over the land and drove out the landowners. There was enormous destruction of property particularly the houses of the estate owners. Many were murdered in the process often by peasants who, as Keyes wrote, "once the Tsar had ceased to be their Little Father, they could be bribed by promises of land to do anything. The soldiers, when their officers had failed, were certain to resolve into peasants and workmen more dangerous for their military training."[159] Thus, the failure to institute far reaching land reform over the previous fifty years and in particular, the Tsar's failure to support Stolypin's attempts at change created an environment where revolutionary upheaval was inevitable once central power failed. The damage wrought to Russian agriculture by this and subsequent actions by the Bolshevik or Soviet governments transformed Russian agriculture from being world leading into a state of decline from which it has yet to emerge.

Keyes ascribes the root cause of the problem to "the agitator class - sneaking through life in overheated rooms, always striving to destroy something of the existing order, it was inevitable that he should be destructive when he broke loose and fail entirely as a constructive force." What impressed him as the "grip the Bolshevik has shown but their organisation is almost wholly Jew and German."[160]

As for the aristocracy, Keyes clearly had sympathy for individuals - not altogether tactfully bearing in mind that he was writing to his wife describing one Princess as "an extraordinarily attractive but rather naughty little lady" - and he also recognised that they "had lost very heavily in the War but the survivors appear to be under the curse of incompetence. Some of the women are splendid but these all seem to have had English governesses." It is noteworthy how time and again in Keyes' writings he combines shrewd perception with complete moral certitude and racial stereotyping; in this case Russians but earlier with Muslim "swine." There is nonetheless no reason to regard Keyes' attitudes as being anything other than reflective of his class and position and, in many ways, his is a more nuanced approach than many others particularly those of a purely military background.

Keyes concludes by describing one of Buchanan's final press conferences where he faced "some ticklish questions." Keyes was impressed by Buchanan who he described as "a fine diplomat on the old lines… who when the Revolution came; - it never would have come if the Tsar had taken his advice - he proved himself infinitely more adaptable than one could have expected." The press conference was evidently challenging but Buchanan "[put] up a game fight and a clean one, which some of his colleagues are not doing."[161] Although this passage points to the possibility that Keyes was in the Foreign Office camp rather than that of the military missions, it is misleading for, as will become apparent, he was to play a close and active role in trying to overthrow the Bolshevik regime and repeatedly disparaged the Foreign Office doves as being unrealistic.

Chapter 12:

The Genesis of the Russian Bank Schemes

The initial motivation behind the Bank Schemes which were to have three iterations over the forthcoming fourteen months lay in the chaos that engulfed Russia following the Bolshevik takeover. The Schemes were sophisticated in themselves and the position was made more complicated by repeated confusions caused by parallel schemes being operated and a lack of coordination between participants. This in part reflects the divergent approach to the handling of the Bolshevik regime discussed earlier. As will be seen, matters were further complicated by clerical errors and the corruption of the encrypted telegrams passing between Russia and London.

It is perhaps indicative of the complex nature of the Bank Schemes that there is even doubt as to how the concept came about although the origins lay in the emergence of the Cossack Union in South Russia, the Volunteer Army and the Party of Collection. The Cossack Union was an association of the four main Cossack groupings, namely, the Don, Kuban, Astrakhan and Terek under the Don Cossacks' Ataman, General Alexei Kaledin. The Cossacks controlled much of southern Russia and the eastern part of the Ukraine but relations between the various Cossack Hosts were strained and there was also tension between the older more traditional Cossacks and the younger ones who had in part been radicalised during the course of military service. It is of course noteworthy that despite their traditional loyalty to the Tsar and in stark contrast with the 1905 Revolution, Cossacks had declined to confront the Petrograd mob in February 1917 leading to the Tsar's abdication.

The then fledgling Volunteer Army was being assembled chiefly from members of the old Tsarist officer class and was led by the former Chief of Staff, General MV Alexeyev and General Kornilov although their relationship was never good since Alexeyev had been responsible for Kornilov's arrest in the summer of 1917 which effectively brought to an end his attempted coup against the Provisional Government. The Volunteer Army was strong on officers but weak on NCOs and private soldiers. This was typical of the White movement as a whole and was reflective of the marked class divide in the old Tsarist army. One young officer, Roman Gul, travelling to join the White Guards describes the peasant soldiers on his train as "the people who smashed our old mahogany chairs… who tore up my favourite books…. who cut down our orchard and cut down the roses that mama planted; these are the people who burned down our house… I saw that underneath the red hat of what we had thought of as the beautiful woman of the Revolution there was in fact the ugly snout of a pig."[162] This summarises the way in which the national support for change that had informed the February Revolution had deteriorated into class war by November 1917; it would become much worse as the country descended into civil war.

The Party of Collection effectively amounted to a group of politicians from the old regime that wished to "collect" the fragmented parts of non-Bolshevik Russian into a coherent opposition. It was a policy with practically no chance of success as the gulf dividing the component parts from Monarchists to Social Revolutionaries was at least as great as that dividing them from the Bolsheviks. Nevertheless, since the Party of Collection attracted formerly prominent figures such as Rodzianko, erstwhile President of the Duma, Prince Shakhovskoy who had been Minister of Trade and Industry from 1915 until February 1917 and NN Pokrovsky, the last Tsarist Foreign Minister, it had considerable influence not least with representatives of the Allied Governments who preferred to deal with familiar faces.

It is likely that the first approach to Buchanan was on 23 November 1917 when he was visited by Prince Shakhovskoy who outlined a plan whereby a Cossack bank would be established with a view to funding Kaledin and the Volunteer Army.[163] Although this seems to be accurate, another version was put forward in the report of the British Economic Mission to Russia dated 27 August 1918 which records that "the first overtures were made by M.Pokrovsky ex Foreign Minister who had been appointed pleni-potentiary by M. Rodzianko."[164] In any event, the key issues discussed were the problems in establishing the basis of government in South Russia. These were primarily financial rather than economic. If finance was available, then there was a chance of occupying the Donetz basin which would effectively block out the Germans from obtaining coal, minerals and oil as well as access to Siberian grain. From a British perspective, there was also the prospect of assistance being given to the Armenians and Georgians in their fight against the Turks. The latter was, in reality highly improbable given the racial tensions of the Caucasus but reflects the longstanding British preoccupation with protecting Persia and the western flank of India, an area in which Keyes had until then spent the entirety of his professional career and is reflected in his observation that South Russia had had "an added importance ...owing to its adjoining the Caucasus where both Bolsheviks and Germans were carrying out an intensive propaganda with a view to raising Persia, Afghanistan and Central Asia against us. They were already launching ventures towards the Caucasus and Central Asia."[165] Keyes predicted that the Germans wanted a route to India and "the most obvious one was through the Caucasus and the Turkish province of NW Persia." which would ultimately enable it to gain access to North Afghanistan "from which she could always destroy the peace of India."[166] Keyes always had at least half an eye on the implications for British interests in India; in this, he was very much in tune with British preoccupations generally.

The lack of unity between the various White movements were married to a lack of coherence between the various Allied national interests and indeed within the British establishment as a whole. The two camps had at their extremes, Bruce Lockhart urging de facto recognition of the Bolsheviks and the provision of military training and resources with the hope that this would encourage the

Bolsheviks to continue some kind of resistance, however passive, against the Germans and prevent or delay the signing of a peace treaty and, on the other, a more aggressive attempt to overthrow Bolshevik rule and replace it with a government which was more acceptable to Allied interests. The dilemma was fully appreciated by the War Cabinet which concluded that the Allies could opt:

"a. To recognise the Bolsheviks 'and make the best
    arrangements possible with them', or

b. To refuse to recognise them 'and take open and energetic
    steps against them.'"[167]

In reality, the policy of drift as advocated by Balfour was adopted for a considerable period of time which had an initial logic in preventing a German takeover and delaying the Central Powers' access to Russian resources but it also allowed the Bolsheviks time to consolidate power so that by the time the Allies decided upon intervention and indeed overt support for various White forces, the prospects of success were that much reduced. At the time however, the British were scarcely in a position to intervene militarily not only because of extreme manpower shortages but also a fear that an overtly anti-Bolshevik policy might provoke a revolutionary response domestically. The matter was summed up by the Minister for National Service, Sir Auckland Geddes, who presented a paper to the War Cabinet concluding "it would be quite impossible to obtain for the army anything like the number of men demanded for it...to get even a proportion ...it would be necessary to cut down shipbuilding, food producing, or the munitions programme or all three it was not likely that any considerable further number of coal miners could be obtained without a serious strike."[168] Later, in January 1918, Arthur Henderson, then Labour party representative to the War Cabinet reported that Trotsky's name had been cheered on Clydeside. This fear of Bolshevik inspired political and economic unrest gravely concerned the Government at this time, one of its consequences being the withdrawal of the offer of asylum to the Tsar and his family which ultimately led to the bloodbath in Ekaterinburg.

All of the above encouraged the British to take the proposals put forward by Prince Shakhovskoy seriously although the Foreign Office was far from enthusiastic as can be seen from a telegram sent on 26 November which indicated that the "scheme for a Cossack Bank seems at first somewhat fantastic. Does any other scheme suggest itself to you [Buchanan] in which the desired end could be rapidly and safely attained."[169] It is clear that none did and Keyes became involved from the outset. The approach came at a good time for him as he was clearly at a low ebb as can be seen from the letter which he wrote to Edith on 9 December;

"I have been through a very bad time both personally and in my work and have been badly knocked off my feet but things are better and I have been given some really important and interesting work to do…you mustn't expect to hear from me for some time."[170]

Keyes was soon wholly converted to the merits of the Schemes and claimed "to be the first to see the importance of [them] and, with the assistance of Harold Williams of the Daily Chronicle, to have been the only official person who has stuck to it through good and evil. The Embassy, the Foreign Office, the War Office and the Cabinet have all at times wavered or lost heart, and I have had to invite serious rebuffs by shoving in unwanted with my advice."[171] This is the only mention of Harold Williams' involvement in the Schemes but it is not surprising. He had been in Russia for many years and, at a time when journalists enjoyed a more prestigious reputation than now, was regarded as an authority of Russian affairs. He had supported the February Revolution but quickly saw the dangers of Bolshevism and was a vocal opponent. He and his Russian wife fled to England in spring 1918 and he was soon appointed to the Russia Committee where he actively pressed for an early intervention but was overruled by Lloyd George.

Keyes readily appreciated the problems facing Alexeyev and the newly formed independent republics in South Russia. He later summarised the situation as one where the "five little 'republics' were organised on the most primitive basis financially. There was not a single bank with its headquarters in that area; and the head offices of the banks which had local branches in the towns of the South had been suppressed by the Bolsheviks.... all money was hoarded, commercial life came to a standstill, there was no outlet for agricultural produce - unless one were made to Germany - and the little parliaments were helpless. They voted troops and supplies in kind to Alexeyiev; but they had no money and his treasure chest had in it at one time but £190. Money tokens were practically non-existent."[172] As Keyes put it, his chief difficulty "was due to a decree making it a capital offence to deal in foreign exchange." Initially, the way around it was to "sell British Treasury orders" but this was done "on so large a scale that it was impossible to keep secret and four of [Keyes'] seven agents were caught and shot."[173]

Following Buchanan's early discussions with Shakhovskoy, it was clear that the nature of what was proposed was in reality an attempt to undermine the Bolsheviks who in practice constituted the government of a significant part of Russia including Petrograd and Moscow. This ran wholly against diplomatic convention and if discovered, could lead to the loss of diplomatic immunity and the arrest of Embassy staff. Buchanan had also given a press conference on 8 December in which he stated "I wish the Russian people to know that neither I myself nor any agency under my control have any wish to interfere in the internal affairs of [Russia]."[174] This was plainly untrue and whilst Buchanan distanced himself from further involvement at least officially, news of his involvement with Shakhovskoy leaked out and Trotsky became increasingly suspicious and hostile to him. This also explains why nearly all of the meetings which Keyes later had took place outside the protection of the Embassy.

As Keyes described in the reports he subsequently prepared upon the Bank Schemes, his initial conversations were with "two eminent Russians" - probably Rodzianko and Pokrovsky but also possibly VM Vonliarsky who was Rodzianko's cousin and agent who was introduced to Keyes in January 1918. Vonliarsky in turn introduced

Keyes to Karol Yaroshinski who was to play a critical part in all of the Bank Schemes over the next two years. Yaroshinski was of Polish origin (hence why he is also sometimes referred to as Jaroszynski.) His family was well connected and had considerable estates near Vinnitsa in the Ukraine. His father died young and he took over the family land and businesses chiefly a sugar refinery which he rapidly expanded but then branched out into acquiring banking interests commencing with the Commercial and Industrial Bank as well as investing in other banks. He was by 1914 one of the three main bankers in St Petersburg alongside Putilov and Batolin who were collectively known as "the Three Horsemen of the Apocalypse.[175] Not very surprisingly however, to achieve this eminence, Yaroshinski had become very highly leveraged and his shareholdings were heavily mortgaged so that he was regularly short of cash. In 1919, he was described by an impressionable British official, Picton Bagge, as "his present age is 40. He is unmarried and his sole care is his mother… His genius is essentially a creative one. I have heard him compared by competent observers to Cecil Rhodes."[176]

The Russian banking system was different from that in the West in that banks not only had financial influence but also exercised near monopoly control over various important parts of the Russian economy. The ones that are relevant to the Bank Schemes were as follows;

The Russian Bank for Foreign Trade which controlled the grain trade on the Volga as well as Russia's two largest sugar refineries and largest insurance company.

The International Bank which dominated the South Russian grain trade, much of its jute and coal production including coal mines and metal works.

The Azov-Don Bank which controlled the largest platinum mine in the Urals as well as having extensive property holdings in Rostov.

The Volga Kama Bank was particularly influential in the upper Volga

The Russo-Asiatic Bank not only had extensive interests in the Urals and Altai districts but controlled the Chinese Eastern Railway

The Siberian Bank controlled the gold, platinum and grain trade of Siberia

The Commercial and Industrial Bank controlled navigation on the Dnieper and Volga as well as interests in the south Russian grain trade.

Prior to 1914, many of these banks had close ties with German banks. Perhaps for this reason, Yaroshinski was regarded as being anti-German. However, German influence understandably dissipated during the war. By November 1917, Yaroshinski saw the opportunity to gain control of all the above banks and with them a preponderant influence over the Russian economy as a whole. Unfortunately, he singularly lacked the resources to make his move and was on the lookout for financial backing.

The Bolshevik takeover had thrown the Russian banking system into crisis. It was immediately evident that the Bolsheviks viewed the banks with overt hostility and were likely to diminish their influence. It was less apparent that the Bolsheviks would effectively nationalise the entire banking system as well as default on all war loans advanced by the Allies. Equally, it was anticipated that the Bolsheviks would prove unable to maintain their control and would then be replaced by a more conventional (and pro-Allied) regime. Accordingly, shares in Russian banks remained valuable and indeed their value had continued to rise after the October Revolution.

Keyes' involvement with the Bank Schemes almost came to a premature end when on 21 December 1917 he received orders from Lieutenant General George Macdonagh, who was the Director of Military Intelligence, to transfer to Tiflis to assist in Transcaucasia. Buchanan was horrified and on Christmas Day telegraphed London that Keyes doing "work of the greatest importance." He followed this up on 27 December with a further telegram saying that "it is essential that Major Keyes...should stay for this and other important work."[177] It is of course noteworthy that Keyes was under

Macdonagh's command and therefore that his role was in Military Intelligence whereas he repeatedly describes his work as being in propaganda. The two are not mutually exclusive but as will become clear, it would seem that the propaganda post was almost certainly cover.

This special pleading worked and on 28 December, Keyes began work in earnest. Over the following two months, he had numerous meetings with Yaroshinski frequently at secret locations. He describes how "it was impossible to meet anyone connected with financial matters except secretly at night. Flats with entrances to two different streets were generally selected, the interviews always took place after 11 o'clock at night, and it was generally stipulated that I should wear a different fur coat and cap each time. There was anything up to one hundred robberies with violence every night - the victims being generally stripped to his vest and drawers in a temperature of often fifty degrees of frost. Snow was not regularly cleared away, but was piled in great heaps at the side of the street, giving good covert to the armed gangs which infested the town. I was out for twenty two nights out of the twenty eight in February, was attacked three times, twice with revolvers and once with a bomb, saw three murders and several hold ups and got involved in two general melees."[178]

At about this time, Keyes also came into contact with Hugh Ansdell Farran Leech who was to play a crucial role in the Bank Schemes. Leech remains an ambiguous figure and his involvement in the Bank Schemes has been the subject of subsequent criticism. He was the son of a city banker who had studied accountancy at Manchester University and engineering in Hamburg. He moved to Russia in 1912 where he married a Russian and undertook work in the oil industry before gravitating towards finance where he may or may not have acquired great wealth as well as a prodigious thirst for vodka.[179] In 1917, Leech was engaged as a commission agent in partnership with WEG Firebrace but he also ran a British propaganda bureau called "The Cosmos Agency" which had some kind of relationship with the British Embassy although there is doubt about its precise status.

As will become evident, Leech almost certainly was a British secret agent albeit a part time one. This is not surprising since the Secret Intelligence Service maintained a close interest in the Russian oil industry and often recruited Englishmen with an engineering background. Further, the role of the Cosmos Agency was to distribute British government funds that had been paid into an account at the London City and Midland Bank to newspapers in Petrograd and Moscow for publishing pro-Allied articles. The Russian bank used for these purposes was the Commercial and Industrial Bank which, as mentioned above, was controlled by Yaroshinski.

This all raises a number of questions. Keyes was after all ostensibly at least closely involved in propaganda. Indeed, in a letter to Edith dated 26 October 1917, he had stated that he was "to run propaganda for the whole Russian army - a job well worth doing under certain circumstances."[180] He subsequently confirmed his this in an affidavit which he swore in 1927 where he stated that although he worked for "the Anglo-Russian Commission which was a propaganda organisation. The Cosmos Agency was a branch of this Commission but worked in another building.... I believe that Leech who was a British civilian resident in Russia was employed by the Cosmos Agency but I have no recollection of him in that connection." However, later in the same document, he says that he "may have met Leech casually before but never had any conversation with him before I met Yaroshinski."[181] Bearing in mind the relatively small number of British representatives in Petrograd at the time and the close knit nature of their relations in a city under siege - see for example, the way in which they were all thrown together in the period after the Bolshevik takeover - this seems inherently implausible. This is even more the case as the Cosmos Agency enjoyed some kind of facilities in the Embassy itself. Bearing in mind the subsequent unravelling of the Bank Schemes and official recriminations, it is perhaps understandable that he would wish to distance himself from

Leech. This is all the more so when it was later concluded that there was sufficient evidence to warrant the British government showing "very great caution" towards Leech.

This is to leave to one side Leech's alleged connection with British Intelligence even at a relatively junior level which Keyes could not mention in Court documents even he had wished to do so. As will be seen, Leech was to become a convenient scapegoat for problematic issues arising from the Bank Schemes but, at the same time, his conduct probably warranted this scepticism and he seems to have been incapable of recognising a conflict of interest since at various times he appears to have been acting for the British, Yaroshinski and himself - sometimes all three at once.

AE (Teddy) Lessing was someone else who played an undefined part in the Bank Schemes and other intelligence enterprises. Like Leech, he appears to have established connections with British Intelligence before the war started but unlike him, he remained involved with intelligence issues for the rest of his life, He was a Captain in the Grenadier Guards in 1917 attached to General Poole's mission, the British Military Equipment Section. This was originally part of the Russian Supply Committee chaired by Lord Milner but later superceded by the Russia Committee. The Lessing family had extensive business interests in Russia and Lessing himself had many Russian links and was fluent in German, French and Russian. His role included being responsible for issues relating to metals but was otherwise unclear. Keyes was to write of him in connection with the Banks Schemes "during the whole time, Lessing has been floating about in the background in both Petrograd and London."[182] However, Keyes was not to know that Lessing through family and personal connections - his uncle was Edward Strauss MP and, more significantly, he was friends with William Sutherland who was Lloyd George's press secretary - was informally providing Lloyd George with information. Indeed, it became increasingly apparent to Keyes that Lloyd George was pursuing his own private foreign policy initiatives chiefly aimed at avoiding intervention and achieving some form of rapprochement with the Bolsheviks and that Lessing was a major player in them. As will appear later, Keyes' opinions of Lloyd George became ever more hostile and the fact that he did not keep them to himself damaged his subsequent career.

One of Lessing's closest contacts was his cousin Vladimir Poliakov a Russian banker and engineer from Rostov on Don. Poliakov was to play an important but confusing role in the Bank Schemes. He had been an engineer officer during the war but was also a director of the Siberian Bank and advised the British Embassy on financial matters. He too was involved with British Intelligence and worked closely alongside Lessing for General Poole's mission. They used the far from impenetrable code names of "Polly" and "Teddy Bear" in communications which cannot have detained the Cheka for long.

It was also in January 1918 that Bruce Lockhart was sent back to Russia following his earlier return to England in disgrace following an extra-marital affair. He was to act as an agent of influence to try to keep Russia in the war but critically, he also enjoyed Lloyd George's support particularly in his more placatory approach to the Bolsheviks. It was whilst in Petrograd that Bruce Lockhart commenced a relationship with Moura Budberg who was one of the more mysterious figures of that time who was amongst other things lover to Kerensky, Jakov Peters the head of the Moscow Cheka, Gorky and HG Wells as well as being a likely double agent and, if that was not exotic enough, she was also Nick Clegg's great aunt.

The earliest meetings with Yaroshinski and Leech took place at venues around Petrograd in January 1918. Keyes later described how "I first met Leech [when] ... he was sent to me by Yaroshinski upon matters connected with the proposed scheme. I may have met Leech before but never had any conversation with him before I met Yaroshinski. Leech accompanied me to Yaroshinski's flat the first time I went there and joined in the conversation to help Yaroshinski who was rather diffident of his powers of exposition. I did not like this arrangement and after that generally saw Yaroshinski alone."[183]

Leech knew Yaroshinski from his various financial schemes and so it was unsurprising that he effected the initial introduction. On Yaroshinski's part, the timing was fortuitous as he was particularly illiquid at the time and had instructed his agent, Isidore Kon, to seek out someone who would lend him one hundred and fifty million Roubles promising him a commission of two percent for doing so. Kon, who had also been the managing director of the Commercial and Industrial Bank up until 1914, contacted Gregory Benenson, a pro-German banking and oil tycoon, who agreed to advance fifty million Roubles. Leech informed Keyes that Yaroshinski's aim was to undermine German influence which was at best only partially true. Knowing Benenson's reputation, Keyes took the bait and informed Leech that the British Government would provide all of the finance required. Leech passed this message on and the loan to Benenson was cancelled although it was agreed that Kon would still be entitled to a sum equivalent to his two percent commission.

Keyes now had a clear run at Yaroshinski (or vice versa) and an outline proposal was fleshed out whereby the British government would lend two hundred million Roubles to enable Yaroshinski to gain complete control of the Russian Bank for Foreign Trade, the International Bank, the Volga-Kama Bank and the Siberian Bank. He would then establish a Cossack bank which would issue banknotes in South Russia and ensure the proper funding of Kaledin and the Volunteer Army.

Buchanan agreed to support the scheme provided that Krivoshein (former Foreign Minister) and Pokrovsky (former Minister of Agriculture) approved. This approval was forthcoming and approval was sought from London to proceed. In his reports in December and on 17 January 1918, Keyes did not mention Yaroshinski by name as he was under surveillance by the Bolsheviks and referred to him instead to "a financier." This was to cause endless confusion as Bonar Law, the Chancellor of the Exchequer, was unwilling to lend so much to an unknown person. General Knox (Buchanan's Military Attaché) then said that "the unknown capitalist was probably Mr

Poliakov." This led to the War Cabinet responding to Lindley and thus Keyes that "the Government are so anxious to give immediate financial assistance to our friends… that if the advance can be utilised immediately … on the understanding that the unnamed financier is P---, the government will sanction the proposal. You will see therefore that we are prepared to take this course entirely on your advice." This far from fulsome support was to come back to haunt Keyes later when the Foreign Office and Treasury gave serious consideration to resiling from the commitment given to Keyes which would have left him personally and professionally ruined.

In the meantime, matters had been further complicated by an approach made by Yaroshinski to Lindley without Keyes' knowledge. This took place in early January and related either to the Bank of Foreign Trade or the Commercial and Industrial Bank.[184] Whichever bank was meant, its directors, who were regarded as being pro-German, wished to leave Russia and were willing to dispose of their shares in return for hard currency being made available to them outside Russia. Yaroshinski had agreed with them that in return for them handing over six million Roubles in Russia an equivalent sum in Sterling would be deposited in London. Yaroshinski persuaded Lindley of the merits of this scheme as not only would it secure control of the bank but, equally importantly, it would forestall imminent German moves on it. Lindley was convinced and telegraphed London on 11 January "recommending an exchange operation to assist Yaroshinski in obtaining control of the Bank of Foreign Trade."

The Foreign Office, presumably spooked by the prospect of losing control of the bank to the Germans approved the proposal provided that the six million Roubles were provided in cash in Petrograd. There then followed a hiatus whilst further terms were negotiated in relation to the way in which the cash was to be provided as the directors initially could only lay their hands on three hundred and fifty thousand Roubles in cash. Eventually, on 18 January, Lindley was able to confirm that the money was to be transferred to South Russia.

The Foreign Office gave its approval provided that the funds were handed over to General de Candolle who was the British Military envoy sent from Romania to South Russia. The Treasury reinforced this by insisting on having a lien on the Sterling equivalent until confirmation had been received from de Candolle that the funds had been received. There then appears to have been a clerical error which led Lindley to believe that he was authorised to proceed without the preconditions laid down.

In a later letter reporting on the transaction, Robert Chalmers of the Treasury pointed out that "for some reason which is still not clear, Mr Lindley is stated to have made arrangements for remittance to the South East of only five out the six million."[185] This was later to become known as the "missing million." There was no question raised about Lindley's integrity although as will be seen there were plenty asked about Leech but nonetheless, his decision appears irrational at best. To make matters even more confusing, Yaroshinski then informed Lindley and Keyes (who appears finally to have been let in on the act) that he "was in a position to remit to Kieff not only the Roubles, five million but an additional ten million Roubles making fifteen million Roubles altogether. By reason of the clerical error referred to above, Mr Lindley believed himself authorised to accept this offer. At this stage of the proceedings the position seems, therefore, to have been that Mr Lindley, after having refused to purchase for Sterling from Monsieur six million Roubles for payment in Petrograd had now agreed to purchase fifteen million Roubles for payment in Kieff or elsewhere in South-East Russia."[186] Yaroshinski seemingly tried to deliver on his commitments and "messengers with bills on Kieff are said to have been sent from Petrograd but owing to the confused fighting which broke out in the Ukraine at this time and to the disappearance into hiding of Monsieur Yaroshinski, the fate of these messengers is unknown, although one is reported to have been murdered."[187]

Following this up, Lindley sent a telegram to the Foreign Office in early February asking that the Sterling equivalent of ten million

Roubles be credited to an account held by Leech. Whilst either Lindley or Keyes told Yaroshinski or Leech that this had been done, the telegram was never received and when re-sent proved illegible. Finally, on 13 February, a third telegram was sent asking that "the equivalent at an exchange of thirty three or roubles five million should likewise be transferred to Mr Leech." Chalmers later drily observed that "the rate specified would have placed a considerable sum of money into the pockets of Monsieur Yaroshinski or Mr Leech…[but]…no action could be taken … on either of these cables pending receipt of information that the roubles in question had actually been received by General de Candolle."[188]

Leech continued to press for payment but this was resisted on the basis that until evidence was produced showing that Yaroshinski had fulfilled his side of the bargain, "both contracts fall to the ground." In any event, as Chalmers was to report, indications had been received "casting doubt upon his [Leech's] disinterestedness in his capacity as agent between the representatives of His Majesty's Government and the Russian parties to the transaction." Furthermore, Yaroshinski had dropped out of sight and Davidoff to whom the Sterling equivalent of six million Roubles was to be credited had surfaced in Stockholm where he was "suspected in some quarters of working covertly in the interests of German Banks… and it is alleged that the amounts to his credit in London will be used, if possible, for opening credits for Germany." Understandably, therefore Chalmers recommended that the agreement be rescinded by the British Government.

Keyes was frustrated by the mess that had arisen and made clear that he "had nothing to do with the inception of this exchange transaction and indeed did not like the manner in which it had been done as it complicated the scheme with which I was concerned." He later claimed that he had no doubt that Leech was acting as Yaroshinski's agent in all of this, that he had explicitly warned Yaroshinski as much and received a written acknowledgement in return but that this had been destroyed alongside many other critical documents when the British Embassy had to leave Petrograd in March 1918. However, it is apparent that the position was far less clear cut bearing in mind that Leech had and continued to work for British Intelligence and was regarded by it as an agent albeit a part time one. As late as October 1918, Leech was to telegram the Foreign Office offering to arrange meetings should that be of assistance which certainly points to a continued link with British Intelligence.[189] This view was implicitly shared by Chalmers when he questioned Leech's "disinterestedness" since an agent for a negotiating party acting at arms' length could not reasonably be expected to be impartial.

The upshot of all of this was that Yaroshinski secured control of a major bank and had improved his bargaining position with Keyes in respect of the principal Bank Scheme. From a distance, it is difficult to resist the conclusion that Yaroshinski and Leech ran rings around Lindley and this impression continues in relation to their subsequent dealings with Keyes. Both Lindley and Keyes were professional administrators with practically no experience of complicated financial transactions and would inevitably struggle to keep up. Further, the world of Russian finance was very different from that in London; there was clear recognition at the time that Russian banking practices would not be tolerated in the West. In 1919 a report was prepared by the British intelligence services on Yaroshinski which stated that he was "a very educated man, very clever and a perfect gentleman in his manners and speech. These characteristics have all played in his favour and in Petrograd financial circles he is looked upon as A1, but one must bear firmly in mind the important fact that Russian financial men themselves, I mean bankers and company promoters are of such a standard and code of ethics that many a businessman of Western Europe would not like to accept."[190]

The fact that notwithstanding all of the warning signs, they still proceeded is testimony to the sheer desperation of the British at that time. It was common knowledge that the terms which the Germans were offering at Brest-Litovsk in return for peace were punitive and would result in German hegemony over much of European Russia. This would not only mean that troops would be freed up for the long feared offensive in the West but also that the economic blockade would be broken which would reinvigorate the German war effort. The Bolsheviks were the only political party with the willingness to agree such terms and so it was inevitable that attempts would be made to destabilise them.

Furthermore, it was not really understood by the parties at the time that the Bolsheviks' antipathy towards the banking world was so implacable. Keyes himself was to report that "the universal opinion of all financial and economic authorities whom I have been able to consult, not only among those who have remained in the country but including those who have taken refuge in Norway and Sweden, is that the Bolshevik regime, though it may ruin individual bankers, cannot, even if the War continues for another year and they have during that time undisputed control in Moscow and Petrograd, ruin the banks themselves."[191] That this view was to prove very wide of the mark does not mean that it was an unreasonable one at the time in question.

Finally, as will become clear in the next chapter, the British motivation for funding the scheme went well beyond immediate practical considerations and amounted to a full blooded Imperialist move to solve the longstanding Russian threat to India, Afghanistan and Persia by acquiring a dominant interest in a post Bolshevik Russian economy.

Chapter 13:

Bank Schemes January - March 1918

Whilst Lindley's scheme was working itself through, Keyes' attention was on the principal Bank Scheme which he was putting together with Yaroshinski and Leech. He was assisted in this by reason of his promotion to temporary Lieutenant Colonel in January which was largely done to give him increased credibility in discussions with Yaroshinski and more importantly with the former Tsarist ministers such as Krivoshein or Rodzianko.

The importance of creating some form of resistance to the Germans was becoming ever more pressing as the negotiations at Brest-Litovsk progressed and, as a consequence, the increased likelihood of substantial transfers or territories to Germany and the breaking of the Allied blockade. By this time, the Director of Military Intelligence was reporting to the War Cabinet on the increasing number of German divisions being moved from the Eastern to the Western Front and the probability of a major German offensive in the spring in an attempt to achieve victory before the planned massive expansion of the US forces in France could take place. This added urgency to the need for action in Russia but precluded the despatch of meaningful Allied forces.

A further consideration was the prospect of giving support to the nascent new nations forming on the periphery of the old Tsarist Empire. These were invariably anti-Bolshevik although frequently socialist or liberal in inspiration so that they were keen to obtain external support where they could and were susceptible to foreign influence whether that of the Allies or Central Powers. Finland for example, was inevitably drawn towards Germany as it was best placed to support Mannerheim and the Finnish Whites in their struggle against the Bolshevik inspired Finnish Reds but that did not prevent localised Allied intrigue. Recognising this issue, the Allies had met at Versailles on 23 December 1917 with Clemenceau, Pichon (French Foreign Minister) and Foch representing France and Lord Robert Cecil (Minister of Blockade and Assistant Foreign Minister) and Viscount Milner representing Britain. At this meeting, Russia was divided into spheres of influence with France being allocated the Ukraine, Russian Poland and responsibility for dealings with the Czechs. Britain was awarded a predominant influence Armenia, the Caucasus and the Cossack territories in South Russia.

Keyes' own position changed as time went by and he became more and more caught up in supporting the Whites. His initial support for the establishment of breakaway states in the Caucasus which would protect the approaches to Persia, Afghanistan and ultimately India ebbed and by 1920, he was railing at the Foreign Office's continued support for them seeing them as a distraction from the main objective of overthrowing the Bolsheviks. His perception then was that they would never be sufficiently strong to resist Bolshevik invasion without considerable Allied military support and this would never be forthcoming. By that stage, the independent states and, more to the point, Foreign Office support for them, had damaged relations with Denikin's White forces. That, however was in the future, the immediate impact of the Anglo-French accord was to draw the Allies further into meddling in Russia's internal affairs whilst enjoying the privileges of an allied nation - for example by the presence of the British and French Embassies and the various assorted military and civilian missions. This contradiction was to damage Allied credibility as well as increase tensions with the Bolsheviks over the coming months.

It was against this backdrop that Keyes' meetings took place in various locations in Petrograd always in secret and never at the British Embassy. This was clearly a highly stressful time for him not only because he was in physical danger but was also negotiating complex financial transactions with, so far as can be seen, no real expertise in the area - after all, there is a very large difference in distributing subsidies or other commissions in Baluchistan or

Persia and endeavouring to gain control of the economy of a major world economy particularly one in a state of political and financial collapse. In such circumstances, what is surprising is not that Keyes was repeatedly outfoxed by Yaroshinski and Leech but that the Schemes progressed as far as they did. Keyes himself recognised his inexperience in this field and was later at pains to emphasise that "I asked to be relieved of my duties in connection with this scheme as soon as a financial expert could be sent out from England."[192]

The basis of negotiations was altered by Yaroshinski's dealings with Lindley in January 1918. Prior to that, it had been envisaged that upon receipt of a loan of £5,000,000 from the British Government, Yaroshinski would secure control of the Russian Commercial and Industrial Bank, the Russian Bank of Foreign Trade, the Kiev Private Bank and de facto control of the Union Bank and the International Bank. At the time, these were "resisting German efforts to obtain financial control" so, unless the British supported the proposal, the banks would fall into German hands. The Germans were certainly interested in securing economic interests in Russia and there is no doubt that their apparent move on Yaroshinski's interests stirred the British into urgent action. It is not clear one way or another whether the German threat was genuine but it was certainly helpful to Yaroshinski in ensuring that the negotiations moved along swiftly.

Following the Lindley transaction, the proposal changed so that the British "were to lend him for three years two hundred million Roubles at 3 ½% secured by shares valued at three hundred and fifty million Roubles. In return, he was to give us half the seats on a board of four to control in our interests the policy of the above five banks and the Siberian and Volga Kama Bank, which he would acquire and of the Cossack which he would found, seats on the boards of all these banks and on all Companies controlled by these banks."[193] That Keyes was sold on the project is clear from his report to the Foreign Office on 21 January which stated that, "two hundred million roubles at present is five and a half million pounds: this could not be regarded as [a] large sum for blocking German schemes and securing great advantages for British trade....it is however [a] loan on good security. Our man is willing to deposit with us shares of conservative valuation of three hundred and fifty million Roubles in railways, oil, cement, timber, flax and cotton...majority of concerns being in the country outside Bolshevik control."[194]

Keyes later reported, "besides the advantages of keeping these banks out of German influence there were certain other political and commercial advantages."[195] The political advantages were specifically the ability to divert funds to South Russia to enable Kaledin and the Party of Collection to establish a viable financial system whereas the commercial ones were the prospect of establishing an economic preponderance in a post-Bolshevik Russia which would have amounted to the biggest expansion of British influence in a century.

As discussed in Chapter 12, the British Government approved the transaction on the understanding that "the unnamed financier was Poliakov."[196] This led to Poliakov becoming involved in the Bank Schemes and was to cause considerable complication and delay. Poliakov and Yaroshinski had little time for one another with Yaroshinski viewing Poliakov's political opinions "with the utmost suspicion" and Poliakov, in return regarding Yaroshinski as being a typical Russian financier "of the bounder type." That Yaroshinski was plainly a handful is hinted at by Keyes' codename for him of "Livewire."[197] The negotiations were bedevilled not only by their mutual antipathy but also that the underlying purpose of the whole scheme, namely, as a vehicle for ensuring funding reached South Russia was, according to Leech, to be concealed from Poliakov. This may have been the initial intention but it was not ultimately sustainable not least because Poliakov was, at that time, almost certainly also attached to the British Secret Service to some degree as well as being a close connection of Lessing who was on his way back to Russia from London with orders to prevent Poole entering into "half baked schemes."[198]

In any event, Keyes, Poole, Poliakov and Yaroshinski met on 6 February to progress their negotiations; it is not clear whether Leech was also present. Yaroshinski by this time was in a greatly improved position as a result of his dealings with Lindley and now explained that he had the "chance of completing his control of the Union and International Banks and of an arrangement with them for acquiring the Siberian Bank." He anticipated that £500,000 "would probably suffice unless German action forced up the price of the shares of the Siberian Bank."

He added that the Volga Kama Bank was no longer a viable target but a decision had to be made that day "owing to the departure of certain directors."[199] It is difficult to know how genuine the German threat was - Keyes certainly believed that it was - but it was clearly useful to Yaroshinski in putting pressure on Poole and Keyes to make a snap decision in his favour.

After a lengthy negotiation conducted chiefly between Yaroshinski and Poliakov, the amount to be advanced was agreed at £500,000 repayable over three years. The rate of interest payable by Yaroshinski was increased from three and a half to five and a quarter percent.[200] However, whilst Yaroshinski begrudgingly accepted, he made it clear that "this would probably suffice unless German action forced up the price of the Siberian Bank. He also "proposed ...to drop the Volga Kama Bank from the scheme." In return, Yaroshinski was to provide security to the value of thirty five million Roubles in shares and to give the British half the seats on the Board of Control of the new bank group.

The Germans were indeed keen to gain control of the Siberian Bank and Yaroshinkski "had to pay much higher than he expected for the shares." As a result, a further loan this time for £428,571 8s 7d which was almost double the initial investment was made - again at five and a quarter percent. According to Keyes, this was only just in time as "we only forestalled the Germans by one day, as the contract of a Company formed in Norway had already been approved by the principal director and was presented for signature in Christiana the day after the news was received that the shares had been sold in Petrograd."[201]

Keyes later summarised the deal to the Foreign Office as being exceptional value as follows:

"We have thus lent Yaroshinski £928,371:8:7 at 5 ¼% on the security of shares worth 35,000,000 roubles in commercial concerns and share in the Siberian Bank for [which] he is paying 66,000,000 roubles.

The shares in Companies stand in my name in the Commercial and Industrial Bank and the transfer of shares in the Siberian Bank are distributed as follows:

a. Transfer of shares deposited in Russian Banks in original with Poliakov, duplicates with me.
b. Transfer of shares deposited in French and British Banks in original with me, duplicates with Poliakov.
c. 1018 shares deposited with me in Legation in Christiana.

HM Government was willing to advance £5,000,000 at 3.5% on securities worth 350 million Roubles to prevent certain banks falling under German influence and to obtain control of them for certain political and commercial aims. The formation of the Cossack Bank is in abeyance. The Volga Kama Bank has been dropped out, but the control of the other banks has been obtained for less than one million Sterling at 5.25% instead of 3.5% with securities worth 101 million Roubles."[202]

The problem, as might be imagined, was the robustness of Yaroshinski's security. Throughout, he resolutely refused to hand over the bank shares themselves and offered instead forty thousand shares in Russkaya Neft Company, twelve thousand shares in the Ter Akopov Company and thirty thousand shares in the Achinsk - Minusinsk Railway; the first two were oil companies of limited value and the third a railway to some Siberian quartz-gold mines. Later, in July 1918, when the matter was investigated by Sir William Clark of the Department of Overseas Trade, he noted that Yaroshinski was not in a position to offer the bank shares themselves as they "were all mortgaged in carrying on his "pyramiding" operations.[203] In short, Yaroshinski's position was so compromised by his previous business activities that his actual control of his shareholdings was more notional than substantive. It is obvious that Keyes and Poole did not appreciate this and accepted what was offered.

Unsurprisingly, in the circumstances, Yaroshinski had difficulty in progressing his negotiations with NM Denisov the principal shareholder of the Siberian Bank as he distrusted Yaroshinski's ability to come up with the necessary cash. Furthermore, the two men who originated the scheme, Pokrovsky and Krivoshein were not in a position to remedy the problem. Pokrovsky who was not only the former Foreign Minister but also Chairman of the Siberian Bank had been imprisoned and so could not assist and Krivoshein, the former Minister of Agriculture had disappeared. All was not entirely lost however as Poliakov was also a junior manager and director of the Siberian Bank and so became closely involved in negotiations with Denisov.

At this point, the Scheme began to fall apart. To begin with, the speed with which the transaction had progressed would inevitably cause subsequent fall out and this is apparent from the Foreign Office telegram to Keyes on 22 January making it plain that the Government's approval to take this course was "entirely on your advice."[204] So, from the outset, Keyes had to accept responsibility for the Scheme's success and was always likely to be the scapegoat if, as in truth was the most likely outcome, it failed.

On 7 February, Lindley made it clear to the Government that the financier was Yaroshinski and not Poliakov adding his view that the matter should not be "finally settled until is has been thoroughly threshed out and Keyes will probably have to go to London to explain it."[205] This warning carried weight and at a meeting of the Russia Committee on 15 February, the Scheme came under close scrutiny resulting in a response being sent to the effect that "no advance of funds should be made to Yaroshinski until after Major Keyes had returned to England and explained the full bearing of his proposal." Having said that, the committee chairman, Lord Robert Cecil acknowledged that "we could not repudiate any action which had already been taken on the strength of the authority which had been given to Major Keyes, who, it appeared had pledged himself to the extent of half a million pounds."[206]

It is astonishing that such a high level committee should have inaccurate information before it. Although not significant in itself, Keyes had been promoted to Temporary Lieutenant Colonel the month before but, of far greater moment, was the fact that Keyes had actually already pledged almost £1,000,000. This meant that the committee wholly failed to comprehend the gravity of the situation.

Other issues also began to press in on the scheme causing it to fall apart. Critically, the position in South Russia was collapsing. The Don Cossacks who had previously refused to fight had then proceeded to mutiny led by two Cossacks, Lagutin and Nagaev who had joined the Bolsheviks. At the same time, the Bolsheviks who controlled much of the surrounding railway network began an advance on Kaledin's position. He was not in a position to offer meaningful resistance and by early February General de Candolle was reporting that the "South East Union" would not be able to retain control of Rostov and would have to fall back on Ekaterinodar in the Kuban.

If fact, the position was worse than envisaged as there was a split between Kaledin and Kornilov who controlled the Volunteer Army. Kornilov, recognised that disaster was imminent with the Bolshevik forces only fifty miles away at Taganrog and made it clear that retreat to the Kuban was the only option. Kaledin refused to join him so, on 8 February, the Volunteer Army began the epic trek to the Kuban which became known as the Ice March. Before their departure, General Alexeyev wrote "we are moving out into the steppe. We can return only by God's mercy. But we must light a torch so that there will be one gleam of light in the darkness enveloping Russia."[207] On the same day, Kaledin retired to his room in despair and shot himself. On 23 February 1918, Bolshevik forces entered Rostov. The Volunteer Army spent the next few weeks struggling towards Ekaterinodar which it attempted to besiege without much hope of success. On 12 April, Kornilov was killed by a stray shell and General Denikin immediately raised the siege and retreated north to the Don. As a result, by mid February at the latest, the main purpose of the Bank Schemes, namely to give succour to Kaledin and the Volunteer Army had been rendered nugatory at least temporarily.

Things were not improved by Poliakov having to go into hiding to avoid the attentions of the Cheka and the fact that, to circumvent the Bolsheviks' nationalisation of the banks, the date of the critical contracts had been backdated to October 1917. This undermined the whole legal basis for the transaction as it rendered it voidable at any time by either party. This was to make the British even more reliant upon Yaroshinski's goodwill something it already was by virtue of the deal's mechanism. As the British Economic Mission was later to conclude;

"It would appear that eventually all the shares and all the voting power in the Siberian Bank will be in M.Yaroshinsky's hands, and any control that we may wish to exercise over this bank will depend as in the case of the other five banks on M. Yaroshinsky's good faith and goodwill."

Keyes' position was therefore somewhat compromised with events calling into question his good judgment. There is also more than a whiff of him being smartly manipulated by both Yaroshinski and Leech with any help which Poliakov might have been able to provide being compromised by the fact that until quite late on, he was kept deliberately in the dark about the true purpose underlying the Bank Scheme. There is also uncertainty about whether Keyes was responsible for the original decision to fund Kaledin and the Party of Collection; as he puts it in one of his reports "I was ordered to devise means of financing Alexeev" but this is contradicted by another report in which he claimed that "it was in December '17 that this business really started, and I claim to have been the first to see the importance of it."[208] Either way, he was an out and out an enthusiast for the project. On the other hand, he played no part in the next move made by the Allies which was to commence preparations for direct intervention both from Murmansk and Archangel in the North and Vladivostok in the East. However this all lay in the future and, on being ordered to return to England, Keyes was still of the opinion that the Scheme would receive formal endorsement and backing. He must also have welcomed the opportunity to leave Russia and to spend time with his family as other than what Edith described as his "secret leave" in 1917 when they briefly met whilst he was en route for Russia, he had not been in England since 1914.

First, Keyes had to secure his exit from Petrograd which was far from straightforward. At that time, the Germans were advancing towards Petrograd with little in the way of effective resistance from the remnants of the Russian Army. Indeed, the Allied embassies were to flee Petrograd on 28 February with the British returning to London and other Allied nations moving to Vologda which was three hundred miles to the north east of Moscow. At about the same time, the Bolsheviks moved their capital from Petrograd to Moscow which was well out of reach of the German advance.

Petrograd was by then effectively lawless with whatever order existed being provided by the Cheka. It was therefore no straightforward matter to obtain permission to leave the country and particularly not for someone in Keyes' rather ambiguous position even if he were not also under suspicion for being involved in espionage. Poliakov going into hiding was clear evidence that the Bolsheviks were becoming increasingly aware of the Bank Schemes and this would compromise any claim that Keyes might have to diplomatic immunity. At this juncture, Keyes was saved by Bruce Lockhart who recounts in his memoirs how he sought to obtain visas from a Bolshevik official, Lutsky, who was in charge of the passport department. He clearly revelled in his power and his rudeness made Bruce Lockhart "boil with rage." Lutsky also picked out Keyes' passport as being suspicious. Bruce Lockhart managed to take advantage of a diversion to slip the passport from the rejected pile so that it was approved and stamped. It is noteworthy that he picked Keyes out as the one to save presumably because he knew how vulnerable he was to charges of espionage. As it was, Keyes and other British officials managed to leave that night on the train to the Finnish border.[209]

Chapter 14:

The Bigger Scheme?

Almost all the available documentary evidence points to the Bank Schemes being entirely directed towards the establishment of a viable financial system in South Russia which would enable the White forces there to be able to challenge and ultimately overthrow the Bolshevik regime. A further immediate benefit of the initial Scheme was that it would ensure that the White movement remained firmly in the Allied camp and would not be vulnerable to German influence. This was not only a merit in itself but also put in place a block on any German moves towards Central Asia and ultimately British India which was always the uppermost consideration in British Government circles. Later versions would promote a more buccaneering and imperialist policy which sought to establish a British economic, financial and political preponderance in a post war and post Bolshevik Russia.[210] The Bank Schemes in this format therefore sit easily with the British policy of trying to persuade the Bolsheviks to continue the struggle against the Germans whilst at the same time funding the opposition.

A century after the events in question many government records have still not been released and more will no doubt become apparent when they are. Certainly, there is nothing in Keyes' own papers that contradicts the accepted version of events. However, there is evidence some explicit, some more inferential, that there were other objectives also in play which contradict and undermine much of the official narrative about British relations with the Bolsheviks in early 1918. So far as possible, the version of events set out in the rest of this book is backed by documentary evidence. However in considering the potential existence of a bigger scheme, only limited evidence is available, either because it does not exist or has not been released.

It would appear axiomatic that the nature of the Bank Schemes was such that it was essential that they should be kept secret from the Bolsheviks so far as possible. The reason for this was obvious as an organised and properly funded White movement in South Russia was a mortal threat to the Bolshevik regime. There was also the fundamental illegality of the original Scheme which required the backdating of the various share purchases to give them a bogus legitimacy. This is all supported by Keyes' evidence when he writes of clandestine night time meetings at various secret locations - care was taken to ensure that there was a distance between Keyes as the chief promoter of the Schemes and the Embassy so that Keyes worked from his flat in Morskaya Street 52 rather than the Embassy in relation to the Schemes as opposed to his more legitimate propaganda activities.

With all of that in mind, the existence of evidence pointing to very active involvement in the Schemes by the Bolsheviks and Lenin in particular is extraordinary and gives rise to the possibility of an entirely different narrative existing details of which have still to be released by the British Government. Regrettably, the evidence that does exist is far from voluminous and reveals nothing about the possible motivations behind it.

The principal evidence comes from Foreign Office records kept at the National Archives and in particular one entitled "A memorandum based on original documents relating to the Banking Schemes negotiated by Colonel Keyes."[211] This explains that there were two threads to follow. Proposition A which related to "a loan of £500,000 in London to Russian Commercial and Industrial Bank at 3 ½ % [with] security shares to the value of 35 million Roubles."[212] Yaroshinski then took over responsibility for repayment. "This means that we are entirely dependent on M. Yaroshinski's goodwill and honesty." Proposition B related to the purchase by Keyes of between forty five and fifty five thousand shares from N Denisov in the Commercial Bank of Siberia. Both propositions were therefore part of the coming together of the initial Bank Scheme.

On the other hand, a document in the same file entitled "Russian Bank Control Scheme" focuses instead on the confusion between the Lindley and Keyes' schemes pointing out "hence there is a double thread to follow, viz a) the Foreign Office and Mr Lindley and b) the Foreign Office and Colonel Keyes" adding that because of the backdating of documents ostensibly to avoid the consequences of the Bolsheviks' edict nationalising the banks and prohibiting dealings in their shares, "it is therefore very difficult to establish the chronology of the transactions."[213] Accordingly, it is evident that there was considerable confusion from the outset and this was no doubt worsened by the fact that, as Keyes wrote, many of the more useful documents had been destroyed when the Ambassadors left Petrograd in March 1918.

The first real indication that something more secret was afoot comes in an entry for 7 February 1918 which reads "(369) Lindley says (ref FO118) Y is Yaroshinski, Poliakoff is Commercial Director of Siberian Bank. Believes in Scheme, but not satisfied with system of control; this Keyes is working over with Poole and Bolsheviks'.[214] This raises the immediate and obvious question as to why the Bolsheviks should have any involvement whatsoever in a scheme to fund their overthrow. However, the telegram sent by Keyes on the following day to the Foreign Office reporting on what is most likely the very same meeting makes no reference whatsoever to liaison with Bolsheviks. The telegram is a useful summary of the then current position and therefore is worth setting out in detail.

"Y[aroshinsky] has continued his policy of acquiring Banks but on slightly different terms and called my attention to the want of £500,000 immediately. At a meeting with Poliakoff and General Poole yesterday, we agreed the following. We pay Y £500,000 in London as a loan at 5 ¼ %. He transfers in my name in one of his banks one tenth share originally offered worth as far as can be estimated, 35,000,000 roubles and as soon as banks are opened will allow us to select in place of any of these shares which have depreciated in value owing to Bolshevik action such shares as we wish.

Unless as is reported, Germans as condition of peace demand Banks be re-established in which case (? I could) pay higher prices for shares of Siberian and Volga Kama Bank."

Keyes' telegram is therefore consistent with the original understanding of the Bank Schemes and does not, of itself, raise any suspicions that something else might have been going on.

However, the matter becomes murkier still with the entry for 19 February 1918 (522) which states that "Keyes reports German attempts to buy up Siberian Bank. Y therefore with assistance of our board has secured control. Y had to buy out certain holder in Moscow Bank at request of Lenin £500,000 did not suffice to acquire Anglo Russian Keyes promised him another £500,000 if he acquired Siberian as security he gives us all shares up to 55,000. Asks us to make further payment." This was clearly a summary possibly of a telegram which explains its terse nature. However, in the report on the Russian Bank Control Scheme, a slightly different version is put forward as follows:

"On same day [19 February], Col. Keyes reported that the Germans had tried to secure [sic.] Bank. Yaroshinsky had therefore secured control with assistance from our board. (He had to buy out certain holder in Moroccan [sic.] bank at the request of Lenin!) Keyes had promised Yaroshinsky another £500,000 if he acquired Liberian [sic.]. As security, Yaroshinsky has given all shares up to 55,000."

Leaving to one side the confusion over the names of the banks and it does seem inherently unlikely that any of the parties named would be interested in the ownership of banks in North and West Africa, the obviously remarkable thing is Lenin's apparent involvement. It certainly sits in stark contradiction with Keyes' own report that during December and January he had various meetings with Alexeyev's agents and "the interviews were very secret, generally held in a new place every night, preferably in a flat with two exits, and I used to borrow different fur coats and caps as often as possible. Had the Bolsheviks tumbled to what was going on they would certainly have shot all concerned."[215] The obvious question was whether there was another aspect to the Bank Schemes that was even more complicated and where the need for secrecy was even greater.

It is possible that the Foreign Office was previously unaware of what was taking place but it is more likely that it was getting more and more concerned about where the Schemes might be going as, on the following day, it telegraphed saying that there should be "no further advances to Yaroshinski until Keyes was back in England and can explain."[216] As has been seen in Chapter 13, this led to delays in payments being made. Keyes was to summarise it laconically as "the Treasury got cold feet when I had spent a million and called the show off."[217] In fact, as will appear in Chapter 15, he had a very hard time of it being caught up in a turf war between the Foreign Office and the War Office and with the potential of being left with personal liability for the entire loans which must have been extremely difficult for him.

The air of mystery is increased by the opaque reference in the Russian Bank Control Scheme document that "the big scheme has been held up for various reasons (evidently correspondence of which no details are at present available had passed between Colonel Keyes and the Foreign Office." As this is within a Foreign Office file, it is difficult to explain why at least the gist of its contents were not included unless there were security reasons for not doing so.

There is evidence of Bolshevik involvement in the trading of Russian bank shares as a Foreign Office telegram refers to the pro-German financier, Benenson, seeking to persuade the British to agree to the exchange of securities for Roubles. The author discouraged any involvement since "opinion is that Benenson and Gookovski (Bol Commissar for Finance) have an agreement and Benenson is working with Bols on a large scale."[218] Isidor Gukovsky was Commissioner of Finance of the People (Narkofin) between March and August 1918 which is close to the time in question. If the report is correct, then the Bolshevik with responsibility for finance and banking was himself engaged in secret transactions with one of the leading Russian bankers. It is, of course, possible that these were being corruptly carried out by Gukovsky in his private capacity but it is more likely bearing in mind the comments concerning Lenin that they were officially sanctioned.

On 27 July 1918, Dominick Spring Rice was to write to Colonel Peel about the dealings in shares in Russian banks by the Germans who were permitted to do so by the Treaty of Brest-Litovsk adding that "there are the usual wild rumours of eminent Bolshevik leaders having taken large commissions from these transactions."[219] This again supports albeit anecdotally the possibility of a consistent involvement by the Bolsheviks in behind the scenes transactions either for personal gain or to raise resources.

One of the other aspects of the Bank Schemes that raises questions is precisely why Keyes and Yaroshinski became distracted by the proposed purchase of the Siberian Bank at all. As might be expected from its name, it had no presence in South Russia and accordingly would be a poor conduit for funds to the Volunteer Army. This point was clearly picked up by Sir William Clark, Leslie Urquhart and Henry Armistead of the British Economic Mission which was sent to Russia in June 1918. The Mission's activities are covered in greater length in Chapter 17 but their conclusion on the acquisition of the Siberian Bank is worth quoting here;

"With reference to the purchase of the Siberian Bank shares we think that two alternatives may need to be considered:

a) To repudiate Colonel Keyes' contract and to cut the loss to Rs 15,000,000 already paid. This course will probably not be regarded by HM Government as suitable or politically desirable.

b) To meet the payments at due dates and to improve as far as possible the position of HM Government....

In our opinion, when once the original object of the scheme had disappeared, and it was decided not to proceed with the formation of the South Eastern Bank...a serious error of judgment was committed in carrying through a modified and altered scheme under which £500,000 was lent to M. Yaroshinsky on very insufficient security...

It is not clear to us why the Siberian Banks was brought into the scheme at all. It was not a bank operating in the sphere of the South Eastern Federation and its financial condition was such that it could not hope to open branches in the South East."[220]

The most likely explanation for how these concerns came about is that the terms of the original Schemes were never explicitly set out and neither the Economic Mission nor the Treasury ever fully appreciated that the secondary limb was to ensure that the Germans did not gain control of Russian Banks. In the case of the Siberian Bank, this is borne out by Keyes' own explanation that "the Germans were making strong efforts to capture certain banks, and that we forestalled them by one day only with the Siberian Bank as the contract for the sale of the "controlling packet" of the bank was presented for signature in Christiania [Oslo] the day after the chief director had heard that his agent had sold us the same shares in Petrograd."[221] It is probable that had the complete story behind the Schemes been fully explained, then Keyes would not have had to endure the threat of being left with personal liability for at least half a million pounds an astronomic sum for a government official.

What is far less clear is what, if any, part the Bolsheviks played in the Schemes. It does seem likely that there was a clandestine Bolshevik policy of sanctioning share transactions provided that an effective commission was paid even though this ran entirely contrary to official edicts. This is, not of itself implausible as the Bolsheviks were comfortable with taking financial advantage or receiving support from their otherwise bitterest enemies. This is obvious from the substantial funding of the Bolsheviks by the Germans prior to their takeover of power.[222]

It must also be the case that the Bolsheviks were aware of the extreme fragility of their grasp on power at that time. Leaving to one side their extreme weaknesses outside of the major cities and even there vocal opposition was growing daily, they must have perceived that at any time, the Germans might weary of Bolshevik attempts to drag out the negotiations of Brest-Litovsk. Should that have occurred, there were no effective forces available to prevent a wholesale German takeover. In those circumstances, it was logical for the Bolsheviks to seek to maximise the financial advantages that power gave them whilst it lasted whether for future political reasons or personal gain is not clear. This was certainly uppermost in the minds of the Bolshevik leadership when they believed themselves to be threatened by Denikin's advance in 1919 (see Chapter 19).

There was also the double headed and fundamentally contradictory British policy of trying to encourage Bolshevik resistance to the Germans whilst at the same time sponsoring White resistance. In furthering the first limb of this strategy, it is unlikely that the British would baulk at paying commissions or subsidies to individual Bolsheviks in return for support. However, this would have to be kept totally secret since, if knowledge were to leak into the western and particularly British press, it would fatally undermine British policy about the Bolsheviks and their domestic supporters.

There is no direct evidence for this but it could also be that the actions of Teddy Lessing and Vladimir Poliakov were directed to these ends. Keyes himself never understood what was going on commenting that "during the whole time Lessing has been floating about in the background in both Petrograd and London."[223] As Lessing enjoyed direct access to Lloyd George, who at all times favoured a more accommodating policy towards the Bolsheviks, it could be that either they were conducting parallel contacts with the Bolsheviks unbeknown to Keyes or that Poliakov's role was to act as contact between Keyes, Lessing and the Bolsheviks. Much later, Poliakov was to tell his grandson that he had had personal dealings with Lenin and Stalin whilst 'working as a translator for the British Mission [in Petrograd]' which may be further evidence of his acting as an intermediary in clandestine discussions.[224]

Intriguingly, in the same recording, he adds that Stalin's mother was engaged by his grandfather's family as a cleaner for their holiday home in Georgia. Either way, what is clear is that Keyes grew to be increasingly disgusted by the actions of Lloyd George in relation to the Bolsheviks and his willingness to abandon support for the Whites, particularly Denikin.[225] Certainly, Lloyd George's own relaxed approach to making personal gains from official positions of power would have meant that he would have had no scruples about sanctioning secret payments to the Bolsheviks. Links such as these could also explain the ease with which Keyes was able to obtain Trotsky's consent to travel to Vologda during the summer of 1918, as his status could already have been apparent; indeed, they may already have met.

There is a flourishing sub-genre of books written about British attempts to obtain the freedom of the Romanov family from Bolshevik imprisonment, many go on to assert that some of them survived the massacre at the Ipatiev House, Yekaterinburg, usually, one of the four daughters, Anastasia, Tatiana, Olga or Maria but, on occasion, the Tsar himself. This speculation founders comprehensively on the DNA evidence deriving from tests on bones found nearby that points conclusively to the murder of the entire family. However, that does not mean that there were no attempts made by the British Government to secure the family's release so that they might go into exile. It is conceivable that these links with Lenin formed part of a scheme to achieve a release without the ignominy of publicly agreeing to pay a ransom, as this would have been tantamount to recognition and also politically dangerous at a time of considerable political and social unrest at home.

Further inferential support for British involvement in potential plots to free the Tsar and his family come from Yaroshinski's own dealings with the Romanovs which had begun when he had helped fund convalescent hospitals where the Empress and her daughters had worked prior to the February Revolution. After the Bolshevik takeover, Yaroshinski was persuaded by a fervent Monarchist and anti-Semite, Nikolai E Markov, generally known as Markov II to become involved in schemes to secure their release from their then exile in Tobolsk. Some time in February 1918, Yaroshinski advanced one hundred and seventy five thousand Roubles to Monarchist groups.[226] Unfortunately, the monies were dissipated in a miasma of Monarchist plotting with most of it being retained by an agent based in Tobolsk, Captain Boris Solovëv. As a result, only thirty five thousand Roubles actually reached the Romanovs.[227]

It is therefore difficult to resist the temptation to link this payment either to the schemes advanced by Lindley or Keyes as the timings certainly seem to match. If so, then conceivably, the British were playing yet another double game; negotiating with the Bolsheviks whilst at the same time funding a Monarchist rescue bid. However, other than as stated above, there is little evidence presently available.

There is also evidence of Yaroshinski's involvement in another plot this one allegedly the brainchild of Smith Cumming, head of the SIS and which also involved Henry Armistead of the Hudson Bay Company and a Norwegian shipping magnate, Jonas Lied who enjoyed close connections with an associate of Lenin's, Leonid Krasin.[228] Lied had opened up a northern route to Siberia and with it transformed the Siberian river trade. He was well connected in Russian commercial circles and had received honorary Russian citizenship. The plan evolved but initially was for the Tsar to escape down the River Ob where he would be met by a British torpedo boat. Armistead was to be a member of the British Trade Mission to the Bolsheviks in the summer of 1918 for which see Chapter 15.

The most likely explanation is that Keyes' accounts are entirely accurate and there was the need for secrecy in relation to the proposed establishment of a south eastern bank as this would pose a direct threat to Bolshevik rule. The position in relation to the Siberian Bank was different and it is possible that the Bolsheviks, knowing that the shares were on the market and being sought by both the Germans and the British determined to control the sale process for their own financial benefit. This was clearly sensitive and might also explain the reference to correspondence not being provided to the authors of the Russian Banking Control Scheme report by the Foreign Office. The potential connection between the Schemes and a deal to secure the rescue of the Tsar and his family can only remain an elusive possibility.

At this stage, all that can safely be said is that there is clear evidence that even now the full picture has not been disclosed.

Chapter 15:

London March - June 1918

Keyes must have been in two minds during his journey back to England; it would surely have been a relief to be leaving the near anarchy of Petrograd and the prospect of spending time at home must have been enticing but he must also have known that he was returning to answer potentially hostile questioning on the wisdom of his agreements with Yaroshinski and the viability of the Bank Schemes. It also cannot have escaped his notice that he had pledged the British Government to make payments of £928,571 and that should it fail to endorse his actions, he might be found personally liable.

En route, he stopped at Oslo where he had a meeting with Denisov and at least one of his associates who requested that Keyes "alter his payment [£308,571.8.7] to one and a half million francs to his credit." Denisov and, by telegram, Poliakov were "very anxious and puzzled as to why payments have not been made and Poliakov ... also made very strong observations as to damage [that] delay in payment will cause to British credit.[229]

On reaching London, Keyes immediately sought to convince a suspicious Treasury and Foreign Office both of the merits of the Schemes and also that they needed to honour the agreement which he had already made. It is hard not to feel sympathy for him at this juncture, as it was clearly a worrying and frustrating time. He had done what he had been instructed to do in extremely difficult circumstances and where he himself was manifestly out of his depth in dealing with complicated financial transactions and was now having to justify his actions to a sceptical audience blessed with the benefit of hindsight.

The position was that he had committed the Government to making the payments and had participated in the giving of an assurance to a M. Gavriel who was one of Denisov's representatives and a minor shareholder in the Siberian Bank, to the effect that Yaroshinski "was receiving payments which would enable him to meet their claims and that the names of certain of them and the amounts due had been telegraphed in Embassy cipher."[230] Keyes was later adamant that once payments had been made to Yaroshinski, it was then up to him to distribute the proceeds to the Siberian Bank shareholders and also that Leech was, at all times, Yaroshinski's agent and not that of the Government. This certainly became the Government's stated position in defending a number of Court cases later brought by the shareholders who had not received payment. The situation was manifestly not as clear-cut as Keyes later asserted not least because Leech was connected with the British Intelligence and had previously been entrusted with the placing of British propaganda in the Russian press. He had also somehow managed to connect himself in some undefined way with the British Embassy and used its facilities to send telegrams using the Embassy cipher. As well as having to explain himself to the Treasury, Keyes was also receiving increasingly impassioned telegrams from Leech enquiring whether the payment had been made. Keyes therefore "visited the London City and Midland Bank on one or two occasions" to seek to resolve issues.

As part of the Treasury investigation, one of its officials, Robert Chalmers, was instructed to investigate the Scheme and he reported in April 1918. Chalmers looked at both the exchange transaction organised by Lindley and the Bank Schemes. He was substantially more critical of the Lindley transaction than the Bank Scheme itself largely because there was no credible evidence available that any funds had actually been transmitted to Kaledin and the Volunteer Army and none whatsoever that they had been received by General de Candolle in Kiev as had been stipulated by the Treasury back in January. He also noted that Mr Davidoff who had been the principal vendor of the shares in the Russian Commercial and Industrial Bank which had been acquired by Yaroshinski by virtue of the Lindley transaction and "at whose disposal it is asked that the Sterling equivalent of Roubles 6,000,000 should now be placed in London" was "now in Stockholm and is suspected in some quarters of working covertly in the interests of German Banks."[231] He was therefore naturally reluctant to sanction payment of a considerable sum to a likely German agent.

Chalmers acknowledged that he was hampered by the fact that many of the key documents had been destroyed when the British Embassy had been evacuated in March. Indeed, Keyes repeatedly lamented their loss in a number of subsequent documents on the basis that they would have fully vindicated his actions. From the evidence available to him, Chalmers reserved his most serious criticism for Leech of whom "certain indications casting doubts on his disinterestedness in his capacity as agent between the representatives of His Majesty's Government and the Russian parties to the transaction" had been received. He also made clear his suspicion of Leech or Yaroshinski's actions in the Lindley transaction pointing out that the exchange rates they had negotiated with Lindley "would have placed a considerable sum of money into the pockets of Monsieur Yaroshinski or Mr Leech."[232] It is not apparent whether Chalmers was aware of Leech's probable dual role but this seems unlikely. In fact, Leech increasingly came to be a convenient scapegoat for the failure of the Bank Schemes particularly when he became caught up in litigation with former bank shareholders during the 1920s. The extent to which the Government underwrote his position is uncertain but, as can be seen from the Affidavit that Keyes produced at the Government's behest in 1921, he was at pains to assert that Leech was at all times and for all purposes Yaroshinski's agent and not that of the Crown.[233] It is evident from all the contemporary evidence that Leech's position was far more complicated than that.

During March, Keyes had produced the first of two reports on the Banks Schemes, this one was one for the Russia Committee. The second report was produced after the withdrawal from South

Russia in 1920 when the question of the Bank Schemes was looked at once again this time probably by the Foreign Office or, less likely, the Treasury. Issues surrounding the Schemes and satellite litigation arising from it were to haunt Keyes for the rest of his life and certainly blighted his career. This, however, was in the future and in his first report, he recognised that with the death of Kaledin and the establishment of German hegemony in the Ukraine that the "immediate political advantages of the scheme are thus considerably curtailed and we are left, for the present, with little more than the economic and financial possibilities, except in Siberia." Keyes also repeated that the race that he had had with the Germans to secure control of the Siberian Bank was won "by one day only." As mentioned in Chapter 13, whether or not this race was real or a negotiating tactic utilised either by Yaroshinski or Denisov is not certain.

Overall, however, Keyes remained of the view that the fundamentals underpinning the Scheme remained in place and that the potential prize to be won of not only denying the Germans' access to resources but also gaining control of substantial portions of the Russian economy was easily worth the investment made. He asserted that "Russia with her enormous untapped natural resources, given order and a fair chance of development is the one European country that will be able to pay her share in the War within a reasonable time - even further, that it is the development of Russia's natural wealth that will play a large part in helping Europe to recover." In hindsight, such views appear sadly misguided but, at the time, they were entirely tenable particularly bearing in mind the commonly held view that the Bolshevik regime was plainly doomed.

In support of his thesis, Keyes added that "the universal opinion of all financial and economic authorities" was that the Bolsheviks would not be able to destroy the Russian banks and that "whatever the new form of Government in Russia, the banks must play the leading part in her reconstruction."[234] Although manifestly wrong, Keyes' view is interesting in that it reflects the overwhelming sense of incomprehension about what the Bolsheviks intended to do as well as the ruthless nature of their determination to stay in control which dominated British and French thinking at the time. In those circumstances, bearing in mind the Allied schemes for overthrowing the Bolsheviks which were in the process of being formed at the time, this was an entirely rational analysis.

Keyes' protestations were ultimately accepted and on 30 March, the Foreign Office finally asked the Treasury to approve the acquisition of the Siberian Bank as well as the loan of five hundred thousand pounds to Yaroshinski. As part of this, £337,500 of the loan to Yaroshinski was paid to Leech's account at the London City and Midland Bank which certainly placed Leech in a position of some strength in his subsequent dealings both with the British Government and Yaroshinski.

Whilst all this was going on, the Bolsheviks were gradually increasing their influence in Siberia and in particular Vladivostok which gave added urgency to the British need to conclude the acquisition of the Siberian Bank so that by the end of April, they had legal, if not practical, control of the Russian grain trade as well as a large part of the Russian economy. To give effect to this, it was increasingly apparent that British interests required the removal of the Bolsheviks if need be by military intervention. Whilst this knowledge was not widely shared amongst the Allies, the French certainly were aware in broad terms of what was afoot as they began asking a series of awkward questions of Colonel Byrne (General Poole's liaison officer in London) which Byrne deflected by referring them to Keyes who in turn was instructed to impart no useful information about the Siberian Bank to them.

At the same time, the Allies were facing a strategic defeat on the Western Front as a consequence of Ludendorff's long awaited Spring Offensive which finally began on 21 March to devastating effect. By 24 March, Sir Henry Wilson was recording in his diary that "at 5.30 Foch telephoned asking me what I thought of the situation and we are of one mind that someone must catch hold or we shall be beaten... At 7o'c meeting at Downing Street of Lloyd George, Bonar Law, Smuts and me. There is no mistaking the gravity of the situation.... we are very near a crash."[235] Over the coming month, the Allies were pushed back further and further towards the vital railway and communications centre of Amiens. There was a desperate shortage of troops at the front but Lloyd George was reluctant to release the reserves held back in Britain because he was fearful that they would be slaughtered in pointless military operations - by this time, his faith in Haig had been fatally undermined and their relationship was non-existent. In the end, the crisis produced the solution that should have adopted much earlier, namely, a unified command with Marshal Foch appointed as military supremo. This facilitated the smooth transfer of reserves between the French and British sectors of the front and, together with the growing American presence, enabled the great Allied offensives of summer 1918 to take place.

The absolute priority of being able to hold back the Germans in the West prohibited making a sizeable military commitment in Russia and also inclined the British towards looking more sympathetically upon reaching some form of accommodation with the Bolsheviks even though competing forces continued to push for overt British support for counter revolution. This inherent tension in British thinking did not go unnoticed by the Bolsheviks and Bruce Lockhart records in his diaries that on 11 March, he was told by Trotsky that "we were accusing him.... of Germanophilism, while his best friends were running him down for having placed too false hopes on a pro-entente policy. He said that our democratic government was pitiable, that our diplomacy throughout the war had been distinguished by a total lack of decision and that our FO was like a man playing roulette and scattering chips on every number."[236] This was a perceptive summary of British policy which, whilst it probably made sense in 1918, became increasingly incoherent following the defeat of the Central Powers and unfortunately did not ever really change until the final ignominy of the catastrophic defeat of the White forces in South Russia in 1920.

The more hawkish side of British foreign policy led to increasing support for intervention both at Murmansk and Archangel in the north of Russia and Vladivostok in the east. The motivation behind this was characteristically blurred. Following Turkey's entry into the war and the blocking of the Bosphorus to Allied shipping, the British were denied access to the Black Sea and they therefore had to concentrate upon the north Russian ports of Murmansk and Archangel to ship supplies to support the Russian war effort. This had led to the establishment of a sizeable depot principally at Murmansk (see Chapter 9). Following Finland's breaking away from Russia, a civil war broke out between the Finnish Whites and Reds. The Whites under Mannerheim, himself a former Russian army officer, were in receipt of considerable German military support and by the end of March 1918 had established effective control. The British were concerned that the White Finns aided by the Germans would seize control of Murmansk and possibly also establish a U boat base there which would also have the effect of closing off Archangel to the British as any convoys would be extremely vulnerable to attack. This would leave Vladivostok, thousands of miles to the east as the only possible avenue for Allied intervention. For once, there was a community of interest with the Bolsheviks who did not wish to surrender an important port and so a small contingent of British Marines landed on 31 March at the invitation of the local Bolsheviks.

Over the coming months, the British presence was to increase substantially and on 23 June, a force known as "Syren" was landed at Murmansk under the ultimate command of General Poole who had been appointed British Military Representative on 11 May 1918. Syren consisted of a disproportionate number of relatively senior officers and NCOs many with an intelligence background who it was hoped would work with local Whites to form a coherent anti-Bolshevik force. Most of the key documents surrounding the mission are unavailable but it is obvious that the true intention went beyond the officially stated purpose of protecting the British storage depot from attack by the Finnish Whites. The second military element was a mission to Archangel known as "Elope" which took place in August 1918 and is covered in more detail in the next chapter.

Also in March 1918, the Japanese made their threatened move on Vladivostok. This had been long anticipated as the British had been lobbying for Allied intervention for some months and, indeed had been providing support to Ataman Grigori Semenov as far back as February. Semenov became an embarrassment, as he was an unsavoury warlord who raided the Trans-Siberian railway from his base in China and was, to all practical effect, a brigand. The logic behind intervening in Vladivostok was that it would provide the Allies with a warm water port into which supplies could readily be sent from either Japan or the United States. The Japanese had thus far had a relatively inexpensive and profitable war mostly mopping up Germany's Asian colonies and incorporating them into their Empire. The British, as Japan's ally since 1902 were believed to have the most influence over them and actively sought to entangle Japan in an out and out takeover of the Trans-Siberian railway as far as Omsk but, in the United States, there was entrenched suspicion as to Japan's true motives. In hindsight, it is difficult to believe that anyone seriously considered that the Japanese would advance west for almost four thousand miles to assist in the overthrow of the Bolsheviks in their heartland around Moscow and Petrograd. Leaving to one side the obvious lack of Japanese enthusiasm for carrying out such a role, militarily they would have been extremely vulnerable as they would be dependent upon control of the railway for their supplies. In fact, the Japanese ambitions were largely self-serving and focused upon bolstering their position in Manchuria.

Intervention in Vladivostok was gradually expanded as the Americans were reluctantly drawn into support. However, whilst the Allies retained control of the city and surrounding areas, the hoped for full scale invasion did not come to pass and the city served primarily as a supply base as well as the ultimate destination of the Czech

Legion. Japan remained in effective control but at considerable cost to its economy until it finally unilaterally abandoned its foothold in 1922.

The Czech Legion preoccupied Allied thinking for much of 1918. It consisted of a combination of the relatively small Czech unit in the Imperial Russian army which had been formed in 1914 supplemented by Czech prisoners of war who had been captured whilst fighting for Austria Hungary on the Eastern Front. The Czech Army Corp had acquitted itself remarkably well during the Kerensky Offensive in June and July 1917 and had been supplemented by two Austrian regiments whose rank and file came mainly from Bohemia and who crossed the lines to join it. This success was noted by the Provisional Government which removed all barriers to recruitment so that by the time of the October Revolution it had grown to thirty thousand men.

In parallel with this development, Thomas Masaryk the leader of the Czech national independence movement had realised the importance of there being a defined Czech body fighting on behalf of the Allies. He and his lieutenant, Edward Beneš, had approached the French government with this suggestion in late 1916. They had ascertained that the French were keen to exploit Russian manpower on the Western Front and so readily agreed to their suggestion that the then Czech Army Corps be transferred to France. As it transpired, only a few troops had been shipped from Murmansk by the time of the February Revolution but the genesis of the idea had been formed and the French remained keen on the idea of a transfer either from Murmansk or Vladivostok until 1918.

At that point, the idea formed (chiefly in French minds as they were primarily responsible for the Allies' dealings with the Czechs) that the Legion could be used as a proxy force against the Bolsheviks. This had many seeming advantages as the Czechs were a coherent and unified force and most of all were already on the spot. From a practical perspective too, the ships which would have to be found (chiefly by the British) to transport the Czechs from Vladivostok or Murmansk could instead be used to ship American troops to France.

By May, a plan had formed whereby the Czech Legion was to form a crucial part of an anti-Bolshevik force funded in large part by Britain and France. One of the purposes of Syren and later Elope was that the small British forces landed at Murmansk and Archangel would march south to secure the critical railway junction at Vologda where the railway line from Moscow to Archangel crossed with the Trans-Siberian railway. They would then join with the Czechs and other anti-Bolshevik forces and either march on Moscow or deprive the Bolsheviks access to supplies from Siberia. Lloyd George was to make the position clear in a telegram to Bruce Lockhart on or about 2 July 1918, namely, that "the Czecho-Slovak successes give us an opportunity of restoring an Eastern front and revitalising Russia which may never return. Unless we take the fullest advantage...I do not see how we are to bring the war to a satisfactory end in 1919."[237]

As it happened, this was far too ambitious and anyway the Bolsheviks were alive to the threat posed. Nevertheless, there were times during the summer of 1918 when the Czechs came close to establishing total control over much of the Trans-Siberian railway and they would have been used in an outright assault upon the Bolshevik heartlands if the attempted Savinkov coup in July had not failed so abjectly (see Chapter 16). In the meantime, all parties including the Bolsheviks themselves anticipated their imminent overthrow during the summer of 1918 and both the Allies and Germans promoted their preferred successors. Bruce Lockhart was to report on 12 June that he had been "informed by two high officials in the Bolshevik Government whose names I do not mention for reasons of safety, that the Bolsheviks understand that their reign is coming to an end."[238] Accordingly, whilst it might be tempting to dismiss the various plots that the British conceived as being amateurish and doomed to failure, they were taken very seriously at the time.

What in summary appears to be the case was that the British, desperate for any means to reinvigorate opposition to the Germans in the East were willing to become entangled in schemes to overthrow the Bolshevik regime whilst at the same time endeavouring to persuade the Bolsheviks to cooperate with them. Whilst on the face of it, these were mutually contradictory objectives, it is hard to see what else the British could sensibly have done. The Bolsheviks were known to have been in receipt of German financial support and were in no position to resist a renewal of the German advance. The Bolsheviks were also the only party in Russia that was prepared to agree the terms imposed at Brest-Litovsk. It therefore made sense to seek to find a way of replacing them with a regime that would be more overtly pro-Allied. At the same time, there was a community of interest between the Bolsheviks and the British over preventing any further German incursions into Russian territory and, from a British perspective in particular, moves to seize control of the Russian fleet.

It is obvious that the Bolsheviks were well aware of this Janus-like quality to British policy and, to some extent it mirrored their own policy priorities which were to bring the war to an end whilst preventing the Germans from becoming so preponderant that they would themselves overthrow the Bolsheviks. Both Trotsky and Lenin were well aware of the risks of being caught in the middle of a war between the two competing forces of imperialism and sought to tread a careful path between them both whilst at the same time ruthlessly consolidating their control over the Bolshevik heartlands.

General Poole sailed to Murmansk in early May arriving on 24 May to establish a base there. A follow up ship left on 18 June which landed the Elope forces at Murmansk on 23 June. In his account of the voyage, Keyes refers to the ship as being "*The Mandela*" but it is likely that it was actually "*The City of Marseilles*" along with a destroyer escort, *HMS Cochrane*.[239] It is hard to know why Keyes added this minor deception when writing of events that took place twenty years' previously particularly bearing in mind the far more obviously sensitive material that he did reveal.

Keyes was fortunate in sailing in a modern ship of over 8000 tons so there would have been ample comforts available. The force sailed from Newcastle having embarked in London where the troops had been informed that they were sailing for America so as to justify the range of hot and cold weather equipment that they were carrying. As well as troops, *The City of Marseilles* also carried a British commercial mission which was ostensibly to advise on the "best means of restoring and developing British trade relations with and interests in Russia and of countering enemy schemes of commercial penetration." In fact, its task was to sabotage Bolshevik trade negotiations with the Germans by offering certain supplies at an economic price pending an overt attempt to overthrow the Bolshevik regime.[240]

The mission was headed by Sir William Clark, Comptroller General of the Department of Overseas Trade and previously Lloyd George's secretary at the Treasury. He was assisted by Leslie Urquhart, chairman of the Russo-Asiatic Corporation which had extensive mining interests in the Urals and Altai. Other member included Henry Armistead of the Hudson Bay Company and F Lambert of Messrs James Whishaw which had a long trading history with Russia. The Mission was advised by Dominick Spring Rice, assistant city editor of the Morning Post and a Captain in the Royal Army Service Corps and who was probably also reporting back to the Treasury.[241]

Keyes' mission is not certain but it is possible that he was one of the senior officers whose orders were to form a coherent anti-Bolshevik force which would be based in North Russia and supplied from the British depot in Murmansk. More likely, however, his mission was intelligence based and almost certainly involved the latest iteration of the Bank Schemes,

Keyes wrote about the voyage and it is plain that it was nightmarish.[242] Implicit in his account is the likelihood that this was the ship carrying the Elope force as Keyes refers to the destination being kept a secret until the ship was out of port, that there were seven hundred officers and men on board and that it never got dark. All of this points to the account relating to the June voyage. Interestingly, he did not mention the commercial mission at all even though Spring Rice was a key component of it and with whom he shared a cabin.

Keyes explained how "a few days out" influenza had struck the ship and soon order in the ship began to break down as more and more passengers and crew fell ill. He wrote of the differing attitudes to death of the Christians, Muslims and Hindus, the latter two being exclusively crew members. It is noteworthy that Keyes wrote admiringly of the Muslims - with whom he would have been far more familiar bearing in mind his service in Baluchistan and Bahrain - and reserves his scorn for the Hindus who "showed none of the reverence of the Christian and Mohammedan burials but a loud wailing while the last offices which they could render their dead were pathetically bungled." This preference for Muslims was a common attitude amongst the British in India and reflected the fact that they were monotheistic with a reverence for scriptures as opposed to the polytheistic Hindus.

Some way in, Keyes and Spring Rice both succumbed to influenza and were clearly very ill indeed for a couple of days with Spring Rice being "in a bad way."[243] Upon his recovery, a brother officer fortified Keyes with a whisky and soda which might, as it were, scotch the rumour of his teetotalism although there is possible evidence to the contrary in that Sidney Reilly later took a marked dislike of Keyes because he had refused to share a drink of champagne with him to celebrate his (Reilly's) promotion but that was more likely to have been a sign of Keyes' distaste for Reilly than alcohol.

Whilst the ship was in the Arctic Circle, it was followed by a school of whales which both Keyes and the ship's captain mistook for a German submarine. Once he had got over the shock, the Captain told him about his problems with the ship's crew who were all Lascars and were struggling to cope both with the cold weather and influenza. As with many of Keyes' accounts, it transpired that fortuitously he was able to sort the problem by using his particular skills, in this case having knowledge of the obscure Punjabi dialect which the Lascars all spoke. As a result, Keyes was able to ascertain that the Muslims were perturbed by being unable to work out the direction for Mecca when the sun never set which he immediately sorted out for them. Matters with the Hindus were more complicated because they were suffering from "sheer funk' as well as being concerned about having to share lavatories with the Muslims and being terrified by the whales. Once again, however, Keyes sorted it all out to everyone's satisfaction.

Chapter 16:

June - July 1918

Keyes' arrival in Murmansk coincided with what was perhaps the time of greatest uncertainty for Russia and the Bolsheviks and there was a widespread belief amongst all the involved parties including the Germans that the regime was about to collapse. That it did not was down in part to a combination of ruthlessness on the part of the Bolsheviks but chiefly to a confusion of aims both amongst the Allies and the Germans.

The Bolshevik position did indeed appear perilous. By the terms agreed at Brest-Litovsk, much of Western Russia had been lost along with Finland and the Baltic provinces and with this a substantial proportion of Russian industrial capacity and population. The peace had not prevented further German depredations particularly in the Ukraine and South Russia where the German backed Hetmanate was in place from April 1918. The Ukraine remained in a state of chaos with Bolshevik insurrections and Allied backed wrecking campaigns conducted to deny the Germans access to Ukrainian resources. As a concomitant, no supplies were sent to the Bolsheviks either.[244] This not only denied them access to Ukrainian grain and other foodstuffs but also the Donbass coalfields. The impact upon the Bolshevik controlled area was therefore serious and there were increasing shortages of food and coal which not only caused hardship for the civilian population but also led to reduced economic activities generally. As a consequence, factories either closed or reduced production substantially and the workforce, faced with shortages and malnutrition increasingly returned to the countryside. This was both natural and readily foreseeable as many workers had only moved to the cities in the previous twenty years and most had retained contact with their local village or *mir*. However, the migration of population was unprecedented and caused substantial economic dislocation.

To put this in context, the population of Petrograd passed the one million barrier in 1900, rose to 2.4 million in 1916 but then collapsed to 740,000 in 1920. There was a similar trend in Moscow where the population was 1.175m in 1900, rose to 1.817m in 1915 but then fell back to 1.028m in 1920.

At the same time, the Volunteer Army and the Don Cossacks were in control of the Kuban and much of South Russia and the Caucasus and, to make matters worse for the Bolsheviks, Siberia was either in chaos or under the control of the pro-Allied Czech Legion. On top of that, the British had just landed in Murmansk and were threatening to establish a power base in North Russia. As a consequence, all of the major grain producing areas were outside Bolshevik control as well as most industrial capacity and there was a real risk of starvation. The Allies attempted to exploit this weakness yet further by plotting to blow up strategic bridges over which supplies were reaching Petrograd. All of this made the Bolsheviks desperate and the activities of the Cheka became ever more ruthless.

The Volunteer Army was more or less stranded in South Russia although beginning to re-establish itself after its winter march into the Kuban following Kornilov's death. It was still dominated by General Alexeyev although his health was failing and he was to die in September 1918 at Ekaterinodar. On Alexeyev's death the movement came under the control of Anton Denikin, another former Tsarist general, who was to remain in command until his resignation in April 1920.

The Volunteer Army retained close links with the Don Cossacks who by the summer of 1918 were led by General PN Krasnov. Following his election by the Don Cossack Host, Krasnov sought out support from where he could most easily find it and this led him into an alliance with the Germans in Ukraine. This alliance continued until the Armistice at which point Krasnov sought to switch his allegiance to the Allies. In fact, his position had always been ambivalent and his links to the Germans were primarily motivated by the need for military supplies and a shared antipathy towards the Bolsheviks (at least in the Ukraine on the Germans' part). By June 1918, he had forty thousand men under his control and fifty six guns and one hundred and fifty nine machine guns which made the Don Cossacks a significant threat. Krasnov passed on much of the weaponry he received from the Germans to the Volunteer Army summing the position up by saying "the Volunteer Army is pure and undefiled. And I, Ataman of the Don, accept with my dirty hands German shells and ammunition, wash them in the waters of the quiet Don, and hand them over clean to the Volunteer Army."[245]

In accordance with the spheres of influence agreed between the British and the French, the Ukraine was subject to extensive political meddling by the French although they failed to prevent the establishment of the pro-German Hetmanate in April 1918. The British with their particular concern to protect India from Bolshevik infiltration had responsibility for the Caucasus and Transcaspia and where possible sought to control the transport routes to India. This led to the sending of an expedition under the command of Major General Lionel Dunsterville which was accordingly known as "Dunsterforce."[246] Its mission was to train local anti-Bolshevik forces and later to attempt to gain control of the Baku oil fields. The British also took the lead in the planned intervention in North Russia of which Keyes was peripherally involved.

The French had primary responsibility for Allied dealings with the Czech Legion and, in particular in denying the Bolsheviks access to supplies from Siberia. The Legion was also intended to be a critical player in a proposed coup to be led by Boris Savinkov (1879-1925) in July 1918. Savinkov was another middle class revolutionary whose political views had been tempered by experience. He was responsible for the assassination of the Minister of the Interior, Vyacheslav von Plehve in 1904 and also plotted the assassination of Grand Duke Sergei Alexandrovich for which he was sentenced to death. He escaped from prison in Odessa and fled abroad. Over the following years he became increasingly disillusioned with revolutionary tactics and became fiercely anti-Bolshevik. He returned to Russia from France in April 1917 and served as Deputy Minister of War under Kerensky. However, he was an inveterate schemer and was closely linked to the failed coup by Kornilov in September 1917. After spending time with Kornilov in south Russia, he returned to Moscow possibly because Kornilov had tired of him. In Moscow, he formed a new grouping, the Union for the Defence of the Fatherland and Freedom which chiefly consisted of ex-Tsarist officers.

In part at the Allies' behest, Savinkov's group became linked in some way to the National Centre itself an organisation of anti-Bolsheviks that sought to coordinate resistance by the various White factions. The risings which he orchestrated in July 1918 were intended to coincide with the Allied intervention and an advance towards Vologda by the Czechs but commenced prematurely and were put down with characteristic brutality by the Bolsheviks.[247]

At the same time, the British and French were busy actively seeking to persuade the Japanese to participate more substantively in moves to overthrow the Bolshevik regime and to extend their influence westwards along the Trans-Siberian railway. As mentioned in Chapter 15, the Japanese had their own objectives and were reluctant to become involved in what was in effect regime change. Further, the practicalities of supplying a force dependent upon the highly vulnerable railway line militated against the scheme's success leaving to one side, the inevitable Russian hostility towards the Japanese which was a legacy from the Russo-Japanese war.

A further complicating factor was that the Americans were highly suspicious of the proposed Japanese intervention which aroused their anti-imperialist instincts. They also had well founded fears that in addition to seeking the overthrow of the Bolsheviks, the British and French had ulterior commercial interests in play. The British were reluctant to act without American backing and support and the Japanese probably used this American hesitancy as an excuse for not doing what they did not want to do anyway.[248]

The British desire for American support became ever more urgent during the summer of 1918 when the Czech Legion was achieving its greatest successes. Lloyd George was to summarise the position pithily in a telegram which he sent to the Ambassador to the United States, Lord Reading, on 3 July which stated "I hope that you will do all you can secure complete American co-operation for policy of intervention in Siberia…the President's arguments against it especially his fears as to effect on Russian opinion of intervention mainly Japanese have weighed strongly with me in the past. Today however, conditions have greatly changed and I am now convinced that if we do not act at once Russia and Western Siberia will be in German hands before winter. The Czecho Slovak successes give us an opportunity to of restoring an Eastern front and revitalising Russia which may never return. Unless we take the fullest advantage of this opportunity of reconstitution of an Eastern front, I frankly do not see how we are to bring the war to a satisfactory end in 1919…unless action is taken at once Czechs may be overwhelmed and chance of establishing ourselves in Siberia and Northern Russia before winter sets in may disappear."[249]

This summary of the position makes plain that the principal British objective was to do all possible to revive a viable opposition to Germany in Russia or at least to block further German expansion eastwards. Implicit in all this was that the Bolsheviks should be replaced with a government which would seek to revive hostilities against the Germans. From today's perspective, Lloyd George's fears appear inherently implausible; there was never a realistic prospect that the Germans would deplete their forces in the west to enable such an adventure to take place. Equally, it is highly unlikely that any Russian government would be able to reconstitute the army with a view to recommencing hostilities against Germany as the situation had deteriorated well beyond that point. However, the fear was clearly real and is illustrative of the pessimism prevailing in Allied circles at a time when the Western Front was being repeatedly pushed back by the formidable German offensives during the summer of 1918.

British hopes of a revived Eastern Front seem overly optimistic and it is probable that the best that might have been obtained was a replacement government that would at least be unequivocally anti-German and which would take all steps short of war to prevent any further German expansion. In truth, that is not very far from what was ultimately obtained from the Bolsheviks particularly as the summer progressed and the German onslaught in the west was succeeded by the prolonged Allied counter-offensive which commenced at Villers-Cotterets on 17 July and continued through to the Armistice in November. Inevitably, German failures in the west caused their influence to wane in the east.

Behind all this was an overt hostility to the Bolsheviks and a desire to secure their destruction. This was informed by the illegitimacy of Bolshevik rule with its lack of democratic backing and the establishment of a ruthless and murderous secret police force. It was also a defensive move as there was a real, albeit overstated, fear of the Bolsheviks exporting the revolution to the West and the best way to combat this was by securing their extirpation. There were genuine concerns about imminent revolution in Britain particularly provoked by the actions of the radical left on Clydeside culminating in January 1919 in the "Battle of George Square." Earlier, fear of revolution had also persuaded George V to press for the withdrawal of an offer to provide the Tsar and his family with the offer of exile in Britain which ultimately consigned them to death. On an even more self-serving basis, there was a desire by the Allies possibly excluding America, to gain positions of influence not only over a potential new Russian government but also over Russia's resources which were seen as a way of recouping financial losses in fighting the war. The Allies expressed outrage at the terms imposed upon the Russians at Brest-Litovsk but a post war Russia dominated by the Allies might equally have been exploited and denuded of its resources.

The German policy towards Russia was also incoherent. Having largely precipitated the Bolshevik coup both by arranging for Lenin's presence in Petrograd and by financial subventions, they had become increasingly disillusioned. On the positive side, only the Bolsheviks would have agreed to the terms of the Treaty of Brest-Litovsk which enabled the Germans the prospect of access to vital raw materials and agricultural produce as well as the opportunity to build up their forces in the West and mount the repeated offensives of the summer of 1918. It is by virtue of the treaty and other subsequent encroachments particularly in the Ukraine that the Germans were able to make progress towards breaking the blockade and securing access to desperately needed supplies and industrial resources.

Against that, they were fully aware of the gulf that lay between them and the Bolshevik political system although it was, in many ways, less extreme in substance than in theory. Germany was, by 1918, effectively a military dictatorship consisting of the duumvirate of Ludendorff and Hindenburg with the Kaiser ruling in name only. They had instituted a policy of *Kriegssozialismus* or war socialism whereby the entire economy came under the control of the government - in this case the army and Ludendorff in particular. It was in effect a militarised form of state socialism which controlled prices, directed labour and industry as well as instituting a strict rationing system. Civil rights and liberties were circumscribed although industrialists were alarmed by the government's insistence upon trade union involvement in decision-making. Increasing state intervention was widespread amongst all the combatant nations particularly where rationing was imposed but the economic effects of the British blockade and Germany's exclusion from all markets other than central Europe and Scandinavia had resulted in it being imposed in Germany to a far greater extent than in Britain or France. The degree of control increased as the blockade tightened with the British gradually closing loopholes by bullying neutral countries, particularly Holland, Norway and to a lesser extent, Sweden into limiting their trade with Germany.

Lenin clearly took note of the German model which in many ways was a more efficient and all embracing version of the Tsarist system. In addition, the Bolsheviks all subscribed to a fundamental belief that state coercion was the only way in which the revolution was to be brought to a backward and politically undeveloped country.

As from May 1918, the Bolsheviks introduced War Communism by which the entirety of society was to come under the control of the Party. The first iteration of this was the Grain Monopoly which sought to stamp out free trading and bring the entire grain trade (at least insofar as it was within Bolshevik control) under Party direction. This move was in part an attempt to address a practical problem caused by White and Allied attempts to starve the regime into submission but it was also ideologically motivated and formed part of the war against the market. This proved to be disastrous and led to resources being committed to enforcing grain seizure and increasing hostility between the Bolsheviks and the peasants who hoarded grain or sold it privately. The peasants turned overtly hostile to Bolshevik rule as a result and increasingly took arms against them; their semi-anarchic forces, some of whom were known as the Greens became another factor in the collapse into civil war.

The Germans looked on this with concern. The replacement of the Bolsheviks might lead to a resumption of hostilities which would in turn require the diversion of German resources back to the Eastern Front. However, the Bolsheviks had made no secret of their intention of exporting the revolution throughout Europe with Germany an obvious first target. The increasing militancy of the German workforce caused alarm to the German government in much the same way that the British government was concerned by the militancy of its own workforce. However, the threat was greater in Germany not least because of real deprivation - the Turnip Winter of 1916-17 had led to the civilian population living at a subsistence level. There was also evidence that fraternisation with Russian troops had resulted in German troops becoming radicalised. Ludendorff was to complain about troops transferred west from the Eastern Front infecting other units with Bolshevik ideas.

All of this predisposed the Germans to look for support amongst the anti-Bolsheviks. However, most of these were by now close to the Allies and many in receipt of Allied subsidies. The Germans therefore sought out the ultra-monarchists as potential proxies as well as providing arms to General Krasnov of the Don Cossacks. On 9 June 1918, the same day that the Gneisenau Offensive started in the west, Ludendorff found time to send a memorandum to the Chancellor, Hertling, recommending that the Bolsheviks be overthrown by German military force. Ludendorff was also certain that Germany's only way to break the Allied blockade was by seizing resources from Russia and the Ukraine. His contempt for the Bolsheviks was evident from his comment that "we can expect nothing from this government although it lives by our mercy. It is a lasting danger to us which will diminish only when it recognises us unconditionally as Supreme Power and become pliable through its fear of Germany and concern for its own existence."[250] He added that Germany should recognise the instability of Bolshevik rule and forge links with Monarchist groups. This reinsurance policy would ensure that Germany was not "left high and dry" should the Bolsheviks be overthrown.[251]

The fractious relationship between Germany and the Bolsheviks became even more troubled with the assassination of the German Ambassador, Count Wilhelm von Mirbach on 6 July by members of the Left Social Revolutionaries possibly with the connivance of the Bolsheviks.[252] This was followed on 30 July by the assassination of Field Marshal von Eichorn, the German commander in the Ukraine, by two other Left SRs. The Mirbach assassination was exploited by the Germans to secure concessions from the Bolsheviks that enabled them to fortify their Embassy with what were almost certainly German or Volga German troops in Russian uniform.

On 19 July, a report was submitted to the Foreign Ministry in Berlin by Counsellor Reizler based at the Moscow Embassy. Riezler's views were the mirror of those of the Allies. He summarised the current situation as being "in a country split by escalating civil wars, it is almost impossible to come to a conclusion about the possibilities open for our politics. But since the whole situation is forcing us to take a course which is to our advantage, on a ship that is thrown about in storms, I shall have to try ...The Bolsheviks are dead. The corpse is alive because the grave-diggers cannot agree who should bury him. The battle which is going on at the moment between us and the Entente on Russian soil, is no longer a battle over the favour of this corpse. It has now already become the battle over the succession, over the orientation of a future Russia."[253]

The Germans were therefore torn between making the best of what they had achieved and continuing to support (or at least not actively destabilise) the Bolsheviks or throwing their full support behind the pro-German element of the Monarchists. This decision was becoming unavoidable as the German-Bolshevik trade talks dragged on and also as the Bolshevik terror took hold and the various officer groups who would be natural supporters of a counter revolutionary coup (both pro-German or Allied) were being rounded up. The Germans were conscious that the Allies had established close and friendly links with most of the anti-Bolsheviks and this tendency would increase with time. They could also see that Bolshevik policies were creating shortages and economic dislocation both of which alienated the peasantry and urban workforce who but for the terror would already have risen up. Against that, the Germans could offer the one thing that the Russian peoples really craved which was peace. Before anything could be concluded, German deliberations were overtaken by events in the west.

In July, there was, however, widespread anticipation not least by the Bolsheviks themselves of an imminent German seizure of power. However, by then, Germany's position in the west was looking increasingly vulnerable and with it a pressing need for reinforcement. This, in turn, meant that troops could not be spared for further expansion in the east. Accordingly, the Germans recognised that their best hope of retaining any meaningful influence in Russia was by cleaving to the Bolsheviks however distasteful that might be. In any event, as the Allied counteroffensive developed during August and September, it became increasingly apparent that the Central Powers were on the point of collapse so the potential for forging alliances with anti-Bolshevik parties fell away.

Keyes' arrival in Murmansk pitched him into the middle of these schemes and plots. The principal reason for his presence was to assist in the tidying up of the first part of the Bank Schemes as well as looking into the possibility of their revival. It is almost certain that he was to work closely alongside Spring Rice and Sir William Clark but he also had instructions from British Intelligence as well. On 25 June, he, alongside Clark and Spring Rice and Francis Lindley who, as has been noted, had been sent back to Russia to act as High Commissioner based in Murmansk, attended a meeting with General Poole and Leech to discuss the Bank Schemes. Leech was reassured by Keyes that the monies outstanding to Yaroshinski arising from the first iteration of the Bank Schemes had now been paid into his London bank account which must have come as a great relief. Leech explained that Yaroshinski's mood was "one of anxiety to know whether he enjoyed the confidence of His Majesty's Government" and was worried about whether the banks under his control could continue to meet demands for withdrawals by depositors "demands that had been growing since the Bolsheviks had controlled the banks in December 1917."[254]

They then discussed the issue of the Board of Control whereby, in return for the £500,000 invested, the British and Yaroshinski were each to have the right to nominate two board members. Yaroshinski wished to retain ownership of his shares in the five banks acquired in January (see Chapter 12) but would surrender management of the banks acquired to the Board of Control. As Lindley explained "for the sake of his own credit, however, he wishes to keep them [the shares] in his own name, so far as this is compatible with the main scheme. The Board of Control would leave the management of the banks as at present, but would hold the undated but signed resignations of all directors. It would then proceed to foster the interests of His Majesty's Government and of Mr Yaroshinsky through the medium of these banks, and presumably Mr Yaroshinsky thinks that His Majesty's Government would save the banks from any mishap they might meet, owing to his speculative activities."[255]

As is implicit from Lindley's report, there was increasing scepticism about the wisdom of the Schemes and the reliability of Yaroshinski and Leech. Lindley was informed by another member of the mission that Leech "was regarded completely as a man of straw before the war" although there was also evidence of him negotiating for the acquisition of a ship repairing business, possibly in Murmansk, "to the capital of which he was to contribute up to £60,000."[256] Equally, there were doubts about Yaroshinski's true wealth which Leslie Urquhart (another member of the mission) had been told was no more than two million Roubles. Spring Rice was suspicious of both of them and expressed the view that "care should be taken that they be not allowed to lower British credit by being too publicly associated with any financial scheme on which His Majesty's Government may embark."[257]

All of this supports the later and convenient view that Leech was at all times Yaroshinski's agent and that accordingly the British Government was under no obligation to stand behind commitments which he had made in pursuance of the Bank Schemes. This was certainly the line adopted by the British and indeed Keyes himself in the various court cases brought against Leech in the following years. In a witness statement, albeit unsigned, in the Keyes Papers, Keyes states unequivocally that "Leech was clearly not acting for and on behalf of His Majesty in connection with the [loan to Yaroshinski of £500,000]. He was, as far as the Embassy and myself were concerned, nothing but the agent selected by Yaroshinski to receive part of the money which the Government had promised to pay Yaroshinski." That being said, in the same document, Keyes also states that, on his arrival in Petrograd, he worked for the "Anglo-Russian Commission which was a propaganda organisation. The Cosmos Agency was a branch of this Commission...and I believe that Leech who was a British civilian resident in Russia, was employed by Cosmos Agency." Bearing in mind the way in which the word propaganda was often interchangeable with intelligence and that the Anglo Russian Commission was headed by a Major (later Lieutenant Colonel)

CJM Thornhill who was Chief of Intelligence to General Poole and later General Ironside, it is hard to avoid the conclusion that the position was far more complicated than presented by Lindley and Keyes and that Leech's position was ambivalent to say the least.[258]

This is borne out by Lindley's own report of the meeting when he records that Leech "dilated on his loneliness in Petrograd as a British agent since the departure of the embassy." It seems obvious that if Leech were not in fact, a British agent, Lindley would have made the point here. After all, as the former Counsellor at the Embassy, he was in the position to know and even if he did not, there were a sufficient number of members of British Intelligence close at hand, particularly Captain WMA McGrath and Keyes himself, who could have put him right. It is therefore reasonable to conclude that Leech did indeed have links with British Intelligence although probably not as strong as he later represented.[259] The failure to address this obvious conflict of interest was to bedevil the later history of the Bank Schemes and Keyes must accept some responsibility for allowing the confusion to arise.

Lindley's return caused Bruce Lockhart to conclude that "London had no confidence in [him]" and he 'returned [from Petrograd] to Moscow in a state of dejection."[260] He also was well aware that the underlying purpose behind the arrival of Poole and the Economic Mission in Murmansk was to intervene militarily in the overthrow of the Bolshevik regime. His memoirs show him as a consistent proponent of cooperation with the Bolsheviks and as being hostile to intervention up until late June or early July 1918 when he changed tack entirely. He ascribes his volte-face to the fact that he "lacked the moral courage to resign and to take a stand which would have exposed me to the odium of the vast majority of my countrymen."[261] Bearing the mind that Bruce Lockhart's default position was one of unbounded self-belief, this acknowledgement of weakness does not ring true and it is noteworthy that prior to leaving Petrograd, he had a meeting with Captain Cromie, the British Naval Attaché and Captain McGrath. Cromie, like McGrath was also a member of British Intelligence.

In his memoirs, Bruce Lockhart records that "in one sense McGrath was reassuring. Some weeks before, in a moment of depression, Trotsky had suggested that I was merely a tool, used by the British Government to keep the Bolsheviks quiet while it was preparing an anti-Bolshevik coup...McGrath, however, had set my mind at rest. The intervention plan, he said, was not very far advanced and England had no policy at all as far as Russia was concerned." Whilst it is fair to say that the British had no coherent policy concerning Russia, intervention was by then clearly an inevitability as Bruce Lockhart cannot fail to have known. A more likely explanation therefore is that McGrath and Cromie passed on instructions from London which Bruce Lockhart was entirely willing to follow.

According to his later witness statement, Keyes had travelled to Russia "to see how Yaroshinski was progressing the scheme."[262] He added that "by a coincidence I met Leech in Murman and we travelled in the same carriage from Murman to Kiev." This statement is almost certainly misleading in that Leech's presence in Murmansk was far from coincidental and, anyway, the discussions about the Bank Schemes took place during a formal meeting and not in a train carriage. Equally, the statement itself is contradictory. To begin, there is no evidence that Keyes (or for that matter Leech) went to Kiev at that time and there was no practical reason why they should. Further, the statement goes on to say that on his arrival at Petrograd, Keyes "received a message from [Leech] that he had had to go into hiding." However, the train route from Murmansk to Kiev went through Petrograd and so, if Keyes had travelled with Leech, they would have arrived together and there would have been no need for messages. What seems more likely is that both of them did travel to Petrograd whether together or separately is unclear but that Leech's going into hiding happened some time following his arrival.[263]

Sir William Clark's mission travelled at about the same time as Keyes and possibly on the same train as they were later all together in Petrograd. As well as examining economic opportunities, the mission had been given the task of investigating both the economic merits of the Bank Schemes and the actions of *Tovaro Obmien* which was the corporate vehicle operated by the Allies to deny the Germans access to Russian resources. Keyes must have been somewhat uncomfortable knowing that his activities in early 1918 alongside those of General Poole and Frank Lindley were to be submitted to such close scrutiny. This sensitivity no doubt accounts for the repeated statements made by him that he had "asked to be relieved of [his] duties in connection with [the Bank] Scheme as soon as a financial expert could be sent out from England."[264]

As well as his other activities in Petrograd, Keyes saw Poliakov to assess the prospects of reviving the Bank Schemes. They must also have seen a senior member of the British Embassy staff that remained there (the British Embassy having returned home and the other Allied Embassies having evacuated to Vologda in March) because Spring Rice was informed that Keyes and Poliakov had made it clear that Leech's connections with the British Government were "the object of much discussion in Russian financial circles." Spring Rice concluded that "something must be done to prevent [Leech] damaging British credit by posing as a British agent."[265]

Clark was aware that active Allied intervention both in North Russia and Vladivostok was imminent and had intended to link up with Savinkov's insurgency then taking place in Yaroslavl. He was therefore particularly interested in the prospects of the Siberian Bank as this still had branches outside Bolshevik control which could be particularly useful in securing Allied economic control of Siberia following the landing of an intervention force in Vladivostok. Accordingly, whilst in Petrograd, he too had a meeting with Poliakov who was effectively in control of the diminished rump of the bank as Yaroshinski was still in hiding.

Poliakov had, of course, been included in the Bank Schemes at the behest of the British Government and had conducted the negotiations with the Siberian Bank's former owner Denisov on Keyes' behalf. He sought British Government funds to enable the Siberian branches to renew trading operations. Clark was sceptical about the bank's resources and Poliakov admitted that shortly before its nationalisation by the Bolsheviks in November 1917, its directors had removed a number of shares in the Amur Transport Company which controlled the Amur Railway – an alternative option for the eastern section of the Trans-Siberian railway - which represented one of the bank's most valuable assets.

Clark approached the Bank Schemes with a considerable degree of scepticism and was inclined to regard Poliakov as 'at least evasive" and concluded that he had received a secret commission either from Denisov or Yaroshinski or perhaps both. This was a reasonable suspicion bearing in mind that Poliakov had been a junior director of the Siberian Bank prior to its acquisition by Yaroshinski and had then proceeded to act for Yaroshinski and Keyes in the purchase of its shares from Denisov. However, Poliakov insisted that he had advised against the proposal at the time and he was later supported in this by General Poole who had known him for some time and had been inadvertently responsible for his inclusion in the Bank Schemes in the first place.

Clark's reservations about Poliakov remained and he recommended that he be replaced by Spring Rice whose own investigations into the Bank Schemes were damning. Spring Rice pointed out that Yaroshinski had acquired an option to purchase the forty four thousand shares in Siberian Bank for sixty six million Roubles (equating to fifteen hundred Roubles a share) which would redeem his loan from the British Government. In other words, should the British hopes of replacing the Bolshevik government with one which would de-nationalise the banks thereby restoring the Siberian Bank to its previous financial power be fulfilled, then the value of the bank would increase well above the share price of fifteen hundred

Roubles. At that point, Yaroshinski would undoubtedly exercise his option. Therefore, the structure of the deal gave the British all the downside risks with none of the up.

To compound matters, Clark's insistence that possession should be obtained of Denisov's actual shares from Yaroshinski was impossible to fulfil both because Yaroshinski could not be found and, more importantly, because the shares themselves were heavily mortgaged and therefore not in his control. Spring Rice also emphasised that the capital in the Siberian Bank had been increased to one hundred and twenty thousand shares prior to Yaroshinski's acquisition so that he (and thus the British) did not even have majority control. Spring Rice concluded that Denisov had thereby grossly misled Yaroshinski.

As well as Spring Rice, Clark was also suspicious of Leech's actions and believed that he had profited from both sides in the transaction commenting that "in several directions, his activities were not in the interests of His Majesty's Government, more particularly later on when he acted as Mr Jarosynski's representative." This is interesting in that it tacitly implies that before he became Yaroshinski's agent, he was working or someone else - logically, the British. Once again, there is evidence that whilst Leech may well have been motivated by self-interest and was more than content to profit from his ambiguous position, he was, in some, possibly informal, way, a British agent. Once it became clear that the Bank Schemes were flawed, Leech became a convenient scapegoat and thereafter the British were at pains to deny any connection. Keyes' position in this is complicated by the fact that he too was in the firing line for a decision made hurriedly and in circumstances of great pressure. He seems to have maintained a line that continued to support the merits of the Schemes whilst emphasising that he had requested professional help. At the same time, he too was happy for responsibility for the inherent flaws which Clark and Spring Rice had so cogently identified to rest with Leech. This is disingenuous as, even though Keyes was clearly out of his depth negotiating complex financial deals, he was highly experienced in conducting negotiations and would instinctively known the importance of establishing clarity of roles. Accordingly, if Leech's position was ambiguous, then it plainly suited Keyes that this was so.

Having conducted his investigation, Clark concluded that the Bank Schemes had lost their rationale the moment that it became clear that "it was decided not to proceed with the formation of a South Eastern bank [and that] a serious error of judgment was committed in carrying through a modified and altered scheme under which £500,000 was lent to Mr Jarosynski on very insufficient security, and a large number of Siberian Bank shares were bought by His Majesty's Government at a very high price and a free option thereon given to Mr Jarosynski."[266] This damning conclusion put the blame not only on Poliakov and Yaroshinski but also on General Poole, Lindley and Keyes himself. Implicitly too it criticised London and the Russia Committee for sanctioning the scheme in the first place. Whilst these criticisms were entirely justified at least when viewed from the situation that obtained in July 1918, they did not take into account the original priority which was not only to find a way of transmitting desperately needed funds to the Volunteer Army in January and February but also to deny the Germans access to commercial assets. It also appears that Clark had not consulted Lessing who, after all, was both a cousin of Poliakov and had direct contact with Lloyd George.

Clark took the view that the Bank Schemes would be of little practical use in the planned Allied interventions in North Russia or even Vladivostok. In order to regularise the position he urged that Spring Rice be instructed to travel to Petrograd to retrieve "any further information which may be required and any documents bearing upon the deals." This was easier said than done as only limited documentation existed and anyway much was destroyed when the British Embassy moved from Petrograd to Vologda in March. Keyes was certainly alive to this point pointing out that "by the time, the beginning of March that the Allied Embassies had to leave Petrograd in a hurry, burning their archives (several important papers of mine were burnt)."[267] Further, with Yaroshinski in hiding and the heavily mortgaged share certificates themselves probably remaining in the various other banks, there would have been only limited documentation capable of being retrieved. If that were not enough, the fact that the relevant contractual documents had been ante-dated rendered them of scant legal value in any event.

Clark's suggested strategy in relation to heading off German attempts to gain control of the Russian economy was to imitate their methods by taking investments from Russians who by then recognised that their own banking system was wholly compromised rather than buying roubles. Clark therefore suggested the establishment of a British Bank of Russia which could take deposits and issue Roubles backed by British guarantee. Whilst in the throes of rewriting British financial strategy in Russia, Clark also turned his attention to *Tovaro Obmien* and blocked the imminent purchase of cotton and flax for four hundred million Roubles.

The British Economic Mission left Petrograd shortly before 21 July 1918 to attend trade talks with the Bolsheviks in Moscow. Bruce Lockhart whose own position was by now hopelessly compromised was given the task of introducing the mission to the Bolshevik Commissars for Trade and Finance (Chicherin, Bronsky and Gukvosky). These talks unsurprisingly proved inconclusive although the Bolsheviks almost certainly used their existence as leverage in their own ongoing discussions with the Germans. In fact, the trip to Moscow was not only pointless it was actually damaging to British interests as the Americans regarded it as a blatant attempt by the British to secure economic advantage rather than advancing the Allied war aims. This was to have the consequence of further diminishing American willingness to sanction the proposed Siberian intervention.

Whilst in Petrograd, Keyes had meetings with Alexander Krivoshein whom he had previously met back in December 1917. Krivoshein, as a former Tsarist minister, was a prominent anti-Bolshevik and was now in control of one of the Monarchist factions.

His sympathies were with whoever he believed most likely to overthrow the Bolsheviks and the Allies were concerned that this might lead him to become increasingly pro-German. Their fears in this regard had been exacerbated by his former colleague and co-conspirator, Pavel Miliukov who had been Foreign Minister in the government formed by Prince Lvov following the February Revolution. Miliukov was by this time leader of the Right Centre and was in Kiev where he was actively working with the Germans. Keyes took part in these meetings with the intention of persuading Krivoshein not to switch sides to the Germans but also to see whether the Bank Schemes could be revived with the intention once again of transferring funds to the Volunteer Army in South Russia. Keyes was clearly successful as he recorded that Lindley "sent me on from Murman to try and get through to Petrograd and Moscow by Lake Onega, and, if possible to interview certain people in connection with the financial scheme and try to get the Monarchist party onto the right lines again. I had the most adventurous journey… Krivoshein when I convinced him that the Allies were really going to do something, undertook to sit on the fence a little longer and come down on our side if we really played up."

The National Centre had emerged from the Moscow Centre which had formed the most important political force opposing the Bolshevik following the revolution in October 1917. This was led by Krivoshein and Victor Chernov who had been chairman of the Constituent Assembly and the former Minister of Agriculture. The Moscow Centre had split into three following the Treaty of Brest-Litovsk. The Right Centre led by the Cadet leader, Miliukov moved to Kiev and sought and obtained German support. The Left Centre was an alliance of the Left Cadets and Right SRs. The remainder formed the National Centre which continued to have close links with and support from the Allies. It also enjoyed close links with Alexeyev in south Russia.

The National Centre also included liberals such as Peter Struvé who, like Savinkov, was another Marxist who had moved to the mainstream and was a prominent anti-Bolshevik. Struvé was living in Moscow under an assumed name during the summer of 1918 but had to flee to Finland following the failure of the attempts to overthrow the Bolsheviks. He was later based in South Russia where he edited a pro-White newspaper and, following Denikin's resignation in 1920, he became Baron Wrangel's Foreign Minister.[268]

The National Centre at least publically advocated the creation of military dictatorship although many of its supporters were actually Monarchists. It is likely therefore that it if had actually successfully overthrown the Bolsheviks then there would have been a period of considerable uncertainty in establishing precisely what sort of government would actually be put in its place. At that time however, the National Centre was an obvious recipient of Allied support and encouragement. Later, following the collapse of Savinkov's attempted coup in July 1918, the National Centre disputed that it had links with him but this seems to be directly contradicted by Bruce Lockhart when he informed London that "Centre has come to complete agreement with Savinkov's League."[269]

In his memoirs, Bruce Lockhart explicitly states that "until the decision was brought to my notice I gave no support to the Whites either in cash or in promises" but this is a further example of the way in which his memoirs are directly contradicted by contemporary evidence.[270] On 7 July, he had actually written to the Foreign Office requesting "power immediately to spend up to ten million Roubles in supporting those organisations which may be useful to us in the event of intervention." Bruce Lockhart called upon Keyes for assistance in raising funds for the Centre and on 25 July he reported that "to prevent further repetition of incidents such as Miliukov decided today after consultation with Colonel Keyes to give half million Roubles and that substantially more would be required urgently."[271] He followed this up on 28 July when he notified the Foreign Office that he had "agreed after consultation with Colonel Keyes to give one million while the French Consul General gave [the other]." Not only was this done without sanction from London

1. Kate Keyes & Family
Standing: Norman, Madeline, Kate & Roger Middle: Dorothea, Adrian &
Katherine Front: Charles Valentine, Terence & Phyllis

2. Quetta 1897

3. Terence and Edith Keyes on their wedding day; 15 May 1909

4. Sir George Buchanan

5. Bolshevik Patrol 1918

6. General Frederick Poole in North Russia; 1918

7. Sidney Reilly

8. Captain Francis Cromie

9. General Denikin and a tank detachment of the White Army; 1919

10. General Denikin and senior officers of the White Army,
Kharkiv; June 1919

11. Terence Keyes, Rosemary, Lavender, Edith and unknown; 1920

12. Old St Petersburg

13. Evacuation of Novorossisk 1920

14. Lord Curzon

15. Terence Keyes and Lion; early 1930s

16. Bolshaya Morskaya 52, St Petersburg

17. Astoria Hotel, St Petersburg

18. Former site of the British Embassy, St Petersburg

but Bruce Lockhart went on to indicate that a further 91.5 million Roubles would be required - ten million for Alexeev, eighty one for the National Centre and the remaining five hundred thousand for VV Shulgin who was a prominent anti-Bolshevik then based in Kiev.[272]

Keyes' own account broadly backs this up but with notable differences. He regarded Bruce Lockhart as "a very ambitious young Consul who had shown lots of initiative" but who was also "a very shameless opportunist... I don't think that he had any convictions." Whilst this analysis is easy to share bearing in mind the way in which Bruce Lockhart was inclined to self-mythologising, it was probably coloured by Keyes' distaste for "Lloyd George's Machiavellian games" in trying to negotiate towards reaching an accommodation with the Bolsheviks whilst at the same time plotting their overthrow.[273] There was also the professional's distaste for Lloyd George's tendency to operate through back channels and for failing to keep the Consul General, Oliver Wardrop, fully informed. His view was however tempered with an admiration for Bruce Lockhart's willingness, whilst operating effectively on his own to "deal with the enemies of the Bolsheviks [the National Centre] when he was entirely in their [the Bolsheviks'] power.[274]

Shulgin had formed the *Azbuka* in 1917 as a vehicle for providing the Volunteer Army with military and political information about German and Bolshevik activities in Ukraine. It eventually became the Kievan branch of the National Centre. He also edited the *Kievlyanin* newspaper which had drifted from out and out Monarchism to supporting the National Centre. The paper was also notoriously anti-Semitic reflecting ideas that were commonplace amongst the Whites and on 8 October 1918, it published an article written by Shulgin entitled "Torture by Fear" which tacitly supported pogroms on the basis that "the Jews formed the basis of Bolshevik power."[275] It was, of course, true that a large proportion of the Bolsheviks at that time were of Jewish origin but it is hard not to suspect that the innate anti-Semitism of many Whites pre-dated the October Revolution. The concept of the Jewish Bolshevik was to have an extremely long life although, ironically Stalin had a strong anti-Semitic streak that became overt towards the end of his life and over time purged the Russian communist party of many of its Jewish members.

Keyes and Bruce Lockhart then attended a secret meeting with members of the National Centre and the French Consul. At this meeting, their desperate need for funds became apparent but neither Bruce Lockhart (who did not have access to funds) or the French (who did) had instructions to release them. Keyes describes how he "was determined to turn on the tap, even if I could only get a trickle at first, so I drew the Frenchman aside and said that if he would ante up with a million roubles, I would make Lockhart do the same. He agreed, and so did Lockhart, who I undertook to find the money within twenty four hours. We then drew up a budget of ten millions for Alexeiev and five millions for various other organisations which we considered it necessary to support. I found Lockhart his million and, as the Frenchman was anxious to put his millions into the pot, I volunteered to go to Vologda and obtain the consent of the Allied Ambassadors to the budget and to our using French money."[276]

This evidences a substantial commitment to support the National Centre and also a further willingness by Keyes to act without authority from London. Bearing in mind the awkwardness that he had faced on his return to London in the spring, his actions show enormous self-belief and a willingness to take risks. It is perhaps also a reflection of the way in which Keyes was accustomed to act in India where self-reliance was a key attribute of a Political Officer. It also shows the close connection (denied in his memoirs) between Bruce Lockhart and British Intelligence and this is borne out by a memorandum sent by him on 5 November 1918 in which he acknowledges that his point of liaison with the National Centre in Moscow was Lieutenant Webster, an officer of the Royal Naval Reserve who had been posted to Moscow as Passport Control Officer - a common cover for intelligence operatives. Bruce Lockhart's connections with

Keyes, McGrath and Webster, amongst others point to the fact that his role went well beyond the purely diplomatic.

It was very likely in furtherance of these aims that Keyes "was caught in possession of roubles to the value of £25,000 by the Cheka."[277] In his account, Keyes states that this took place in "the summer of '19" but this is clearly incorrect as by then he was well established with the British Military Mission in South Russia. He described how, when he was arrested, he was not only carrying the currency but a revolver as well. If either of these were found he would in all likelihood be tortured to find out the names of his agents and "a whole series of allied officers through whom the money could be traced back." He was taken to the Cheka's Moscow headquarters where he was to be examined by "a typical, stupid, old fashioned policeman...they called Comrade Lebedinsky"[278]

Whilst standing in the long queue awaiting interview, Keyes was able to transfer the money from his jacket to the Burberry he was wearing as it had open pockets and then along with the revolver, he deposited it on a chair at the other end of the room where it was promptly sat upon by an old woman. As a result, when he was later searched nothing was found. Then, putting on an accent, Keyes managed to convince Lebedinsky that he was an Irish revolutionary come to see how "you're making your Revolution and I'm afraid I can't congratulate you! I've never seen such disorder. This won't look very well when I see your Commissariat." As a result, he was not only released but also able to retrieve the raincoat and "walk straight from the Cheka to [his] rendezvous." This was not the only time when he was arrested that summer although no details are available about the other occasion.

Like so many of Keyes' stories, it is hard to know how much credence should be given to his account. As has already been shown, he was perfectly willing to embroider facts so as to create a good story and this is a good story. He also liked to present an image of himself as being unflappable and well able to get better of others - particularly foreigners. That said, the basic facts of his accounts all ring true and it is entirely possible that in the chaos of July 1918 when Bolshevik rule was being assailed on all sides that a harassed official might be fooled by a show of outrage and an Irish brogue.

The danger which Keyes and his agents faced is brought out in more reliable evidence, namely, one of his reports on the Bank Schemes prepared in or about 1920 when he states that "the only way in which I could get money down to the Volunteer Army was by sending women agents with their skirts lined with thousand rouble notes. A few only of these got through. I was arrested twice myself and had much difficulty getting out of the country."[279] He does not record the fate of those who were caught but it was probably torture and execution by the Cheka.

Keyes managed to get to Vologda by an extraordinary route as Bruce Lockhart obtained Trotsky's authority for him to travel, ostensibly so that he would persuade the Ambassadors to travel back to Moscow. Keyes was therefore introduced as "a person of influence over [the] High Commissioner and... was given a clear the line pass to Vologda." He even travelled in the same coach as some Bolshevik delegates and "had a loathsome journey with these wild creatures and had to play my old game of being an Irish revolutionary."[280] By these means, he was able to obtain the Ambassadors' consent and even managed to talk his way back to Moscow even though his pass was one way only. Of course, if the connections with the Bolsheviks were as close as appears from the evidence in Chapter 14, then Trotsky's assistance might be more easily explained.

At the same time that all this was going on, Cromie, the British Naval Attaché in Petrograd, was engaged in schemes preparing the way for the anticipated Allied intervention from Murmansk. Like many other British representatives in Russia at that time, Cromie was a complex figure. He was by profession a submariner who had been sent to Russia in 1915 in command of a fleet of three submarines which later fought alongside the Russian Imperial Navy. His command had grown to seven submarines by the October Revolution but was stranded at the naval base at Kronstadt and came under direct threat following the Treaty of Brest-Litovsk. When the Allied embassies fled to Vologda on 28 February 1918, Cromie was left in Petrograd in charge of a skeleton staff. By this time, the Germans were practically at Petrograd and Cromie was informed by the Bolsheviks to hand his submarine force over to them for onward transmission to the Germans. Instead, with great initiative, he organised the scuttling of his command practically in sight of the approaching Germans.

Thereafter, he became increasingly engaged in intelligence matters particularly where naval considerations were concerned. He worked closely with Bruce Lockhart and George Hill in bribing the leaders of the Russian Black Sea fleet to agree to scuttle rather than hand over ships to the Germans. It was a sign of the confusion prevalent at the time that he, at one stage, had friendly meetings with Trotsky to achieve this end as the Bolsheviks were also concerned that the fleet should not fall into German hands which is why they had arranged for it to move from Sebastopol to Novorossiysk. Subsequently, in June, when the Germans threatened that town, they ordered that it be scuppered.

Mostly, however, he was involved in schemes to overthrow the Bolsheviks and by July he was reporting to Admiral Reginald 'Blinker' Hall head of British Naval Intelligence that he had assembled a force ready to rise up when the British intervention force approached Petrograd adding that he had "nine river gun-boats at [his] disposal but dare not give them definite orders until I am sure of a base, but they could take Petrozavodsk [a city on Lake Onega, approximately halfway between Murmansk and Petrograd] any day. There is some danger in having so many irons in the fire but I think that I have enough friends to get me out even if it comes to flying. Evacuation has come to a standstill as far as we are concerned, but we will push the official lot as much as possible. We continue to delay trains of mines and guns for the north at very small expense."[281]

Like Bruce Lockhart, whose affair with Moura Budberg was notorious, Cromie also seems to have been equally successful at forming non-political links with the Russian aristocracy and was conducting an affair with a Sonia Gagarin. As will appear below, Cromie was prescient in worrying about the risks involved but ultimately too optimistic about his prospects of successfully fleeing Petrograd when the need arose.

In the light of all of the above, the decision to murder of the Tsar and his family at Ekaterinburg on the night of 16-17 July begins to make sense. Gunfire from the Czech and other White forces could be heard in the distance and indeed the town fell on 25 July. There is considerable doubt about where responsibility for the murder should lie. Traditionally, the local Bolsheviks have been blamed but it seems likely that Lenin and Sverdlov were also aware and approved of their actions. In his diary for 1935, Trotsky gave his account of what happened: - "my next visit to Moscow took place after the fall of Ekaterinburg. Talking to Sverdlov, I asked in passing: ' Oh yes, and where is the Tsar?" It's all over,' he answered, 'He has been shot." And where is the family?' 'And the family along with him? All of them?' I asked, apparently with a touch of surprise. ' All of them!' replied Sverdlov, ' What about it?' He was waiting to see my reaction. I made no reply. 'And who made the decision?' I asked. ' We decided it here. Ilyich believed that we shouldn't leave the Whites a live banner to rally around, especially under the present difficult circumstances...' I did not ask any further questions, and considered the matter closed. Actually, the decision was not only expedient but necessary. The severity of this summary justice showed the world that we would continue to fight on mercilessly, stopping at nothing."[282] The fact that the diary was composed some seventeen years after the events in question and at a time when Trotsky was terminally estranged from the Soviet regime does cause some questions about its veracity but there would appear to be little to be gained by him in making this up - particularly as he approved of the actions taken.

Keyes was clearly closely involved in much of this and there have been suggestions that he may have had links with some scheme to rescue the Tsar. If so, this could have been a further reason for his contact with Trotsky and journey to Vologda. However, there is no evidence for this; only extrapolation from the reference to contacts with Lenin and other Bolsheviks discussed in Chapter 14. Keyes' assessment of the overall political situation was pithily and realistically expressed in a letter to Edith from Moscow on 15 July when he wrote "that eighty percent of the country is against them [the Bolsheviks] but they have the talent, the guts and the machine guns."[283] Ironically, of course, many of those machine guns were British in origin and had been shipped out to equip the Tsarist armies.

The position therefore by the end of July 1918 was one of total confusion. The Allied force, Syren, that had landed the previous month in Murmansk was beginning to move south along the railway whilst, at the same time, the second limb of the intervention, Elope, was sailing to Archangel where a rising against the Bolsheviks had been procured. This was led by Captain Georgi Chaplin who had served in the Tsarist navy and had been given a British passport and papers in the name of Commander Thompson. The original idea was that the two force would move south pushing the Bolsheviks back and the Elope force would then link up with the Czechs although this was already clearly no longer feasible as the Czechs' attention was increasingly drawn towards Siberia. The Syren force was also hampered by the need to guard its flank against possible moves from the German backed Finnish Whites who had the potential to cut the force off from its supply base. The greatest problem, however, was that the combined force was hopelessly inadequate to the tasks it had been set consisting as it did chiefly of second rank troops who were not fit to fight on the Western Front. As stated in Chapter 15, it contained however, a disproportionate number of officers, many with a background in intelligence which reveals the forces' true intention which was to encourage local anti-Bolsheviks to rise up under Allied leadership. This danger was immediately appreciated by Bruce Lockhart who wrote to London that the "Centre warn us that if our intervention is to be successful it must be made in force and that the support we will receive from Russia will be in proportion to the number of troops we send. This seems to me such an elementary truth that I must once more point out the serious danger we run in imagining that we have only to send out officers to form and command troops composed of those Russians… willing to serve us."[284]

The problems facing the Syren and Elope force were shrewdly summed up by one of its officers, Lieutenant Colonel Byrne; like Keyes another Indian army veteran. He wrote that "we have come here to form and train a Russian army with which we can threaten Germany and compel her to withdraw troops from the Western Front, and to do this we have landed in a country whose de facto government is at peace with Germany but which is threatened by counter-revolutionary forces whom we favour and intend to assist; at the same time we expect Moscow not to interfere with our plans."[285]

Whilst this had been going on, the Bolsheviks were in the process of ruthlessly shutting down Savinkov's premature rising. It is unclear whether the mistiming occurred as a result of delays by the Allies in the commencement of both Syren and Elope or because the details of the plot had come to the attention of the Cheka necessitating it being brought forward. At the same time, in Petrograd, Cromie and others were making preparations for seizing power at the crucial moment. Keyes was similarly engaged in Moscow as well as organising funding for the National Centre and the Volunteer Army in South Russia. The British and French were also trying to inveigle the Americans to support a largely Japanese led intervention from Vladivostok but were meeting increased resistance from a sceptical President Wilson.

The Germans were similarly confused and conflicted in their own thinking with support for a Monarchist coup favoured by Ludendorff being balanced by the German Foreign Office's preference for an accommodation with the Bolsheviks. In furtherance of their desire for Russian produce to break the Allied blockade, the Germans had been drawn far further into Russia than the boundaries set at Brest-

Litovsk and with that move had become further entangled in the confused politics of the Ukraine and also the Caucasus where there were rising tensions between German and Turkish ambitions.

The Bolsheviks meanwhile were aware that they were in a struggle for their very survival and strove largely successfully to avoid having to commit to either side as they were well aware that to do so would almost inevitably lead to their overthrow. Although militarily weak and starved of critical resources both as a consequence of concessions made to the Germans at Brest-Litovsk and by sabotage incited by the Allies, they nonetheless were able to retain control largely as a result of the terror which Lenin had brought down upon opponents of the regime. The conclusion in Keyes' letter to Edith of 15 July was an accurate summary of the Bolsheviks' determination to keep power.

Chapter 17:

August - September 1918

The various plots that were developing in July came to fruition in August 1918 and, whilst for a while the Bolsheviks' position looked highly precarious, by the end of September the crisis had passed and their grasp on at least central Russia was much firmer. This was not to occur without much drama and bloodshed as the Bolsheviks unleashed a wave of savagery against their opponents and the loss of life was extensive, as indeed was the dismantling of the few remaining civil rights enjoyed by the suffering population.

At the beginning of the month, the Bolsheviks and Germans were still in negotiations in Berlin over a new Russo-German trade deal. These negotiations were complicated by the fact that both sides had conflicting agendas. The Bolsheviks, recognising the danger that they would face by coming down unequivocally either for the Germans or the Allies continued to play for time. The risks here were obvious and direct; if the Bolsheviks came under German influence, then they would lose credibility with the Russian peoples and would also unite the many sided anti-Bolshevik forces. It would also mean that the Allies would have no option but to pursue a full blooded anti-Bolshevik campaign whereas at that time, they were having to adopt a more nuanced policy for fear that they would drive the Bolsheviks towards an accommodation with the Germans.

Equally, if the Bolsheviks were to reach an accord with the Allies then they would face the immediate threat of invasion by the Germans in circumstances where there were only poorly organised units available to meet them. It has to be remembered that although the Germans had reduced their presence on the Eastern Front following Brest-Litovsk, they still had considerable forces stationed throughout Western Russia and the Ukraine and were, in any event, in easy striking distance of Moscow and within seventy miles of

Petrograd. Ludendorff had six or seven divisions ready to march on Petrograd whenever directed and so long as General Krasnov, Ataman of the Don Cossacks, could protect the their flank, a number of other German divisions could easily move north along the Rostov-Voronezh railway. There is little doubt that such a move would have succeeded as the Bolsheviks were ill equipped to resist it and the White forces were too fragmented themselves to do much either.

The Bolsheviks' only plan for survival therefore was to continue to play the Allies off against the Germans and await more propitious circumstances. The Bolsheviks were also aware that Ludendorff's offensives in the west had not brought about the hoped for victory and that Allied counter-attacks were beginning to push the Germans back from their over extended positions in France. The increasing likelihood that the Central Powers would lose the war was more and more apparent particularly after the crushing defeat suffered by the Germans on 8 August at the Third Battle of Amiens where fifty thousand Germans were taken prisoner and the German lines widely breached. This was the opening of the Hundred Days' Offensive during which the Germans retreated back towards their 1914 start point and, in the face of political collapse, were forced to seek an armistice. Inevitably therefore, German credibility with the Bolsheviks decreased during this period as it became obvious that the war was lost. Nevertheless, back in August, the position was far less clear-cut and, as will appear below, the threat to the Bolsheviks from the Allies was serious and urgent and this predisposed the Bolsheviks to maintain good relations with the Germans. They were also keen to limit the scope for further German moves upon the already much shrunken Russian heartland as well as to secure access to Ukrainian grain, coal and other raw materials which were being blocked with German connivance.

German policy towards the Bolsheviks was also divided. The German Foreign Office was in favour of continuing the alliance and keeping the Bolsheviks in power largely on the basis that, other than the Monarchists, the Allies had formed connections with all other opposition groups. Ludendorff, on the other hand, hated the Bolsheviks and was willing to sanction military action to secure their removal. He was particularly concerned about the increase in revolutionary activity within Germany and the army in particular. He attributed this to Bolshevik agitation although the acute deprivations caused by the Allied blockade also had an impact upon domestic morale. Ultimately, the German Foreign Office view and that of the Kaiser prevailed since, as Hintze, the Foreign Minister explained, "any other government - we have to be perfectly clear about this - is either immediately or within a short time a friend and ally of the Entente. We do not have any friends worth mentioning in Russia; whoever informs Your Excellency to the contrary is deceiving himself... We have milked them [the Bolsheviks] for all they are worth; our quest for victory requires us to continue to do so as long as they remain in power. Whether or not we like the idea of working for them is unimportant as long as it is useful to do so."[286]

The Germans were thus caught out by the consequences of their actions in 1917 in supporting the Bolsheviks and, in particular, procuring Lenin and his followers' transportation back to Russia from exile. They were now bound to continue to support an alliance with the Bolsheviks and to seek to obtain as many of Russia's raw materials and produce as possible mostly by establishing puppet regimes particularly in the Ukraine but also the Baltic states. In the meantime, they were fully aware that the Bolsheviks were in turn encouraging revolution in Germany at a time when military reverses and pressing shortages were making the German peoples and their armed forces susceptible to Bolshevik propaganda.

The Allied position was equally complex. The British and French appreciated the threat posed by the Bolshevik regime and were determined to see that it was overthrown. In the first instance however, their priority was to encourage a revival of an active Eastern Front or, failing that, to prevent the Germans being able to break the blockade by getting hold of Russian resources and military materiel (particularly Russian naval assets). There was therefore a need to tread carefully as too overt a hostility would force the Bolsheviks and Germans together but not enough would allow the Germans to denude their forces in the east yet further as well as to break the blockade. As has been seen earlier, there were two aspects of British policy at work, the active interventionists on one hand whose chief proponent in the British cabinet was Lord Robert Cecil and those who preferred a more nuanced and placatory relationship with the Bolsheviks. The former were chiefly of a military background such as General Poole and the various intelligence officers on the ground whereas the latter's chief mouthpiece was Bruce Lockhart who, although relatively junior in terms of years' service continued to enjoy great influence not least with Lloyd George himself. Balfour as Foreign Secretary persisted in following his policy of drift. In hindsight, it is clear that by June 1918, the British had decided upon intervention and, as a consequence seeking to procure the Bolsheviks' overthrow. In his memoirs, Bruce Lockhart maintains that he continued to lobby against intervention until almost the last moment but it is now evident that his position had changed long before then. It is obvious from everything that Keyes wrote that he was vehemently anti-Bolshevik and very firmly in the interventionist camp.

There was also a tension between the Allies over their policy towards Russia. The British did not support the Bank Schemes just in furtherance of their war aims but also with a view to establishing British dominance over trade and commerce under a new anti-Bolshevik regime. The French similarly had plans to secure repayment of their war debts from Russian resources. In the Far East, the motivations of the Japanese for agreeing to participate and indeed lead the Vladivostok intervention were coloured by their ambitions upon Manchuria. The Americans were suspicious of what they saw as imperial aggrandisement and were happy to pursue what could be termed a higher humbuggery whilst at the same time not having suffered the crippling financial losses borne by Britain and France.

As far as Vladivostok was concerned, the British and French remained eager for the Japanese to participate fully and advance up the Trans-Siberian railway as far as Irkutsk and even Omsk to support the Czechs. Leaving to one side the practical difficulties of maintaining a force along a four thousand mile long railway line, the Japanese were anyway only really interested in extended their influence into Manchuria. The Americans were, even then, inclined to Sinophilia and, if anything, viewed Japan more as a potential rival power in the Pacific than an ally in Russia. President Wilson therefore was most reluctant to agree to anything more than establishing local control in the Vladivostok area. This lack of unity in aims was to hamper the intervention from the outset.

The Czechs meanwhile had probably reached the peak of their effectiveness and were beginning to lose faith in the Allies particularly as there were difficulties in supply and consequently morale was beginning to falter. The Czechs' difficulties were exacerbated by the fact that various White forces had arisen from the chaos in Siberia. Originally, the most important was that run by Semenov who, with assistance from the Czechs established a power base in Chita on the Chinese border. As mentioned in Chapter 15, Semenov had received financial and other assistance from the Allies but proved to be little more than a bandit. Later on, Admiral Kolchak was forced to recognise his suzerainty over the Chita military district but other than accumulate wealth, he did little to advance the White cause. Semenov's credibility with the more orthodox White forces was not helped either by his willingness to accept help from and work with the Japanese or from his association with the unhinged Baron Roman von Ungern-Sternberg a fervent Monarchist from what is now Estonia who, not without reason, was known as "the Mad Baron."[287]

In the summer of 1918, the more orthodox White forces were split between those based at Samara who were mostly SRs and therefore supporters of the Constituent Assembly and a more monarchist inclined force based at Omsk. Relations between the two were strained with each showing an unwillingness to support the other both militarily and in terms of supplies. At the behest of the Czechs and the French Mission, conferences were held at Chelyabinsk in July and August to try and convince the contesting forces to form a unified body but without success.

The Bolsheviks took advantage of this disunity where possible but also suffered a major defeat on 8 August when Komuch forces (ie Samara based Whites) seized Kazan with Czech help and with it managed to gain control over much of the Russian Imperial gold reserves. These reserves became known as "Kolchak's Gold" and although a substantial proportion was surrendered to the Bolsheviks on Kolchak's capture in January 1920, the whereabouts of the residue has been the subject of endless subsequent speculation.

In South Russia, attempts were being made to transmit funds to the Volunteer Army and Keyes and Bruce Lockhart were closely involved in the process. They were greatly impeded by the Cheka's penetration of their networks and by the difficulty in getting supplies to the Volunteer Army whilst access to the Black Sea was blocked by the Ottomans. The Volunteer Army itself was successfully advancing north again and on 15 August, it took Ekaterinodar and then on 26 August, Novorossiysk. This represented significant progress following the defeats in February and the subsequent Ice March from Rostov to Ekaterinodar.

At the same time, the British expedition known as Dunsterforce was advancing from Hamadan in Persia approximately two hundred miles towards Baku on the Caspian in a force consisting of three hundred or so officers and NCOs driving Ford vans and armoured cars. The purpose of the mission was to secure control of the Baku oilfields to deny them to the advancing Turks. Dunsterville reached Baku before the Turks and joined with the local forces, mostly Armenian but also various White forces under the Centro-Caspian Dictatorship. They managed to hold off a much larger Turkish force from 26 August to 14 September and also wrecked much of the oil installations before departing. After capturing the town, the Turks murdered up to ten thousand Armenians in revenge for a massacre by Bolsheviks and Armenians of a similar number of Azeris in March 1918. The Turks failed to derive any advantage from their conquest of Baku before the Armistice of Mudros brought an end to hostilities between the Allies and the Ottomans on 30 October 1918.

A parallel force was also despatched to Turkestan under General Sir Wilfrid Malleson and assisted the Trans Caspian Government based around Ashkabad. This too intervened in support of anti-Bolshevik forces primarily with the intention of preventing penetration of the area by the Germans and Turks as well as seeking to limit Bolshevik influence. It was another move by the British to protect the borders of India from potential disruption and was a continuum of British policy in the area modified to take into account the Bolshevik threat. This became increasingly serious following the Bolshevik takeover of Central Asia in 1920 and the British took pains to limit the penetration of their ideas to the subcontinent. A very clear illustration of this was the lecture given by Keyes to the staff college in Quetta in 1922 which addressed the threat posed to British interests by the Soviet government. Keyes was passionate in expressing his concern at the threat to British India posed by Bolshevik penetration and the spread of what he regarded as seditious propaganda.

Whilst Dunsterville and Malleson were busy in Central Asia, the main focus of Allied effort remained in the north with the Syren force pressing south from Murmansk and the Elope force establishing itself at Archangel. As mentioned in Chapter 16, the intention was that they would both move south along the lines of the respective railways with Syren moving towards Petrograd and Elope towards Vologda where, in theory anyway, a planned meeting would take place with the Czechs. The Syren force's position was made easier by the news from the British Consul in Helsinki that the Germans had begun evacuating their forces from Finland. This was encouraging as it meant that the threat to the their flank from German troops and Finnish Whites was very much reduced. However, progress was still not as fast as intended and, critically, General Maynard who was the officer commanding, reported that in a month's recruiting, he had only managed to raise twelve hundred potential troops. This was far fewer than had been anticipated and showed that the local Russians were unwilling to commit themselves to armed insurrection presumably because they were only too well aware what might happen to them if it failed. This reluctance to enlist undermined the whole premise of the Syren mission as it had always been anticipated that it would provide the vanguard and leadership of a much larger Russian force which is why it included a high proportion of officers often with an intelligence background. Without local recruits, the force was unbalanced and inadequate.

In Archangel, the Elope force was less dependent upon attracting local recruits as it was intended that it would soon link up with the Czechs. Nevertheless, local conditions made military campaigning difficult. Unlike Murmansk, Archangel could not function as a port all year and in 1918, the thaw had only come in June which was later than usual. This naturally delayed the arrival of the Elope force. Then, once it had landed, it had to advance up the River Dvina which, although broad, was shallow and difficult to navigate. River transport was also plagued by swarms of mosquitoes taking advantage of the brief summer period.

One of the additional stories annexed to Keyes' own relates to an operation by the Elope force namely, Michael Keyes' recollections of stories told to him by his father in the late 1920s. It describes the easy capture of a railway junction by the Elope force on its advance south from Archangel. The gist of the story is clearly intended to entertain a child at bedtime but what is significant is that Keyes placed himself in the middle of the story acting as translator between the captured Bolshevik commander and the British Brigadier General in command. The events in the story must have taken place sometime after the landing of the Elope force at Archangel on 2 August. Keyes had of course arrived back in Russia on or shortly after 23 June when the Syren force had reached Murmansk. He had then travelled to Moscow after a stopover in Petrograd. He was in Moscow during July and almost certainly still there throughout August as a letter to Edith was sent from there on 15 August.[288] It is also wholly implausible that having been so involved in matters of vital national importance, he would have been ordered to travel over nine hundred miles simply to perform translation duties. This is particularly the case as the Elope contingent contained so many officers with an intelligence background. It also had two specialist interpreters in Alexander Proctor and the diplomat and author, William Gerhardi. Keyes' presence was therefore superfluous leaving to one side the logistical issues.[289] The far more likely explanation is that the story was based upon an account that Keyes had heard but that he was certainly not present.

At that time, the government of Archangel was notionally in the hands of Nicolai Tchaikovsky - another aristocratic former revolutionary who had moved rightwards although in this case, his revolutionary fervour was also tempered by a Tolstoyan religious faith. Tchaikovsky was, if anything, a socialist and was therefore gravely put out when General Poole forbade the display of any form of the red flag. He was even more dismayed by Poole's decision to treat Archangel as if it were a particularly backwards province of the Empire of which he was the Governor and as well as ignoring the local regime also commandeered the best property for his headquarters.

The sense of loss of control was increased on 9 August when the Allied ambassadors arrived at Archangel from their temporary home in Vologda. It was also reflected in orders sent by the CIGS, Sir Henry Wilson, to General Poole on 10 August to the effect that the Syren force was to march south and link up with the Czechs and then gain control of the Archangel - Vologda - Ekaterinburg railway which, together with the river connections, would enable rapid supply from Archangel whilst depriving the Bolsheviks of one of the principal routes to Siberia. Wilson added that if it transpired that the Czechs had moved east to link up with other Czech forces in Siberia, then the Elope force was to establish a fortified bridgehead at Archangel. To achieve this, he too was to encourage recruitment from the local Russians.

It is therefore quite clear that the British and French were actively seeking to procure regime change under the pretence of preventing Germany from gaining control of Russia. This was a different objective from that adumbrated by President Wilson and, whilst in many ways, far more realistic in its assessment of the position on the ground, was to cause increasing tension amongst the Allies. The American position was reflective of their own distaste for imperialism at least when practiced by others and the fact that both the British and French governments were unwilling to have an open breach was a sign of their increased dependence upon American resources and manpower. This encouraged them to act in an underhand way which, once discovered (as was inevitable) further alarmed American sensibilities.

It was all ultimately to lead to a divergence in policy following the abortive peace conference between the Allies, the Whites and the Bolsheviks scheduled to take place at Prinkipo (an island off Constantinople) in January 1919 when the Americans continued with peace talks with the Bolsheviks and William Bullitt, the US chief foreign policy adviser, recommended that the Bolsheviks be recognised and a peace treaty negotiated. The British and French blocked this and continued with support for the Whites. It is interesting to speculate how the Bullitt initiative might have played out and the possibility exists of a divided Russia with a White Ukraine and South Russia and Bolshevik control of the Russian heartlands and Siberia. However, the perennial dispute between Russia and the Ukraine over borders indicates that it never could have been sustainable in the long term.

At the heart of the various schemes lay attempts by the Allies to overthrow the Bolsheviks in both Moscow and Petrograd. These were planned to coincide with the advance of the Syren and Elope forces as well as a westwards movement by the Czechs with the intention of joining forces at Vologda before advancing on Petrograd. In the meantime, the Volunteer Army was to advance northwards to put pressure on Moscow. Keyes was closely involved in the financial side of the Moscow plots. In particular, he was responsible for arranging for money to be smuggled to the Volunteer Army and, as mentioned in Chapter 16, he organised several female agents to attempt the journey with very mixed success.

In Petrograd, Captain Cromie remained in charge of a skeleton staff at the Embassy. He was also in possession of up to £1,000,000 which had been earmarked for bribes to friendly contacts to ensure the destruction of the Imperial Baltic fleet should the Germans advance to Petrograd. This money was now to be used to encourage a rising in Petrograd to coincide with similar risings in Moscow and the Allied advance from Archangel and Murmansk. The Bolsheviks were aware that Cromie was in possession of considerable funds and also that he was engaged in plots to secure their overthrow. To try and forestall any attempted coup, shortly before 5 August, they arrested approximately seven thousand former Tsarist officers and civilians and imprisoned them either at the grim Peter and Paul Fortress in Petrograd or at Kronstadt both of which were safely under their control. In order to persuade Cromie to disgorge himself of the £1,000,000, the Commissar of Petrograd, Moisei Uritsky, offered to hand the prisoners over in return for its payment to him. It is unclear whether this was a genuine offer or a ruse but it was not taken up.

Cromie was also becoming more and more isolated as the Bolsheviks tightened control over the telegraph system and freedom of movement. He nonetheless concluded that the regime was tottering, reporting in a telegram to General Poole that the "position of Soviet power in Petrograd is becoming rapidly untenable... it is evident that they are in touch with the Germans. Lenin is at Peterhof and a yacht under Swedish flag [is] ready to take him away."[290] This was partially correct as, whilst there is no evidence about Lenin's imminent flight, the Germans were certainly in close touch with the Bolsheviks and were supportive of a plan to assist them in fighting the British in North Russia. This was to form part of their ongoing trade talks which were to reach fruition on 27 August and which was to be the cue for the Allied sponsored risings in Moscow and Petrograd.

The British link between Moscow and Petrograd was Sidney Reilly who was the driving force behind both plots. Reilly was and remains something of an enigma, part confidence trickster and fraudster, part spy. Even his real name remains uncertain, with Reilly being one of the least likely options - it was probably Rosenblum but there is doubt even there. After a long career, including arms dealing, informing for Special Branch and possibly being implicated in murder, he formally became part of the Secret Intelligence Service in 1917 before being posted to Russia in the summer of 1918. The extent to which he was following orders in what follows as opposed to acting on his own initiative is questionable as there are indications that he was not fully trusted by British Intelligence. Having said that, he must have been valued at a senior level as he was awarded the Military Cross on 22 January 1919 although there is also evidence that the British were happy to let Reilly carry the can for their failed plotting. Reilly's end was characteristically mysterious. He and Savinkov were enticed back to Russia in 1925 ostensibly to forge links with an anti-Soviet organisation known as The Trust. This was, in fact, an OGPU front and they were captured and interrogated. Savinkov allegedly committed suicide by jumping from a window in the Lubyanka in May 1925. Reilly was probably executed on 5 November 1925 but rumours of his survival lingered on for many years.

What is clear is that Reilly showed great resourcefulness over the summer of 1918. He established contact with a Colonel Friede, a former Tsarist officer who was Bolshevik Chief of Staff in Moscow.

Friede was a Latvian and had no great sympathy for the Bolsheviks. He therefore assisted Reilly not least by passing on information and obtaining a post for him with the Cheka posing under the rather unimaginative name "Relinsky." In his other guise, Reilly was also operating under the name of M. Constantine.[291] It is testament of the unreliability of all evidence about Reilly that in his memoirs he describes Petrograd as "his birthplace" which it manifestly was not, the most likely candidate being Odessa.[292]

Officially, the links between Reilly and the legitimate British presence in Russia at that time have been denied and certainly, in his memoirs, Bruce Lockhart takes pains to distance himself from Reilly's scheming. As with Bruce Lockhart's dealings with Savinkov and the funding of the Volunteer Army, this does not bear close scrutiny and he and Reilly, with Keyes sitting somewhat uncomfortably between them were fulfilling the Moscow part of a coordinated plan with Cromie handling the Petrograd end.

Following the collapse of the Savinkov rising in July, the British continued with a plan to suborn the Latvian guards who were regarded as being susceptible to bribery. The Latvians were regarded by the Bolsheviks as an elite force not so much for their revolutionary fervour but for their efficiency and, as a result, they were the regime's chosen guards. The Latvians' position was not dissimilar to that of the Czechs. They were also the former subjects of an imperial power who wanted to create and then safeguard a new national homeland. Unlike the Czechs, circumstances favoured them keeping on good terms with the Germans as much of what was to become Latvia was under German occupation. Therefore, on the face of it, the Latvians had no particular ideological connection with the Bolsheviks and were regarded as capable of being turned.

In June, two Latvians, Jan Bredis and Jan Schmidken (or Smidchen) approached Cromie indicating that they might be able to persuade the Lettish (Latvian) forces to desert and support a Bolshevik overthrow. Cromie then put them in touch with Reilly who was convinced of their good faith and sent them in turn to see Bruce Lockhart in Moscow. At the same time, through another source, Cromie was negotiating with two other would be Latvian agents, Steckelmann and Sabir and ostensibly persuading them to destroy a railway bridge to the Finland Station so as to delay any German advance upon the city. It is likely but not certain that they were all agents provocateurs and were reporting back to the Cheka from the outset but there is a possibility that Bredis and Schmidken were actually awaiting events before deciding which side to support. Steckelmann and Sabir seem to have been Cheka agents throughout. Whichever it was, the Cheka had a reasonably good idea of what was going on from an early date.

Bredis and Schmidken had not totally convinced Bruce Lockhart and he had requested an interview with one of the senior officers in the Lettish forces. They reported this back to Joseph Peters, a fellow Latvian who was deputy head of the Cheka and who arranged for Lieutenant Colonel Berzin, the commander of the artillery that guarded the Kremlin to be sent. Berzin in turn met Bruce Lockhart and then Reilly both of whom appear to have been convinced that he was genuine. In fact, it is possible that Berzin was also playing a double game and was ready to switch sides if it became clear that the Bolsheviks were about to fall. However, whilst Bruce Lockhart sought to distance himself officially from what was afoot, he was trapped into giving Berzin written permission for the Latvians to cross the British lines. This was to come back to haunt him later.

On 17 August, Reilly held discussions about sending troops to Vologda who would then turn the town over to advancing Allied forces. Reilly's plan also included the Latvians seizing control of Lenin and Trotsky and parading them through Moscow without their trousers. This particular aspect of the plot has been dismissed as fanciful but bearing in mind the attitude of the British at the time with agents called "Teddy Bear" and "Polly" and Keyes putting on an Irish accent, this is not as far fetched as it might appear.

The trigger for the coup was to be the publication of the peace terms agreed between the Bolsheviks and the Germans which were imminent and would inevitably cause widespread revulsion with the populace. Before then however, Reilly was pressed to attend a meeting at the American Consulate in Moscow. He was clearly unwilling to do so as it was inevitable that the building was being watched by the Cheka but eventually he agreed. The meeting was attended by the American Consul, de Witt Poole and Colonel de Vertement, the French Consul General. Extraordinarily, the meeting was also attended by Rene Marchand who was the Bolshevik sympathising Moscow correspondent for Le Figaro. Out of the blue, Marchand asked Reilly for his name. Reilly writes that he "mumbled the first that came to [his] mind, probably Rice." Later, Marchand gatecrashed a private meeting between Reilly and de Vertement.[293] Reilly was right to be suspicious as Marchand reported all that he had heard - which was only part of the conversation relating to the destruction of bridges in Petrograd to the Cheka who were by now getting a very clear insight into what was planned.

Reilly himself summarises the scheme as follows:

"It was arranged that upon the signal being given, their Lettish bodyguards were to arrest Lenin and Trotsky and parade them publicly through the streets, so that everyone should be aware that the tyrants of Russia were prisoners. At the same time, the provisional army was to mobilise under General Judenitch [Yudenich] and the provisional government be instituted. As soon as affairs in the city were sufficiently quiet - a matter of a very few days- an army was to march off to cooperate with General Savinkov against the Red forces which were still in the field against him. Another force was to be despatched to Petrograd where a simultaneous rising was to take place and Uritzsky, the head of the Tcheka, to be arrested."[294]

The Russo-German trade treaty was signed on 27 August and the Bolsheviks agreed to sell part of the Baku oilfields to the Germans as well as paying a substantial indemnity and handing over the Black Sea Fleet. In return, the Germans were to cease support for Krasnov and the Don Cossacks, permit the Bolsheviks access to the Ukrainian grain and coal market and tellingly provide military assistance to the Bolsheviks, operating under nominal Bolshevik command, in clearing North Russia and Vologda of the Allies and British in particular. This was the catalyst that Reilly required and he then needed to ascertain when Lenin and Trotsky might be together before unleashing his planned coup. Fortunately, he learned that there was to be a meeting of the Central Committee at the Grand Theatre on 29 August. Berzin confirmed that his Latvians would close all the exits and facilitate the arrests. At that point, the meeting was put back until 6 September. Reilly decided to use the extra time in visiting Petrograd to ensure that preparations were all in hand there travelling under another of his other aliases, "M. Massimo, a Turkish and Oriental merchant."[295]

The disorganisation and under-resourcing of both the Syren and Elope forces now came into sharp focus. For the schemes prepared by Reilly, Bruce Lockhart and Cromie to work, it was imperative that supporting forces were near at hand to take advantage of the disruption. However, both Poole in Archangel and Maitland in Murmansk had plenty of their own problems not least a shortage of food and supplies so that they could not adequately feed the areas under their control and this, in turn, impacted upon their ability to recruit local forces. Everything stemmed from the fact that the Allies had sent out a token force of second line troops which was wholly insufficient for the task in hand. At the same time, Czech priorities had changed so that there was no realistic prospect of Allied and Czech forces meeting at Vologda as had been planned.

It is as unclear how the Cheka intended to bring matters to a head as it is precisely how much they actually knew. It is possible that Dzerzhinsky intended to use the Latvians to draw the Allied forces into an exposed position before striking but it is equally possible that he was uncertain as to the Latvians' true allegiance and therefore would not want them to be in a position to link up with the Allies. As it was, other events intervened.

On 29 August, presumably based upon Marchand's disclosures, the Cheka struck and raided the French Deuxieme Bureau and arrested all French agents other than de Vertement who fled over the rooftops. The same day, Reilly's Moscow base, the flat of his ballerina mistress, was raided and some details of his schemes revealed when, with extremely bad luck, another agent, the sister of Colonel Friede, arrived whilst the Cheka were still present carrying with her enough detail of the proposed plot to cause them real alarm. Reilly himself discovered on the same day that his cover as Massimo had been blown and that various places where he stayed in Petrograd had been raided.

In the morning of 30 August, a junior officer or Junker called Leonid Kannegisser parked his bicycle outside Cheka headquarters in Petrograd and went in. Shortly afterwards, Uritsky, who was also the head of the Petrograd Cheka arrived. Kannegisser shot and killed him and then fled on his bicycle. He was pursued by the Cheka and abandoning his bike, took refuge in the English Club. He was captured, tortured and shot shortly afterwards. Kannegisser had strong connections with Savinkov who may well have ordered the assassination. He also had personal motives for wanting Uritsky dead as he had signed the death warrant of Viktor Pereltsveig who was Kannegisser's lover. It is unclear why he took refuge in the English Club; it could be coincidence or, more likely, there could have been British involvement in the assassination.

Immediately, Lenin heard about the assassination, he ordered Dzerzhinsky to travel to Petrograd to oversee investigations and also to raid both the British and French Embassies and Consulates in both cities. However, later that day, Lenin was himself the victim of an assassination attempt when he attended a meeting at the Mikhelson factory in Russia. The would be assassin was Fanny Kaplan, a former anarchist who had become a SR. Lenin was critically wounded by three bullets and was thought to be on the point of death but he pulled through and by 25 September, he had recovered enough to be sent to convalesce at Gorki outside Moscow. His supposedly miraculous recovery was used to create a Lenin cult attributing to him the type of semi-divine powers previously ascribed to Tsars. Indeed, he was referred to as "the People's Tsar." To his credit, Lenin, unlike his successors, disliked this cult of personality which clearly offended his Spartan world view and took pains to scale it back upon his recovery

Following the assassination attempt, the Bolsheviks not unsurprisingly perceived themselves to be in imminent danger and so lost all restraint and what became known as the "Red Terror" began. Over the coming months there were mass arrests of suspected White sympathisers many of whom were executed. Guilt was decided chiefly upon class and perceived opposition to the regime so that Zinoviev could write in mid September "To overcome our enemies we must have our own socialist militarism. We must carry along with us ninety million out of the one hundred million of Soviet Russia's population. As for the rest, we have nothing to say to them. They must be annihilated."

The Terror was from start to finish managed by the Cheka which had grown significantly since November 1917 so that it had a staff of at least one thousand in Moscow alone by this time. One of its founders, another Latvian, Martin Latsis was to write, "Do not look in materials you have gathered for evidence that a suspect acted or spoke against the Soviet authorities. The first question is what class he belongs to, what is his origin, education, profession. These questions should determine his fate. This is the essence of the Red Terror."[296] The arrests that took place in the following weeks ripped the heart out of the White resistance movement in Moscow and Petrograd; not only were many supporters incarcerated but those who remained at liberty were terrorised into inactivity. Whilst resistance would have existed anyway and there is no direct evidence of Allied involvement with either Kannegisser or Kaplan's assassination attempt, the fact that the Allies were up to their necks in inciting a revolt and the Bolsheviks knew this almost certainly added a viciousness born of desperation. It was another example of

British policy not being thought through and causing damage to those it most wished to support.

One immediate effect of the Terror was the arrest of Bruce Lockhart in the early morning of 31 August. He was taken to the Lubyanka where he was interviewed by Jacov Peters, temporary commander of the Cheka during the period following Mirbach's assassination in July. Peters interviewed Bruce Lockhart with some delicacy which Bruce Lockhart puts down to his diplomatic status and friendship with the Commissar for Foreign Affairs, Georgi Chicherin.[297] Peters pressed Bruce Lockhart about his connection with Fanny Kaplan, which Bruce Lockhart denied. The matter was pursued further when Kaplan was brought into the same room as Bruce Lockhart and his assistant Captain William Hicks presumably in the hope that they would give a sign of recognition. This indicates that the Cheka was still uncertain about the precise nature of the Allied schemes which in all likelihood did not involve Kaplan at all. Bruce Lockhart describes her at this moment as being "dressed in black and her eyes, set in a fixed stare, had great black rings under them. Her face was colourless. Her features, strongly Jewish, were unattractive. She might have been any age between twenty and thirty five."[298] He is being particularly ungallant here. She was in fact twenty eight and had spent eleven years in Tsarist prison camp following a failed attempt to assassinate the Governor of Kiev in 1906 in which her eyesight was permanently damaged. She was therefore nearly blind and may not have been able to recognise Bruce Lockhart even if she knew him. [299]

More significantly, Peters questioned Bruce Lockhart about Reilly but without obtaining anything useful. At this point there was an interesting development. Whilst most of the other Consulate staff were imprisoned together in the Butyrka prison, Bruce Lockhart was first released and then when re-arrested after five days was kept in relative comfort at the Kremlin. More to the point, his mistress, Moura Budberg was also arrested and only released following a begging letter from Bruce Lockhart. She was then allowed to visit him regularly and bring him private correspondence. Budberg's role in all this is extremely complicated not least because she was at one time or another connected with both British and Russian intelligence operations. The possibility exists either that Lockhart cooperated with Peters in return for favourable treatment for Budberg and himself or, alternatively, that she secured Bruce Lockhart's release in return for future cooperation. Either way, she was almost certainly an NKVD agent during the 1920s and 1930s. Perhaps unsurprisingly with that background, she was to become a close friend of Guy Burgess. A MI5 officer later reported with unconscious irony that "Budberg is not a desirable acquaintance for someone like [Burgess]."

The Bolsheviks maximised British involvement for publicity purposes describing it as "the Bruce Lockhart Plot." This was probably to give him more credit than was his due as the origins of the schemes lay in London. However, in the immediate term what it did lead to was the wholesale disruption of British influence in Moscow both with arrests and the flight of others.

Keyes had been involved in assisting Reilly with the suborning of Berzin and was able to secure the funds necessary for bribes to the Latvians. He worked closely alongside Bruce Lockhart probably in much the same way as he had with Buchanan the previous winter by dealing with matters from which the professional diplomats required some distance; in December 1917 it had been the Bank Schemes and in August the proposed coup. Probably because he was aware of what was going on, he advised Sir George Clarke to leave urgently and tagged along with the Mission party when it departed for Vologda along with an escaped Canadian prisoner of war.

They travelled to Petrograd where Keyes spent "a few hours" with Cromie assisting him to raise money to "finance his scheme for preventing the Baltic fleet from falling into the hands of the Bosche." This is possible but more likely it was intended for the planned rising. The precise date of this meeting is not certain although Keyes mentions that it was a few days before Cromie's murder so it is likely to have been in late August. From Petrograd, with the assistance of "a stout hearted little ancien regime conductor", they avoided the Bolsheviks' ban on travel to Vologda but on arrival were blocked as the various Allied Ambassadors had already left for Archangel to meet up with the British landing there. Somehow, the conductor was able to get them onto a train to Archangel and they had a nervous journey as if they had "bumped into retreating Bolsheviks they would certainly have scuppered the lot of us."[300]

In the meantime, there were even more dramatic developments in Petrograd. In the morning of 31 August, Reilly states that he had arranged to meet Cromie at a cafe at noon but Cromie did not turn up. Later on, Reilly risked a visit to the Embassy but found it surrounded with Cheka trucks on the street side and covered by the guns of ships moored nearby. This version is contradicted by the memoirs of another British agent, George Alexander Hill who wrote that Reilly remained in a flat belonging to Lieutenant Boyce who was also involved in intelligence matters. Boyce had gone to the British Embassy with the intention of returning with Cromie by 3pm. When he had not returned by 6pm, Reilly, possibly scenting danger, had returned to Moscow. It was only upon his arrival that he learned about Cromie's fate. It is impossible at this distance to work out whose version is correct - Hill's seems more plausible not least because it fits in with the timing of the raid on the Embassy during the afternoon so that there was no obvious reason why Cromie could not have made the noon rendezvous that Reilly planned. It is yet further evidence of the slippery nature of much of the published evidence.[301]

What had happened was that, as a consequence of the information obtained during the raids in Moscow, the Cheka had raided the Embassy. Cromie had tried to hold the Cheka agents back whilst papers were destroyed by the Consul, Woodhouse, and so that visitors could escape. There is some conflict over who shot first but it seems likely to have been Cromie. Three Cheka men were wounded and Cromie killed. Later, in 1924, by which time he was a Liberal MP, Teddy Lessing informed the House of Commons that Cromie "shot two of the assailants before he was shot himself...I was within a few yards of Captain Cromie when he was shot. As a matter of fact, they did not fire first."[302]

At this distance, it is difficult to know exactly what Cromie achieved by this act of suicidal bravery although it is possible that he delayed matters long enough for the most incriminating evidence to be destroyed. On the other hand, it may be that the Cheka already knew what was going on anyway. What happened next is testimony to the fear felt by the Bolsheviks and the incipient cruelty of the times. Cromie's body was mutilated by a mob which the Cheka had permitted into the Embassy building and then flung out of a window onto the street. A different side of Russian sentiment was displayed six days later at Cromie's funeral when the sailors on the destroyers that had provided cover for the raid witnessed his funeral cortege on its way from the Anglican church to the Smolensky Cemetery on Vasielievski Island about a mile a half distant. On realising that it was Cromie and remembering his joint service with the Tsarist navy, they lined the sides of the ship in silent tribute to a fellow sailor.[303]

It is evident, however, that there was much going on at the Embassy on the day of the raid. Lessing's own presence is unexplained but must have been Intelligence related given his connections. At the same time, a meeting was taking place with Sabir, Steckelmann and two British agents Boyce and Hall. Prince Shakhovskoy who had initiated the Bank Schemes was also present and it was only a matter of luck that the White leader, General Nikolai Yudenich was not there too.

It is not really clear whether the Cheka already knew what they would find as a result of Sabir and Steckelmann's information but they certainly uncovered plentiful evidence of the serious threat posed by the Allies' schemes. They also later announced that they had indisputable proof that the British had been implicated in Uritsky's murder.[304] Furthermore, they produced evidence of Allied plans to blow up bridges thereby preventing the Bolsheviks from gaining access to badly needed foodstuffs. This was emphasised when they raided de Vertement's flat and found eighteen pounds of explosive hidden there.

The arrest of Bruce Lockhart and death of Cromie caused an international outcry and the press reported it in lurid terms, one paper stating that a decree had been issued which "ordered the arrest of all British and French subjects between eighteen and forty years of age and that British officials have been arrested on trumped up charges of conspiring against the Soviet."[305] Bruce Lockhart himself described reading of "our iniquities in the Bolshevik press, which excelled itself in a fantastic account of a so-called Lockhart Plot. We were accused of having conspired to murder Lenin and Trotsky, to set up a military dictatorship in Moscow, and by blowing up all the railway bridges to reduce the populations of Moscow and Petrograd to starvation. The whole plot had been revealed by the Lettish garrison whom the Allies had sought to suborn with lavish gifts of money. The whole story, which read like a fairy tale was rounded off with a fantastic account of my arrest. I had been arrested, it was stated at a conspirators meeting"[306]

It is noteworthy that in this case, it is the Bolshevik account is almost totally accurate - as Bruce Lockhart very well knew - whereas the Allied account was highly selective and misleading. The only inaccuracy concerned Bruce Lockhart's arrest was that he was in fact in bed with Budberg when the Cheka raided his flat. It is possible that the Bolshevik press omitted this fact in their reporting less to protect Budberg's virtue than her cover as a Cheka informant.

Faced with the collapse of their plans and the arrest of their agents in a blaze of publicity, the British took what steps they could to salvage as much as they could. In the first instance alongside an official playing down the allegations made, the British sought to obtain some bargaining chips of their own. Accordingly, Maxim Litvinov, the Soviet representative in Britain was detained along with some of his colleagues; his secretary, Mr Wintin, his military adviser,

Captain Oshmyanski and Nicolai Klyshko who was a draftsman at Vickers Limited's Croydon premises.[307] Like Bruce Lockhart, Litvinov's status was opaque and he certainly did not have official accreditation. Also like Bruce Lockhart, he was heavily engaged in promoting his country's interests against the host nation. In this case, he actively encouraged Bolshevism in Scotland and went so far as to appoint a prominent Marxist and anti-war campaigner, John Maclean as the Bolshevik Consul of Glasgow.[308] The legality of his arrest was dubious and the British had to rely upon the catch-all provisions of Regulation 14B of the Defence of the Realm Act ("DORA") which provided that "where it appears to the Secretary of State for securing the public safety or defence of the realm it is expedient in view of the hostile origin or associations of that person, the Secretary of State may...require that person to be interned in such place as may be specified." The open ended provisions of DORA led to it being strongly criticised as an assault upon justice and principles of Habeas Corpus.

Having secured Litvinov in custody, negotiations with the Bolshevik government began to secure the return of British subjects in return for his and his companions' release. These were protracted by reason of the mutual lack of trust but eventually they were landed in Bergen in late September. At that point Lockhart and others were allowed to cross the Russo-Finnish border.

As for the intelligence agents, it was up to them to make their own escape. Reilly, having bravely or rashly returned to Moscow to discover that all his covers were blown including that of Relinsky, the Cheka agent, seemingly offered to give himself up in return for Bruce Lockhart's release. However, he was dissuaded from taking this quixotic and probably pointless gesture by Captain Hill. Reilly then making use of Hill's own fake cover, managed to make his way back to Petrograd sharing a train carriage which had been booked by the German Embassy. From there, he found a berth on a Dutch yacht that sailed to Reval (now Tallinn) which even though then under German occupation must have come as a considerable relief.[309]

Bruce Lockhart and "some forty or fifty French and English" were able to travel over the Russo-Finnish border and then, presumably by train and boat back to England.[310] He adds that the journey home was not an uncomfortable one. Keyes, in the meantime, managed to get on one of the last boats leaving Archangel. He mentions that he "had to travel steerage with soldiers of all Allied nations, an ex-whip of the Galway blazers and a lot of Russian wives of Belgian and Italian workmen."[311] Interestingly, they were escorted by 'a Bolshevik trawler as a German submarine was reported to be in the White Sea. However, this helpful gesture did not survive their disembarkation at Kandalashka, a port with land access to Murmansk, as the trawler proceeded to shell the town causing particular alarm to one of the escaping ships which "was tied up to a barge of dynamite." After "a loathsome time in Murmansk - I was quite ill", Keyes left on an unescorted "ship with over a thousand women and children" the journey being particularly uncomfortable not only because it had to sail into the far north to avoid German submarines but also because of the overcrowding and the need to share a berth with a particularly malodorous fellow passenger. Intriguingly, this story contradicts one later told by Keyes in which he gives an account of travelling through Finland and noting the savage fighting between Finnish Whites and Reds.[312]

Chapter 18:

October - December 1918

On his return to England, Keyes lobbied Milner hard again to establish a joint Persian and Russian section the better to combat the threat posed to India by German moves. Milner was persuaded and Keyes then tried to secure Lloyd George's support. He does not seem to have held back as he also told "them that the piecemeal way in which they were dealing with the question [of the German threat] was fatal, and that our adventure in Archangel was a crime unless we were prepared to push it through with at least two Allied divisions." If that was not blunt enough, he then lambasted the Director of Military Intelligence about the folly of Dunsterville's mission to Baku. Even Keyes acknowledged that he "must have been tactless in [his] denunciation of the crime of this second jumble." As a result, he was not given "the appointment at the War Office that Milner had promised" instead being transferred "much against my will" to the "Ministry of Information as adviser on Russian affairs and 2nd of the Oriental Section"[313].

Keyes' account of his discussions raises the question as to why a relatively junior officer should have direct access to so many influential people. Bearing in mind that he had spent his entire career abroad, these were not social connections and the answer must lie in Keyes' intelligence role whether in connection with the Bank Schemes or something even more secret. It is also interesting that he had no hesitation in taking them to task for the perceived failings of their policies even though he can have had scant insight into the domestic political situation that then obtained and in particular, Lloyd George's preoccupation with the potential of Bolshevik inspired disorder. It may well be that these discussions coloured his views of Lloyd George although they were obviously very different politically in any event. As will be seen later, Keyes' willingness to confront senior politicians was to blight his career this time permanently and ensure that ultimately he was to spend his remaining working life in India.

Keyes' return to London coincided with the last stages of the Allied counter offensive that had begun in July. By October 1918, the German armies in the west were in retreat although far from beaten and the end of the war was clearly imminent. Indeed, Ludendorff and the Kaiser had privately accepted that the end was inevitable in the weeks following the Battle of Amiens which had commenced on 8 August and which was described by Ludendorff as "the black day of the German army."

In London, a strategic rethink was taking place in respect of Russia. Up until then, the primary objective was to do all possible to encourage the Russians to reopen the Eastern Front failing which to limit access to Russian raw materials and other resources. With the war ending, this objective fell away and the Allies had to decide their next steps. The removal of the common purpose of German defeat revealed a fundamental conflict in Allied objectives which was to bedevil relations between themselves and lead to further confusion in aims in respect of Russia and the Bolsheviks in particular.

The division of Russia into spheres of influence in late 1917 with the French predominating in Ukraine and Western Russia including what was to become Poland and the British in North Russia as well as the Caucasus and the borderlands between Persia and central Asian Russia made sense as inevitably the British had dominated the supply routes to Murmansk and Archangel and were also acutely sensitive to threats to India. The position in Siberia was more complicated by the interests of both the United States and Japan.

The concern about the perceived vulnerability of India's northern and western borders was in many ways a reversion to the position prior to the Anglo-Russian Entente of 1907. However, whilst the war was proceeding, it had been exacerbated by the threats posed by both German and Turkish agents that had so preoccupied Keyes in 1916. Following the revolution, the situation became even more acute when both the Germans and Turks moved upon Russian oil resources in and around the Caspian. There was a realistic fear that domination of the area would inevitably lead to threats to India as well as permitting the Germans access not only to oil but also to cotton which was, amongst other things, important in the manufacture of explosives. This had been the primary motivation behind the advances into the area by Dunsterville and Malleson. As part of the same strategy, a further mission was sent to the Caucasus to prevent both German and Turkish threats which, like the others, was of mixed success.

Moreover, one of the first things that the Bolsheviks had done on taking over in October 1917 was to repudiate the Anglo-Russian Convention as well as taking active steps to promote revolutionary activity in India. Lenin himself regarded Britain as the arch-imperialist power and recognised India as one of its areas of vulnerability. He therefore swiftly took steps to radicalise Russian Central Asia and to forge links with revolutionary Indians. These actions, combined with the threat from Turkey and Germany, represented a complete failure of British policy. It had somehow contrived to achieve the worst of all worlds with its Indian possessions being threatened by both Bolshevik Russia and the Central Powers, something that would have seemed inconceivable when the Convention was agreed back in 1907.

To make matters worse, British military power in India was at an all time low with practically all but the poorly equipped forces on the North West Frontier fighting in Mesopotamia. This meant that the British would struggle to control civil rioting let alone a credible military threat. Meanwhile, Mesopotamia itself was threatened since the British had been dependent upon the Russian forces of General Baratov based at Hamadan in western Persia to protect their flank from Turkish attack particularly upon the Persian oilfields around Abadan. Following the Bolshevik takeover, Baratov's forces disbanded and he himself went into exile in India for five months.

The British were therefore forced to intervene in the vacuum left by the Russian collapse which explains the various missions sent into Central Asia and the Caucasus during 1918.

Keyes' entire background put him squarely in the Indian camp and even when he was actively engaged in Moscow and Petrograd, he was aware of the threat posed to British India and would therefore have entirely understood the reasons for British forces being sent into Central Asia. Indeed, bearing in mind his previous activities travelling in Russian controlled areas and confronting German agents in Persia in 1916, it is likely that he would have been actively involved had he not been preoccupied elsewhere. With that in mind, his criticisms of Dunsterville's mission were more likely to have been tactical rather than strategic.

In his lecture to the staff college at Quetta in August 1921, Keyes set out in detail his view of the Bolshevik threat to India based upon his experiences in Russia. This is revealing not only of Keyes' own views but also those of the British establishment in India. The lecture was lengthy and wide ranging but the section that related to the Bolshevik threat was particularly pertinent.

In terms of numbers involved, Keyes indicated that "as for genuine holders of the creed, they are very few in number - probably not more than five thousand though I have heard it put as low as fifty eight by a man who is now one of their inner ring." He adds that unlike the other parties "they had leaders of real dynamic force and organising capacity - mostly Jews."[314] Once again, there is evidence of a grudging respect for the Bolsheviks as well as Keyes' preoccupation with the preponderance of Jewish people involved. Two years earlier he had entered into correspondence with Leonard Cohen a prominent member of the London Jewish community on the subject.[315] Cohen quotes Keyes as saying "it is no good putting your heads (ie the heads of European Jews) in the sand and saying that Jews were not succouring the Bolshevik horror - they are."[316]

Keyes' views were correct in that there were a high proportion of Jewish Bolsheviks but it also elides with an implicit anti-Semitism that keeps cropping up and for example, almost certainly coloured his relations with Reilly. It is difficult to know how much weight to ascribe to it bearing in mind that Keyes was doing no more than reflecting the preoccupations and values of people of his background and class at that time so that for example, an unnamed Foreign Office official was to opine that "Trotsky is mainly the agent of the Jewish conspiracy of Eastern Europe whose chief aim is to destroy European civilisation at all costs and by any means, German, Allied, Socialist or any others." If this was typical of (presumably) informed thinking, it was no wonder that there was a lack of coherence in British policy.

As for Bolshevik penetration of India, Keyes was explicit that "Lenin and Trotsky have said that the road to London lies through Kabul and Delhi" and that 'they have a propaganda school near Bokhara with one side teaching Hindustani to communist agents and the other teaching Anti-British propaganda to Indians."[317]

The collapse of the Central Powers opened up extensive opportunities for the Allies but with them came the risk of internal division. What was exposed was the fundamental disconnection between Allied aims about what was the appropriate way to resolve the entire Russian conundrum. The French and British were both hardwired into an essentially imperialist way of thinking exacerbated by the need to secure some kind of return on the crippling financial costs of the previous four years. The Japanese, whose policies had paid dividends at a limited economic cost, were seeking to maximise the return on their investment in supporting the Allied war effort. They wanted not only to obtain a Pacific empire from the former German colonies such as the Bismarck Islands but also the German concession in Tsingtao. Japanese involvement in Siberia was also intended to bolster claims to the Russian Far East.

The Americans were understandably concerned not to have anything to do with any imperial ambitions particularly by the British and were also disinclined to support regime change particularly after the Armistice in November 1918. This meant that activities particularly in Central Asia were exclusively British and carried out without American assistance. The Americans were also suspicious of Japanese expansionism primarily because they perceived Japan as a threat to US dominance in the Pacific but also because they wished to see an independent and strong China which would be unlikely to occur with a Japanese occupation of Manchuria.

Behind all this was a fear that, even following the German defeat, links forged between the Germans and the Bolsheviks would lead to a German economic hegemony in Russia notwithstanding its military collapse. Both Britain and France were keen to avoid this occurring as well as being acutely aware of the threat to their own war weary populations of Bolshevik propaganda. All of this predisposed them towards continuing to seek the Bolsheviks' overthrow and this, in turn, led them to support both the various White movements and to keep the intervention forces in Murmansk, Archangel and Vladivostok in play.

Against that, there was no public appetite for any further military commitment in terms of troops and, in any event, both Britain and France were financially exhausted which limited their ability to achieve the replacement of the Bolshevik regime. The dilemma was well summarised by Sir Henry Wilson in a memorandum of 13 November 1918 which pointed out that two of the previous British objectives in Russian policy, namely to keep German forces committed to the Eastern Front and to deny them access to Russian resources, had been achieved which left that of achieving influence over Russia and its economy. Wilson went on to identify a series of partially conflicting aims; the desire to root out Bolshevism both for the benefit of Russia and to prevent its spreading both into Europe and British India, the likelihood that any vacuum created by Allied withdrawal would be filled by German influence, the desire to support pro-Allied Whites who would in all likelihood otherwise be destroyed in the Red Terror and the need to secure the safe evacuation of Allied troops already in Russia.

Wilson discounted the idea of removing the Bolsheviks as a policy in itself on the grounds that it was purely political and "we cannot permanently stifle it by military action."[318] The need to prevent German influence remaining in what had been former Russian provinces particularly, Finland, the Baltic States, Poland and the Ukraine was of paramount concern even though Wilson recognised that, in time, they were likely to be re-absorbed back into the Russian sphere of influence. As for providing assistance to Whites, he was of the view that British obligations amounted to providing material support but little else. It would then be up to the rival factions to fight it out amongst themselves.

Wilson saw that German influence could either be limited by putting the Border States under Allied military protection or by increasing the Intervention forces so that they could effectively challenge the Bolsheviks in their strongholds in the larger cities. Whilst, on balance, he favoured this latter strategy, it was fraught with difficulty not least in securing public support for what would in effect be the continuation of the war, the likelihood of American opposition and the logistical and climatic problems of operating militarily in Russia. He therefore concluded that "one course only remains, namely, to do all we can to give our friends a fair start and then to withdraw."[319]

Wilson then conducted a tour d'horizon of the key areas and issues. He believed that the Poles would be able to hold off Bolshevik advances particularly if the thirty thousand Polish troops based on the Western Front were swiftly transferred. He foresaw great difficulty in preventing a Bolshevik seizure of the Ukraine once the occupying German forces were evacuated and that the Czechs were increasingly disengaged and would militate for a return home. Whilst this weakened the position in Siberia, he was optimistic that the Omsk government would establish its authority and so he was willing to recommend that the British give it official recognition. Romania should be encouraged to occupy Bessarabia on its eastern border to create a buffer as indeed took place.[320] The Allies should stand ready to support any governments that emerged in the Baltic States following a German withdrawal and the British should put pressure on Finland to reach an agreement with the dissident Karelians which would protect the British flank at Murmansk. The opening of the Black Sea to Allied shipping meant that significant material support could finally be given to Denikin, who was then in the Caucasus and Krasnov, the leader of the Don Cossacks. Finally, the establishment of good relations with whatever new regime emerged in Turkey should enable the British to retreat from their bridgehead around the Caspian and to allow Malleson to leave Hamadan.

Wilson's hard headed approach was shared by the Foreign Secretary, Balfour, who believed that the British public would not support a "crusade" against Russia even though local British advisers favoured this policy, something he put down to their being "obsessed" with Bolshevik terror. In the circumstances, it is hard to not sympathise with them as they would have been witnessing the massacre of practically entire social classes by the Bolsheviks. This was, in many ways, a continuation of Balfour's pre-existing policy of drift and whilst it made sense for the cogent reasons expressed, in reality, it was the worst of all options as the Whites were generally well equipped and able to fight but insufficiently strong ever to defeat the Bolsheviks permanently. The Bolsheviks were themselves much weakened and only able to continue to fight because of desperation and the utterly ruthless suppression of any internal dissent. As a consequence, the Russian Civil War dragged on at the cost of millions of lives and the destruction of vast swathes of property for a further two years.

One of the immediately pressing issues was whether to give official recognition to the Provisional All Russian Government based at Omsk. This was an unhappy merger between the SR dominated Samara government and the rightist Provisional Siberian Government which contained many former Tsarist officers. However, matters moved swiftly and on 18 November, the Government was overthrown in a coup and Kolchak appointed Supreme Ruler with extensive emergency powers.

There is conflicting evidence about whether the British connived at Kolchak's takeover; certainly two of the British officers left in Omsk after General Knox's departure, Lieutenant Colonel JF Neilson and Captain Stevani, were aware that something was afoot and apparently took pains not to become involved. However, at the same time, Kolchak had close links to the British and his appointment therefore was possibly in line with British intentions. This is borne out by Neilson's comments that he had made it clear to Ivan Mikhailov, a key plotter and later Kolchak's Minister of Finance, that "the current state of affairs was most unsatisfactory and that Admiral Kolchak was the only man capable of saving the country."[321]

Furthermore, Colonel John Ward of the 25th Middlesex Regiment ordered his men to block off the streets of Omsk ostensibly to allow the Ministers of the Provisional All Russian Government time to consider whether to agree to resign which, ultimately, they did. However, it also prevented them from being able to offer substantive resistance to Kolchak's forces. Neilson claimed that this was done without his agreement which again does not seem plausible. It is therefore entirely possible that the British were up to their necks in the coup but could not admit to being so because it cut across policies previously agreed with the other Allies. Ward later claimed to have been unaware of what was afoot and, as a former Labour MP and prominent trades unionist, was furious at having unwittingly played a part in what amounted to a Tsarist coup.

In London, news of the coup seems to have come as a surprise and there was talk of censuring Neilson for his actions. On the other hand, there was no criticism raised about General Knox who, as Neilson's commanding officer, must have had some idea about his actions - certainly, both the French and Japanese thought so.

Kolchak's takeover alienated the old Samara faction of SRs some of whom were arrested while others crossed sides and fought with the Bolsheviks. At the same time, he failed to maintain good relations with the Czechs and Poles. It also led to concern in the British dominated enclave in Archangel. Matters did not improve when, following the uprising in Omsk, many of the captured SRs were massacred.

Meanwhile, in Archangel things were not improving. Francis Lindley, the former Counsellor at Petrograd who was now High Commissioner in North Russia, was dismissive of the prospects of any organisation that relied only upon the former aristocracy and officer class of ever being able to mount an effective challenge. This was an accurate summary of the problems underlying all the major White movements. In order to attract popular support, they had to commit to supporting land reform and recognising the peasants' seizure of land from the aristocracy which was always inimical to their principal supporters. The same was true about recognising the States that had broken away from Imperial Russia. Their support - particularly that of the Finns - would have been of considerable value in overthrowing the Bolsheviks but to achieve it the Whites would have to recognise them as sovereign states which was something they could not bring themselves to do.

In South Russia, the Armistice with Turkey opened up great opportunities as the Allies finally had unfettered access to the Black Sea which meant that they could supply DenikIn and the Volunteer Army properly. Accordingly, as early as 14 November 1918, the War Cabinet had agreed "to establish touch with Denikin at Novorossiysk and afford him all possible assistance in military material" as well as to ensure compliance with the agreement reached with the French in December 1917 over spheres of influence.[322] The British tended to include South Russia in their area which made Denikin of particular interest to them.

Keyes himself claims to have been the prime instigator of the decision to support Denikin. He plainly hated his job with the Ministry of Information and it is unlikely that he was popular there particularly after his "advice which was to sack the lot of the

Russian Section was not taken." He then concentrated upon Turkish related issues which is no doubt why he became preoccupied with the opportunities presented by the reopening of the Dardanelles for supplying arms and equipment to the Volunteer Army. He "was told the W.O. had decided to do nothing" but notwithstanding this, he prepared a memorandum recommending "that steps should be taken to send a propaganda mission to South Russia" and delivered this by hand to Lord Beaverbrook "who was ill in bed."[323] His approach was successful and Beaverbrook "promised to give a copy to Lloyd George."[324] Unfortunately for Keyes, his attempt to get himself appointed head of the mission failed when Sir Henry Wilson gave the post to General Poole who was now back in London. However, he was appointed to Poole's staff as a Political Adviser.

The decision to lend all support short of troops had therefore already been made in the case of Denikin which contrasted with the earlier landing of military forces in North Russia although they were to re-embark for England as soon as practicable. Consequently, it is clear that transferring the considerable number of troops necessary to achieve a White victory in the south was considered to be politically unachievable in a very war weary Britain. Nevertheless, moves were swiftly taken to make contact directly with Denikin and by 23 November, three British officers were at Denikin's base at Novorossiysk where they were greatly feted but also greatly lied to as to the true strength of the forces under Denikin's command. In fact, the officers realised that although strong on paper, the White forces were in fact weak but their account of a potential force of 1.2 million men was seized upon by the British in London to justify the continuing supply to Denikin of money and materials but no troops.

On their voyage to South Russia in mid-November, General Poole and Keyes were also accompanied by a Major Clayton who was to travel to the Caucasus as a logistics expert, Major Edwards and John Picton Bagge who was the British Consul in Odessa returning from leave in England. This fits well with Keyes' role as the interface between Military Intelligence and a more political and diplomatic role and, in time, Picton Bagge was to play an important part in the third iteration of the Bank Schemes. This new position represented an escape from a dreary post for Keyes and he was also promoted to Temporary Brigadier General on 8 December 1918 to cover the period whilst he was engaged on "special duties."[325] It also carried with it the prospect of finally becoming European based and not having to return to India. This was welcome since, as his correspondence increasingly made clear, he regretted the long absences from Edith and his family. He had been in England for less than three months over the past four years and, when he was, had been on duty for much of the time. This trend was to continue and he was not to see his son, Patrick Terence until he returned to England in spring 1920 by which time he was over a year old.

Other members of the party included Ernest Tamplin and two regular officers, Edwards and Namier as well as a Russian Captain called Basilovich. Tamplin already had experience of Russia having been attached to Bruce Lockhart's Mission and had landed at Archangel in August 1918 before swiftly returning to England. They paused en route in Rome which gave Keyes the opportunity to share with Edith his impressions of Italians - "the men like a lot of malicious monkeys and the women are the least attractive of any people I have ever seen." After Rome, they sailed into the eastern Mediterranean calling at Corinth on 29 November and arriving in Constantinople on 4 December. This coincided with the move to hold a peace conference on the nearby island of Prinkipo. The party must have played some part in the discussions taking place about this as well as liaising with French representatives whose ambitions conflicted with those of the British, being focussed upon gaining effective control of the Ukraine. The French moves had failed catastrophically and resulted in the Ukraine being thrown into chaos with not only the Bolsheviks and Whites vying for control but also Ukrainian nationalist forces led by Symon Petliura and anarchists led by Nestor Makhno.

The conference at Prinkipo was strongly supported by Lloyd George who saw in it an opportunity to disengage from Russia. This was particularly important in the run up to the election in December 1918 which no doubt was Lloyd George's principal concern. He therefore took all steps to speed up demobilisation so that Sir Henry Wilson would write; "Lloyd George insisted on men getting leave etc. All bribes, and disgusting as it is against the law."[326] Lord Milner resigned from the government in protest at Lloyd George's actions. British involvement in Soviet Russia was electorally unpopular particularly with organised labour which was another factor in Lloyd George's enthusiasm for a conference that was conveniently scheduled for February 1919 by which time the election would have safely taken place.

What was apparent was that the fundamental inconsistency in British policy was becoming ever more obvious once the principle objective of reconstituting the Eastern Front against the Germans was no longer applicable. This increasingly highlighted the tensions inherent in the inter-Allied objectives with the Americans keen to disengage, the French embarking on a policy of out and out imperialism and the British somewhere between the two. Having said that, all the nations involved demonstrated the usual combination of high mindedness and naked jackalry so that the Japanese offered to send twenty thousand men to assist Kolchak in overthrowing the Bolsheviks in return for north Sakhalin, a portion of Kamchatka and control of the Manchurian railway.

Once the election was over, the practical difficulties of the proposed conference became ever more apparent. The Whites were unwilling to negotiate with the Bolsheviks and it soon became clear that the Bolsheviks were adopting similar tactics to those which they had adopted at Brest-Litovsk, namely, agreeing to negotiate but then dragging things out in the hope that time was on their side and that the delays would enable them to establish firmer control as well as to re-equip the Red Army. As a result, the proposed conference never took place.

Keyes in the meantime had left Constantinople and arrived at Ekaterinodar on 18 December. His mission in South Russia then began in earnest.

Chapter 19:

South Russia 1919: The British Military Mission

The problem facing the Allies in early 1919 remained how to deal with the Bolshevik threat and in particular what support should be given to White forces and which of them would make the most convincing alternative government. Up until the Armistice, the differences in approach between the Allies were subsumed in the overarching objective of opposition to the Germans. As considered in Chapter 18, the splits in Allied interests became ever more apparent as time went on.

In early 1919, the French had established a viable base in Odessa with a mixed garrison including troops sent by the Greek Prime Minister, Venizelos, with the intention of building up credit with the Allies before the forthcoming peace conference in Paris. The French wished to capitalise on their influence in Ukraine to establish a bulwark against Bolshevik incursions into Eastern Europe and also with a view to exploiting the considerable natural resources of the area. French policy lacked coherence not helped by an unwise alliance with Petliura's Ukrainian nationalists who, in the immediate aftermath of the collapse of the German backed Hetmanate, seemed to represent the best hope for a stable future. Keyes was of the view that the French were particularly motivated in their support of Petliura by a desire to gain control of the Ukrainian sugar trade noting too that they "had a tremendous lot of money invested" which would otherwise be at jeopardy.

As it happened, Petliura lost control of Kiev on 3 February 1919 and was then pushed back to Podolia in South West Ukraine. Petliura, although anti-Bolshevik, was regarded as too radical by Denikin and the Volunteer Army and there were intermittent skirmishes between the two forces. It was this inability to cooperate in opposing the principal Bolshevik threat that bedevilled the White movement in general and contributed significantly to its ultimate failure.

Petliura's defeat led to the French losing enthusiasm for establishing a political presence in the Ukraine so that they concentrated instead upon building up the border states, particularly Poland and Romania, with the intention of forming a cordon sanitaire preventing the spread of Bolshevism out of its Russian heartlands. Considerable French resources were devoted to supporting the Romanian and Polish armies. In Poland's case, the French trained Blue Army (so called because it was equipped with French uniforms) was later to play a vital role in defeating the Red Army at the Battle of Warsaw and the French Military Mission of four hundred officers was important in the organisation of the other Polish forces.

In contrast, the British military was less generous in the distribution of supplies but made up for it by the gallantry of its leader, General Adrian Carton de Wiart VC who, in the course of an extensive military career had been shot in the face, skull, stomach, hip and ear and had pulled his own fingers off when a doctor declined to amputate them following a serious wound to his hand in 1915. De Wiart fought alongside the Poles, crashing two aircraft and falling from a train whilst shooting Bolsheviks with a revolver. After the end of the Polish-Soviet war, he was given the use of an estate near what was then the Russian border where he lived until returning to active service with the British army in 1939.[327]

The Americans' desire to withdraw entirely became ever more apparent with the passage of time and the establishment of an increasingly isolationist mood post war. Bearing in mind the importance of US forces not only in the Allied bases in North Russia but also in Vladivostok, their imminent departure undermined any Allied wish to continue with an active military intervention. The Americans were also important politically in preserving the impression of inter-Allied co-operation. Furthermore, it was becoming ever more apparent that American financial muscle could be exerted to restrain actions by its greatly impoverished allies. The

Americans were also inherently suspicious of Japanese intentions which, as discussed in Chapter 18, were nakedly imperialistic.

To a greater or lesser degree, all the Allies shared a dislike of Bolshevism and a fear that it might spread into their own countries. These fears were exacerbated by the Spartacist uprising in Germany in January 1919. There was therefore a tendency to balance a wish to extirpate the threat to world peace against the risk of encouraging domestic upheaval. In Britain, this inherent conflict was personified in the approaches of Lloyd George and Churchill who, following the election of December 1918, had become Secretary of State for War (and for Air).

Lloyd George was the minority leader of a coalition and knew that he had to operate by persuasion for his government to remain in office. He could also see that the rise of the Labour Party corresponded with the split in the Liberals meaning that there was almost no chance of him subsequently presiding over a future Liberal government. He was also was sceptical about the prospects of intervention, fearing that Britain was repeating the mistakes of supporting the forces of reaction against revolutionary France which had led to more than twenty years of conflict. His views in this regard were reinforced by a palpable concern about civil unrest which was entirely justified since, by that time, the Labour Party was supporting a voluble "Hands Off Russia" campaign so that Lloyd George feared an imminent general strike in February 1919.

Temperamentally too, Lloyd George was suspicious that a successful counter-revolution in Russia would reintroduce autocracy and Kolchak's appointment as dictator in December 1918 could have done nothing to allay these fears. Curzon, the Foreign Secretary commented that 'the trouble with the PM is that he is a bit of a Bolshevik himself. One feels that he sees Trotsky as the only congenial figure on the international scene'.[328] All of this convinced Lloyd George that despatching troops to combat the Bolsheviks was fraught with risk not only in Russia itself but also domestically in Britain.

Churchill, on the other hand, was convinced of the need to overthrow Bolshevism before it took root and was therefore far more willing to support the Whites, if need be with British troops. This not only reflected his perception of the threat posed by the Bolsheviks to the world order but also his innately imperialist views on foreign policy. One of the first steps that Lenin had taken following his seizure of power was to repudiate the Anglo-Russian Convention of 1907. This immediately revived the threat to British India which indeed was made far worse by Lenin's determination to spread revolution to India with the express intention of securing the destruction of the British presence. This revival of the Great Game was reciprocated by the British whose preoccupation with Asiatic Russia and the Caucasus became ever more evident the more that a threat was perceived. It is noteworthy that whilst the British were unwilling to send troops to support the Whites in South Russia, there were British detachments in the Caucasus as well as a military mission whose principal aim was to establish an anti-Bolshevik buffer. Ironically, one of the admittedly many reasons for the failure of Denikin's forces in South Russia was that they were distracted by squabbling with the British backed proto-states in the Caucasus, particularly, Georgia.

Lloyd George was well aware of the divergence of views and he had been explicitly warned about the risks inherent in them by an aide, Philip Kerr who wrote that "in my opinion, Mr Churchill is bent on forcing a campaign against Bolshevik Russia by using Allied volunteers, Polish and Finnish and any other conscripts that can be got hold of, financed and equipped by the Allies. He is perfectly logical in his policy, because he declares that the Bolsheviks are the enemies of the human race and must be put down at any cost. Personally, as I think you know, I am against such a policy because, to my mind, it must lead to the Peace Conference taking charge of Russian affairs, and, if they do that it will end in revolution in the West."[329]

Churchill's views were therefore in direct conflict with those of Lloyd George and he had also been a voluble critic of the proposed Prinkipo Conference claiming that "you might as well legalise sodomy as recognise the Bolsheviks."[330] Perhaps unsurprisingly, Churchill's hostility to the Bolsheviks was widely shared amongst the military and, as will be seen, by Keyes in particular. However, it was not shared by a British public that was plainly unwilling to support the sending of troops - especially, conscripted troops - to fight in Russia.

The compromise solution was that adumbrated by Sir Henry Wilson (see Chapter 18), namely to supply the White forces and Denikin in particular with military equipment but no troops. The British Military Mission to South Russia was to coordinate its distribution as well as to take steps to protect British interests politically. It was to be General Poole and Keyes' task to ensure that this took place.

General Poole and his party, including Keyes, had arrived in Novorossiysk in South Russia on 3 December and were made much of by Denikin and the Volunteer Army. Although Poole was not convinced by Denikin, he formed a favourable impression of the army and Baron Wrangel, its cavalry chief in particular. He then travelled on to interview General Krasnov, head of the Don Cossacks. This meeting rapidly became a party with many gypsy girls laid on to accommodate Poole's seemingly well-known susceptibilities in that direction. Perhaps as a result, Poole formed an overly optimistic view of the Don Cossacks' strength and consequent need for generous supplies. This was not entirely his fault as both Krasnov and Denikin were both prone to great exaggeration of their military strength in the belief that this would not only convince the British that they were right to continue support but also to ensure adequate, indeed overly generous, supplies.

Reilly and George Hill had also been sent to South Russia and both, particularly Reilly, formed more realistic views as to White strength. They met Denikin who Reilly described as being "a man of about fifty, of fine presence, the dark Russian type with regular features; he has a dignified, very cultured manner.... he gives one the impression of a broad-minded, high-thinking, determined and well balanced man - but the impression of great power of intellect or of those powers of intellect that mark a ruler of men is lacking."[331]

Reilly had no faith in Krasnov who he described as "a stupid man [but], an impresario of genius."[332] Interestingly, Keyes' own views were practically identical and he reported that Krasnov was "a very clever creature. He found no difficulty in shifting his allegiances from Germany to us and produced a well written but absolutely useless account of the military and economic situation of the Don. He was a first class impresario and was ably seconded by his entourage who did their best to complete our deception with champagne and choked off our curiosity by nearly killing us with cold."[333]

Keyes and Reilly however clashed and had little time for each other. It is entirely possible that Keyes' "great aversion" for Reilly stemmed from a lack of trust in his good faith but it may also have been tinged with anti-Semitism.[334] The dislike was reciprocated by Reilly who wrote in his diary that, on buying champagne for all present to celebrate his and Hill's award of the Military Cross, Keyes had declined the offer so that Reilly described him as "a cad and a fool." It is impossible to disentangle their relationship at this distance but, in later life, Keyes was an evangelical teetotaller so it is at least conceivable although unlikely, that it was all a misunderstanding.[335]

Keyes wrote to Edith on New Year's Day 1919 full of enthusiasm for his new role adding that "we are having a very interesting time here. I spend the whole time interviewing people, generals by the dozen, politicians, bankers merchants etc and am really getting the hang of the general situation at last." He continued to work assiduously on this and by the spring was becoming a key player in the Military Mission. General Poole soon returned to London and was able to report on his findings to the War Cabinet on 13 February. Poole's view was that Denikin was no military genius but he was patriotic and generally respected. He was also well supported by at least two of his commanders, Dragomirov and Wrangel. He also spoke well of Krasnov's Don Cossacks pointing out that he was holding back troops ready for an advance on Moscow. This was sharply contradicted by the Foreign Secretary, Curzon, who reported that the latest information was that Krasnov had been thrown back in confusion by the Bolsheviks. Poole appeared unperturbed by this and recommended that the British should offer equipment including tanks and aircraft but no troops other than a limited number of specialists.

The Chancellor of the Exchequer, Austen Chamberlain, in questioning Poole, neatly summarised the fatal flaw in the Whites' prospects of success whether under Kolchak, Denikin or Yudenich which was that none of them commanded any support amongst the peasants who constituted eighty six percent of the Russian population. Indeed, whilst the peasants were deeply suspicious of the Bolsheviks and particularly resented the seizure of grain, they were even more fearful of a return to power of the landowning classes who would inevitably look to return property back to its previous owners. This was the paradox underlying White policy namely that the only way in which they could succeed was to broaden their political base away from the landed and officer class but that this was impossible without offending their core military support. There were occasional attempts to find a more reformist approach such as that of Petliura or the Samara Whites but they all ended in failure. A similar problem beset White policies towards the former Russian provinces, particularly Finland. In the end, this meant that promising opportunities to overthrow the Bolsheviks were frittered away for ideological reasons.

In the meantime, whilst the British and Allied governments dithered over formulating a definitive policy towards Russia and the extent of assistance that was to be given to Kolchak and, in particular, Denikin, they were overtaken by events. On 19 February, the Bolsheviks successfully launched a surprise attack on the Don Cossacks at Tsaritsyn. Krasnov's forces had shrunk to approximately fifteen thousand men by casualties and, in particular, desertions and they fell back south westwards towards the Donetz and the Volunteer Army. Denikin was able to hold back the Bolshevik advance long enough for the spring thaw to set in which made movement extremely difficult and which therefore brought a temporary respite.

Meanwhile, the manoeuvrings by the French in the Ukraine were coming unstuck. They had initially sought to establish joint Franco-Russian regiments which, naturally, were to be French officered and whose troops were to be paid at a higher rate than the Volunteer Army. This understandably aroused Denikin's hostility and resentment. At the same time, French actions in Odessa were also causing suspicion amongst the Volunteer Army representatives who not only distrusted French motivations but also their association with the mostly Jewish Odessan commercial class. The French in turn were frustrated by the failure of White counterintelligence to prevent Bolshevik sympathisers from spreading propaganda amongst the increasingly restive French forces in Odessa. This extended to the widespread circulation of a French language paper called "*Le Communiste.*" On 2 March 1919, infuriated with local incompetence, French counterintelligence arrested eleven members out of twelve of the Bolshevik Propaganda Committee. These were handed over to the local Odessan authorities and promptly shot which led to an outcry. When the twelfth member was subsequently caught, the French at least ensured that he received a trial of sorts before the inevitable execution.

Reilly reported gloomily on French actions and was concerned about the effect of a breach between them and Denikin. He recommended that Keyes should accompany Denikin to a proposed summit with General Berthelot who was the head of the French Military Mission in Bucharest which shows his regard for Keyes' abilities notwithstanding their personal antipathy.

Whilst the French were pressing on with their ultimately doomed Ukrainian plans, the impasse between Churchill and Lloyd George continued with Churchill making repeated proposals but never receiving a definitive response. On 8 March, Churchill wrote to Lloyd George summarising what he believed to be British policy. So far as North Russia was concerned, Murmansk and Archangel were to be evacuated as soon as the ice melted with British troops being sent out to cover the evacuation. The thirty thousand British troops in the Caucasus were also to be evacuated as soon as possible. Denikin was to be required to give an undertaking not to make any moves upon the new states in the Caucasus in return for which a British Military Mission of two thousand men was to be sent to South Russia along with extensive military equipment including tanks and aircraft. Similarly, the two British regiments then with Kolchak at Omsk were to be replaced by a British Military Mission. He concluded by inviting Lloyd George to let him know if he disagreed. No reply was received, presumably because even then Lloyd George was unwilling to commit himself and so matters proceeded along the lines proposed by Churchill effectively by default. Notwithstanding his silence, it is clear that Lloyd George continued to look to find a way in which peace could be made with the Bolshevik regime as, in his opinion, it was the only way in which stable government would be restored to Russia.

Once again, with the best of intentions, the British had managed to alight upon the worst possible policy. The White forces were to be given sufficient support to enable them to continue to fight the Bolsheviks but not enough to succeed. Equally, the British were to offer advice and support so that they were associated with the Whites' actions including the renewed spate of pogroms in South Russia but not so much that they could have a dominant influence over White military and political policy. As a result, the potential for positive relations with the Bolsheviks with benefits both politically and economically that had seemed at least a possibility if the Prinkipo proposals had been followed through, were permanently lost. At the same time, the White forces were trapped into a dependence upon Allied support and weaponry whilst, simultaneously, feeling undermined and betrayed by the very people who had encouraged them so vigorously whilst Germany remained undefeated. The problems inherent in such a strategy would soon become apparent and would place the British officers and diplomats both in South Russia and Siberia in an extremely difficult position.

By this time, Poole had been replaced by General Briggs and, as Keyes was later to report, "the Government had decided to send Denikin arms and equipment for two hundred and fifty thousand men. They subsequently increased this to four hundred thousand."[336] Keyes settled well into his role and began to see it as a potential escape route from his previous career pointing out "that it weren't for this, it would be India with the certainty of a permanency whilst this work always gives the possibility of a release from India." Later on, he added that "there is every chance of staying in Russia for several months more and of its leading to permanent employment in South Russia."[337] This was only one of several references to his urgent desire to avoid a return to India with the likely further separation from Edith and his children. As events unfolded, this became ever more unrealistic as the British position in South Russia became untenable and Keyes began to make himself unpopular in London.

During March, whilst protracted negotiations were taking place in Paris over the restructuring of Europe and the price to be paid by the Central Powers, the position in Russia was changing fast. Kolchak had captured Ufa and two Bolshevik regiments had defected to him. In the south, Trotsky had been held back by a Cossack rising which was also backed by the Volunteer Army and there were strikes in Petrograd which were violently suppressed by the Latvians who remained Lenin's praetorian guard. Set against that, the Bolsheviks were encouraged by the establishment of a Soviet government in Hungary under the leadership of Bela Kun. This, although short lived, had the effect of alarming the Allies even more about the risks of a Bolshevik contagion spreading into Western Europe. It was this fear that encouraged the French in their policy of building up the new border states which Lloyd George rightly regarded as flawed believing instead that the solution was to create a stable Germany which would stand firm against any future Bolshevik inspired depredations. Lloyd George was also against the imposition of overly heavy indemnities upon Germany indicating that "we cannot both cripple her and expect her to pay." Furthermore, he sought to oppose the creation of substantial minorities (chiefly German but also Hungarian) in the newly created Central European states correctly believing that this would lead to subsequent unrest.

Keyes, in the meanwhile, was with Denikin when the Volunteer Army advanced towards Lugansk in eastern Ukraine with the intention of meeting up with the Cossacks who had risen against the Bolsheviks. After making substantial initial progress, the attack had to be called off when the 2nd Ukrainian and 13th Red Armies counter-attacked. Denikin's left flank in the Ukraine remained unstable because of the chaos brought about by the French dalliance with Petliura and their subsequent shameful failure to hold Odessa which caused untold damage to the reputation of the Allies. The French evacuation of Odessa on 4 April 1919 was extraordinarily badly handled and there is ample evidence of a wholesale breakdown of order as well as the surrender of considerable equipment and materiel to the Bolsheviks. Worse still, many White officers fell into Bolshevik hands and were brutally tortured and murdered. One account given to the British parliament, describes how some officers were "stripped...of their clothes and [were] burnt alive by binding them to planks which were slowly pushed into the ship's furnaces; others had steam jets from the boilers turned on their naked bodies, were scalded all over, then exposed to bitter frost, finally thrown overboard with stones tied to their feet. A diver later reported "all these four hundred officers were standing upright on the harbour bottom like a battalion of men just swaying backwards and forwards."[338]

To make matters worse, the British policy in the Caucasus was causing disharmony with Denikin who disliked the arbitrary way in which the British had carved up zones of influence without consulting him. The failure to establish a policy in relation to the Caucasus that was satisfactory both to the Volunteer Army and the new republics was to lead to considerable later confusion as well as a fatal splitting of Denikin's forces and focus of attention. Keyes was voluble in pointing out the discrepancy in British policy whereby the War Office was doing all it could to bolster Denikin's White forces with their commitment to the integrity of the old imperial boundaries whilst, at the same time, the Foreign Office, working with the French, was striving to establish viable new states at the fringes of Russia as a barrier against further Bolshevik contagion. By doing so, of course, he further alienated the senior echelons of the Foreign Office.

After the fall of Odessa, the Bolsheviks had moved on to the Crimea and by 15 April had surrounded Sebastopol. British and French ships shelled Bolshevik positions but it was clear that the town was lost and so an evacuation process began. This included the destruction of extensive stores and equipment. The morale of the French troops remained shaky and on 19 April, sailors on the battleship *France* mutinied. The loss of the Ukraine and Crimea was a direct result of the incoherence of the French policy and was to create a lawless void which was filled by a number of groups of which the Bolsheviks were the most important but others ranged from what was left of Petliura's Ukrainians, Nestor Makhno's anarchists and a variety of adventurers, deserters and bandits. Ultimately, it led to Bolshevik domination as they were the only force with a coherent policy and the necessary logistical system to succeed on a permanent basis.

Meanwhile, on 13 April, the British delivered twelve tanks and the necessary instructors and No 47 Squadron of the RAF to Novorossiysk. They were the first of many further shipments so that, in time, Denikin's forces were predominantly equipped with British arms and uniforms. The accompanying British troops and airmen were there to train Denikin's forces which would then use them against the Bolsheviks. It later became clear that this was only partially successful and relations between the RAF and the White Russian Air Force was particularly strained.

Militarily, Denikin was in considerable difficulty as the Bolsheviks were advancing both into the Ukraine and also towards Rostov the capture of which would have split the White forces. Many troops both in the Volunteer Army and particularly amongst the Don Cossacks were falling prey to Bolshevik propaganda and consequently were deserting in large numbers. One of the rumours put about was that the British actually supported the Bolsheviks and that the British Military Mission was a fake with Russian officers pretending to be British. This rumour was so prevalent that General Briggs was asked to ensure that none of his mission should be overheard speaking Russian, as this would confirm the widespread suspicions.

The inconsistencies in British policy meant that at the same time that Denikin was receiving substantial supplies, his position was being weakened by the removal of British forces from the Caucasus where they were, in effect, protecting his rear either from Bolshevik inspired risings or tensions with the nascent Black Sea Republics. There was also the gradual pulling out of British forces from the Caspian and Asiatic Russia which freed up Bolshevik forces and also removed the potential for a junction of Denikin's forces in South Russia with those of Admiral Kolchak in Siberia. The latter was in reality the only way in which the White forces would have achieved the strategic coherence that would have enabled them to achieve victory. It was foreseen by the British that their actions in this regard would substantially undermine their ostensible allies but it was recognised that the use of troops - particularly conscripts - in an Anti-Bolshevik crusade was unachievable and could have led to disorder at home. There was particular sensitivity about this as the war economy was being closed down as quickly as possible and with it substantial economic dislocation and consequent unemployment.

Meanwhile, at the same time that they were encouraging Denikin and Kolchak, the British were prevaricating about supporting General Yudenich who was assembling forces in Estonia with a view to making an assault upon Petrograd. The key British supporter of this scheme was none other than Hugh Leech who had escaped Petrograd following the murder of Cromie and subsequent September terror and had relocated in Finland. There he became involved together with Jules Hessen who was the managing director of the Eastern Company of Russia, the largest transport concern in Russia and a key supporter of Yudenich. Between them, they sought to raise £1 million to support Yudenich from Russian bankers in Helsinki but also with Treasury approval.

Leech was in London in March 1919 and visited Sir George Clerk at the Foreign Office on 27 March to brief him on the position in Finland and to solicit Foreign Office support for the Yudenich scheme. He was only partially successful in this and both the British and French remained lukewarm in their support for Yudenich who was suspected of being too pro-German. Leech's actions at this time again strongly point to him being at least a part time British agent and are further evidence that the Affidavit which Keyes swore in later litigation was misleading in characterising Leech as solely Yaroshinski's agent and therefore incapable of binding the British government.

In North Russia, the British still intended to withdraw from both Murmansk and Archangel and the local commander, General Ironside, was working towards those ends. However, to support an evacuation, it was agreed to send three thousand five hundred more troops thus ironically increasing the British commitment albeit temporarily. The overall intention was to train up local forces which would then take over from the British and then hold the area against the Bolsheviks. It was also hoped that a link up with Kolchak's forces moving west from Siberia could still be achieved. Sir Henry Wilson recorded in his diary for 23 March "Winston and I discussed a good punch towards Viatka to join with Kolchak before we cleared out."[339]

It was at this point that one of the more shameful aspects of British activities in Russia took place as Ironside was offered and accepted a considerable consignment of a new poison gas for use against the Bolsheviks. Churchill was initially against the move not for any moral reasons but because he was concerned not to waste the shock value of a new gas when it might be kept back for later. Once he had been reassured that this was probably not an issue as news of the new process was bound to become public knowledge anyway, he readily endorsed its use. The idea being that in heavily forested areas such as surrounded Archangel, artillery was of limited effect but, as Churchill was advised, `gas would ...drift along very nicely and certainly put the wind up someone. I believe that if you got home only once with the gas you would find no more Bolshies this side of Vologda'.[340] The General Staff and indeed Churchill also discounted the risk to civilians on the basis that this had never been a concern in the battles on the Western Front. This was more than a little disingenuous as there were few if any civilians in the battle areas in Northern France which had generally been evacuated whereas there were many inhabited villages in the areas surrounding Archangel.

News of the planned use spread and on 19 May 1919, Colonel Wedgwood, who was then back sitting as an MP, asked whether it was true that it was intended to use gas against the Bolsheviks. The reply on behalf of the Government was that it was as a retaliatory measure "as the Bolsheviks have already employed gas on the Northern front...every precaution is being taken to protect our brave troops against the inhuman methods of the Soviet forces." This was an outright lie and ten days later was echoed by Churchill himself when he said in the House of Commons "poison gas is used against our troops by the Bolsheviks. I do not understand why, if they use poison gas, they should object to having poison gas used against them." There is no evidence of the use of gas by the Bolsheviks who may not even have had access to it.

The gas in question, diphenylamine chlorasine was eventually used with considerable success against Bolshevik forces near Archangel on 27 August when DH9 bombers attacked the village of Emsa and further attacks took place in September. However, they failed to achieve the predicted collapse of Bolshevik resistance and the remaining stocks were dumped in the White Sea when the British later withdrew from Archangel.[341]

Whilst the various moves against the Bolsheviks were taking place in Siberia, North Russia and Estonia, the situation in South Russia was becoming more encouraging for the White forces. The collapse of Ukraine had exposed Denikin's left flank and he faced four Red Armies across the Donetz. However, on 8 May, a small British trained tank force went into action with five tanks and achieved considerable success. Matters then turned in Denikin's favour largely because forces previously allied to the Bolsheviks in the Ukraine, primarily those of Ataman Nikifor Gregoriev and Nestor Makhno's anarchists turned against them whilst, at the same time, there was an ongoing anti-Bolshevik rebellion by the Donetz Cossacks. This enabled Denikin's forces to make considerable progress and Wrangel moved on Tsaritsyn which fell in June. Tsaritsyn, (later Stalingrad) was a critical junction on the Volga and it also opened up the possibility of a link up between Denikin and Kolchak's forces. Its fall was in large part down to one of the Military Mission's tank instructors, the one armed Major Ewen Cameron Bruce who, in contravention of his orders not to participate in actual fighting, led a single handed tank assault which resulted in the capture of the city and forty thousand Bolsheviks.[342] Keyes was particularly impressed by the efforts of the tank crews reporting that "eight thousand men and six tanks saw eighty thousand Bolsheviks off the field...the fall of Tzaritzin was due almost entirely to the gallantry of a British tank instructor.[343]

The role of the British Mission was reviewed and a decision taken by Churchill to replace General Briggs with Major General Holman who was a specialist in administration and logistics. Holman was initially described by Keyes as "an Indian Army man - very clever but a real high handed creature" but they were later to work well together.[344] Holman had submitted a report in May that set out the parameters for future British engagement. The key components included the withdrawal of the existing British instructors and their replacement with specialist detachments of air force squadrons, tank and armoured car units. It was intended that these would ensure that such military aid as was given was done in a concentrated way. The principal change was that the Mission was to focus upon administration and supply. Holman recommended that whilst British supply specialists should take de facto control of Denikin's supply base at Novorossiysk, there would also be sections of the Mission attached to each of the three White armies in South Russia; the Volunteer Army, the Don Army (ie Krasnov's Cossacks) and the Army of the Caucasus. Later on, a further section was based in the Ukraine following Denikin's capture of Kiev in the summer of 1919.

Keyes in the meantime continued to be well regarded and was promoted to Brigadier General on the staff - as he called it "a pukka GSO I which is a very good job for an outsider" and was acting as liaison officer with the Don and Caucasus Volunteer Armies. Later on, he became the diplomatic representative with Denikin which brought them into direct contact on a very regular basis. Keyes liked and respected Denikin who he later described as "a great man and typical of all that is best in Russia" and one who had been let down by the wooden headedness of his supporters who failed to see the need for an imaginative political solution rather than a return to the status quo ante.[345]

In May, General Mai-Mayevski astutely used the railway network to advance deep into the east of the Ukraine, capturing Kharkiv. His success led to him being appointed Chief Commander of the Volunteer Army until his later replacement by Baron Wrangel on 27 November. Mai-Mayevski was an unusual choice notwithstanding his undoubted military abilities as he was obese and untidy in appearance, an alcoholic and stood out as an anti-Semite in a largely anti-Semitic army.

The summer of 1919 represented the high water mark of Denikin's advance. In May he had set out his Moscow Directive which ordered the three White armies under his control to converge on Moscow.

Mai-Maevski and the Volunteer Army would advance towards the west capturing Kharkiv and then Kiev thereby securing the Ukraine before turning towards Moscow. The Don Cossacks now under a new Ataman, Bokaievski, were to advance under the leadership of General Sidorin along the line of the Voronezh-Riazan railway. Finally, Wrangel was to advance from Tsaritsyn towards Nizhniy-Novgorod before marching west.

This strategy would be the subject of serious criticism chiefly from Wrangel but also members of the British Military Mission, particularly General Holman, who were concerned that Denikin was dissipating the effectiveness of his forces by splitting them and also that the further he advanced the harder it would be for him to secure his lines of communication and supply. Denikin's forces were also hampered by the fact that they were seen by the peasants as an officer heavy reactionary force and so commanded little respect and loyalty even though the true nature of Bolshevik rule was becoming more apparent by the day. All these fears were amply borne out in the coming months.

Over the coming months, the hopes of achieving a Bolshevik overthrow rapidly fell apart. Kolchak's forces were decisively defeated at Chelyabinsk on 25 July and fell back eastwards in disorder. This, in turn, rendered any hope of a link up with the British Military Mission in Archangel hopeless and indeed the position there was already precarious following the mutiny of some Russo-British units who had murdered their British officers. Accordingly, Field Marshal Rawlinson was sent to oversee the evacuation which was completed in September in the case of Archangel and October in Murmansk. In the Caucasus, the British had already withdrawn their forces by the end of August.

The British continued to be half hearted in their support for Yudenich and he, in turn was unable to build up sufficiently strong alliances with the border states, particularly Finland and Estonia which were suspicious that any White government would soon evince its innately revanchist tendencies and seek to reassert control over what it would regard as lost provinces. After initial success, Yudenich's final assault on Petrograd reached the outskirts before collapsing in the face of Bolshevik reinforcements (see Chapter 21).

As a result, all hopes were increasingly pinned on Denikin whose advance upon Moscow continued during the summer months. However, the British cabinet remained split over the extent to which support should be offered. This was less to do with sympathy for the Bolsheviks and more about concern for what a White government would be like. The perception was that a dictatorship would be established which would seek to re-establish a unified Russia and possibly would also be a greater threat to India than a weak Bolshevik government surrounded by buffer states. This view although perfectly reasonable in respect of the ambitions of a White government was also unrealistically optimistic in assuming that once the Whites had been defeated, the Bolsheviks would be willing to permit the continued existence of the border states. In fact, the Bolsheviks' views on re-establishing Russia's imperial borders were remarkably similar to the Whites and the coming years were to be dedicated to achieving these ends. It is noteworthy that the only countries to escape from Russian domination prior to 1939 were the more sophisticated and economically developed ones of Eastern Europe such as Finland, the Baltic States and Poland, those in the Caucasus and Central Asia were soon effectively reabsorbed.

The role of the Military Mission was to ensure that the supplies sent to Denikin were safely stored and then distributed as needed. The Mission was also responsible for ensuring that Denikin's troops were properly trained so as to make the best use of the equipment received by them. Whilst Denikin was disappointed that the British would not send troops to support his forces, he had few grounds for complaint about the lavishness with which he was supplied. During the course of the Mission, Denikin received twelve hundred field artillery pieces, over six thousand machine guns, two hundred thousand rifles with over two million rounds of ammunition, over seven hundred vehicles, eighty tanks and armoured cars, two hundred aircraft, sufficient medical equipment for twelve major hospitals and twenty five field hospitals, extensive amounts of signalling equipment and uniforms for five hundred thousand men. As Denikin struggled ever to have more than one hundred and fifty thousand men under his command at any one time, there were plainly no shortages. In fact, Kolchak had been equally generously supplied and following the capture by the Bolsheviks of his base at Omsk, entire regiments of the Red Army were fitted out entirely in British equipment. Having said that, not all equipment was suitable for Russian fighting conditions. Steel helmets and bayonets were unpopular and of limited use in a war of movement with relatively restricted use of artillery and trench warfare.

With the arrival of General Holman, the British had begun to assume effective control of the distribution of equipment after it had landed at Novorossiysk and onward shipment to the frontline forces. This led to a considerable improvement both in terms of speed and efficiency. Prior to that, items of equipment, particularly uniforms were finding their way into private hands. Keyes was later to report on the problems of supply and logistics pointing out that "instead of the large base staff we had asked for...one ordnance and one RASC officer arrived and were unable to cope with the situation. The confusion and corruption at the Russian base was indescribable and the looting was wholesale."[346] One extreme example was the surprising adoption by Novorossiysk prostitutes of a version of a British nurses' outfit but there was also widespread peculation of blankets and other medical equipment.[347]

The other role of the Military Mission was to provide specialist training to the White forces particularly in the effective use of artillery, tanks, machine guns and aviation. The troops sent were mostly volunteers and were instructed not to become actively involved in fighting. However, as with Major Cameron Bruce at Tsaritsyn, there were many examples of this order being ignored; even by General Holman himself who, on a few occasions, took to the air in a DH 9 to "throw some bombs at the Bolsheviks" as well as riding in a tank in fighting near Kharkiv.[348] In addition to seeking adventure, many of the officers saw that the only way in which their specialist equipment would be used properly was if they were physically present to give orders.

The myth of non-engagement was particularly exposed by the activities of 47 Squadron of the RAF which, alongside 221 Squadron was actively and heroically engaged throughout 1919-20. Although training up the White air force formed the major part of its duties, the squadron actively participated in many missions against the Bolsheviks and particularly during the siege of Tsaritsyn. Relations between the British and Russian pilots were frequently strained as the Russians did not respond well to formation flying and routine operations. They were referred to by the British as "the Wanderers" reflecting their unwillingness to obey orders. Over time, 47 Squadron was reinforced with Sopwith Camels and RE 8 bombers and even contemplated a bombing raid on Moscow. By the end of 1919, all were volunteers, often men who did not wish to return to civilian life. The Bolshevik air force opposing them was far less developed but appears to have made limited use of German mercenaries or former prisoners of war. This continuation of cooperation between the Bolsheviks and Germans after the Armistice was to increase substantially following the Treaty of Rapallo in 1922 with Germany gaining secret training bases in Russia in return for shared technology.

Relations between the British and Whites in general were not always easy and there were misunderstandings on both sides. The British were comparatively wealthy as the government exchange rate for the Rouble worked heavily in their favour. On 23 May, it had been decided that men serving in Russia would be entitled to an extra "colonial allowance" so that officers were paid 4s a day and other ranks 2s 6d. The Navy was paid in Sterling which had a local exchange rate of two hundred and fifty Roubles. The army was paid in Roubles at an exchange rate of eighty to the pound. The Treasury eventually agreed to pay a smaller colonial allowance but in Sterling for all troops at a fixed exchange rate of two hundred. This comparative affluence led to tensions and regular fights with the Whites not least because British officers were popular with Russian women not only because of their wealth but because marriage would provide an escape from the strained local conditions. In what might be termed an early iteration of Russian Brides, there were a significant number of Anglo-Russian marriages as a result.[349]

Wartime conditions particularly the close proximity of officers and men in the trenches had led to an increased informality in the British army. This was not the same in Denikin's army which continued to implement the oppressive discipline of the Imperial Army particularly in respect of what were, in essence, peasant levies. White officers thought little of beating their men and also paid scant regard to their welfare. This was noted by the party, including Keyes, that accompanied General Poole in December 1918 one of whom remarked that 'there is the same utter lack of consideration for one's inferiors socially that has always existed, eg, the orgy given by the Kuban Cossacks to Poole which kept a band and waiters until 6am, and such things as keeping motor cars waiting hours in the cold while the officers have a six course lunch."[350]

In general however, most of the officers attached to the Military Mission became highly supportive of the White cause and were described as being "more Russian than the Russians." This epithet certainly applied to Keyes whose pain and anger at British lack of support to Denikin and later Wrangel will become clear in Chapter 21

Chapter 20:

Bank Schemes Part III

Taking into account the difficulties that he had faced with the Treasury in spring 1918, it is unlikely that it was part of Keyes' mission to South Russia to revive the Bank Schemes. Financial matters were clearly not his strongest suit as he readily recognised. If he had realised that he would still be dealing with the fall out of the Schemes fifteen years' later, no doubt, he would have been even less willing to become involved in them again.

The third iteration of the Schemes came about in February 1919 when Sidney Reilly came across Yaroshinski in Odessa. The last contact with Yaroshinski had been almost a year earlier in Petrograd after which he had gone into hiding and therefore not been around to discuss the Schemes with Keyes when he visited Petrograd in June 1918. It was not altogether surprising that he had turned up in Odessa as his family were of Russian Polish origin and their original investments were sugar refineries around Kiev. As Odessa was the entrepot for the Ukrainian export trade, it is likely that he recognised this as a place of opportunity for him. Other than that, little is known of Yaroshinski's activities during 1918 although, as mentioned in Chapter 14, there is an intriguing reference to him being involved in abortive plots to rescue the Tsar and his family.

Reilly lost no time in introducing Yaroshinski to Picton Bagge who was by then back in post as British Consul in Odessa. The meeting was a great success possibly because Picton Bagge had already been briefed by Keyes on the voyage out to South Russia. Either way, he reported to London that he considered "it of the greatest importance that Carl Yaroshinski should be given a visa for England and every facility extended him. His influence is enormous both in Russia and Poland and his interests almost fabulous."[351] The British government did not share his enthusiasm and so Yaroshinski remained in the

Ukraine. Picton Bagge was clearly struck by Yaroshinski as he added that "his present age is 40. He is unmarried and his sole care is his mother. His genius is essentially a creative one, I have heard him compared by competent observers to Cecil Rhodes."[352] This rather preposterous comparison signally failed to take into account the febrile nature of Russia at a time when concepts of property were proving to be entirely illusory in the face of wholesale appropriations. It also reflects the way in which people were seeking comfort in the dream of a restoration of bodies, including corporate ones, which pre-dated the revolution. Having said that, if, as then seemed to be likely, the Bolsheviks were overthrown, it made a sort of sense. It did not, however, pay any regard to the inherent impossibility of the peasants acquiescing in the restoration of land to its previous owners. As that land formed the security for much of the credit granted by the banks, then they would in all likelihood be insolvent and worthless on any restoration that did not replicate the pre-revolutionary system.

Picton Bagge was also at pains to exculpate Yaroshinski from any blame in connection with the difficulties that had arisen with the original Bank Scheme pointing out that:

"I am aware that difficulties have arisen over the purchase of shares in the Siberian Bank negotiated by Colonel Keyes. It does not appear however that any blame is attached to Mr Yaroshinsky and from conversations I had with him and Colonel Keyes on the subject in February, I am convinced that Mr Yaroshinsky is not in any way to blame but anxious to clear up this matter to the satisfaction of HMG."[353] Keyes' own thoughts on this are not recorded nor are they about the reprise of the Schemes as a result of Reilly's plotting with Yaroshinski and Picton Bagge. It is unlikely that he regarded it with much enthusiasm bearing in mind the way in which he had only just managed to avoid being left with personal liability for the £500,000 lent to Yaroshinski (approximately £27m at today's values) when the Foreign Office contemplated arguing that he had acted ultra vires and therefore should bear personal responsibility for his actions. This would have led to him having to defend the threatened litigation from the vendors of the bank shares acquired by Yaroshinski without government backing. It also tends towards the conclusion that the Schemes' revival was a piece of opportunism dreamt up by Reilly once he had encountered Yaroshinski in Odessa.

At least part of the reason for Picton Bagge' enthusiasm came from the activities of the French in Odessa. As mentioned in Chapter 18, by early March, the French had sought to commit the Allies to an alliance with Petliura and the Ukrainian Directorate. They had agreed to the Directorate being given official recognition and to retaining control over the former Imperial Black Sea Fleet. The French would also support Ukrainian claims at Versailles. In return, the French were to be given de facto control over the Ukrainian economy and a veto over its government. The Directorate also agreed to its armed forces being transferred into a new White Russian Army under French control. To give these sweeping powers effect, two Russian banks and the Societe Generale de Paris and the Banque de Paris et des Pays Bas joined forces. If that were not ambitious enough, the French established an Inter Allied Supply Commission which was to manage the entire economy of South Russia and the Caucasus. Whilst this had a Russian President, effective power was very firmly French. Such out and out commercial imperialism seems to have inspired Picton Bagge into thinking in the same grandiose way.

As well as courting inevitable British opposition, the French moves met implacable hostility from Denikin and the Volunteer Army who saw not only a direct threat to their status as the principal White opposition to the Bolsheviks but disliked and distrusted the leading figures in the proposed White Russian Army who were chiefly ex-supporters of Skoropadsky whose evanescent puppet regime, known as the Hetmanate had been openly pro-German. It was only after high level intervention from Clemenceau that reasonable inter-Allied relations were restored.

Picton Bagge's discussions with Yaroshinski convinced him that a revived Bank Scheme would literally pay dividends and he became a passionate advocate. This enthusiasm survived the chaos of the fall of Odessa to the Bolsheviks in the first week of April 1919. The British and French managed to evacuate many of the inhabitants as well as Allied representatives so that Picton Bagge himself sailed to Constantinople and almost certainly arranged for Yaroshinski to accompany him.

Picton Bagge was not alone in believing that the White cause would ultimately triumph but he was a particularly vocal in making his views known, for example, in a telegram to Sir Ronald Graham he wrote that "in my opinion the power of Bolshevism is fast waning and I should not be surprised if the Soviet Government fell before the autumn."[354] His optimism led him - and others - to look to ways in which the British could profit from the improving situation as "at stake is possibly the greatest asset resulting from the World War, namely, the friendship and market of Russia which will revive as a great power within a short time."[355] This very far from ethical foreign policy concentrating upon the potential for commercial gain makes more sense when what was at issue was not only the potential for recovering British debts arising out of the war but also recouping some of the losses caused by the Bolsheviks' nationalisation of commercial enterprises, the British being by some considerable magnitude the biggest foreign investor in pre-revolutionary Russia.

In May 1919, Picton Bagge submitted his report to the Foreign Office. It was based on his discussions with Yaroshinski and others, including Keyes. It is apparent that Picton Bagge saw the scheme in a commercial and imperialistic way that differed markedly from the out and out political motivation behind Keyes' involvement in the previous year. It is hard to tell whether Picton Bagge reached his conclusions on his own or whether Yaroshinski encouraged this line of thinking as a way to revive what had been hitherto regarded as moribund. Equally, it is possible to see the hand of Reilly in such a grandiloquent interpretation.

In a reprise of the earlier Schemes, the essence of Picton Bagge's report was that Yaroshinski should be supported in gaining effective control over the six banks notionally acquired in February 1918 (see Chapter 12). Whether or not control had actually already been obtained was somewhat uncertain bearing in mind the Treasury's havering over making payments. There was also the question of the extent to which the shares were already mortgaged to others not least by Yaroshinski's "pyramiding operations" by which he had utilised the shares in one bank as security to for funding the purchase of another.[356] This had certainly caused William Clark concern in his report of 27 August 1918 (see Chapter 14).[357] Added to that, the documents were all of dubious legality having been backdated to October 1917 and to cap it all, many of them were "at present buried in the ground at Petrograd."[358] Undaunted or perhaps in ignorance of these complexities, Picton Bagge went on to extol the virtue of the Russian Banks project pointing out that;

"As regards the Banks, control of these means not only control of financial institutions as understood in England but also of a great number of industrial and commercial undertakings, mining, forestry and other concessions. The great Russian banks which are but few in number have branches and agencies throughout Russia…such a measure of control would in itself alone be extremely beneficial to British economic interests…. The end to be attained however, is for more imperial control of the banks [which] should mean both the economic and political control of Russia.

In the first place, representatives of British interests will have places on the Board of Directors and so control of the policy of the Banks. In second place, influence can be obtained over prominent politicians and men of standing in other spheres of life by appointing them to the Boards of Management of the Banks at good salaries when not actually in office. In this manner, at no expense to the public purse, Great Britain will secure the advocacy of the influential sector of the Russian political, financial and commercial world….

I propose that British subjects should be given posts both senior and junior in all the Banks and…. as regards the younger men, I would suggest that they be of the public school boy type."[359]

It has to be remembered that Picton Bagge, as the longstanding Consul to Odessa, would have commercial interests very much at heart. However, the direct way in which he pushed the economic and political advantages to the fore belies the more high minded speeches about restoring good government to a former ally. It perhaps also marked the turning point between the more commercially driven aspects of Victorian foreign policy and the more inward looking ambitions of a nation crippled by war debt and desperately trying to preserve the imperial legacy on the cheap. Having said that, Picton Bagge's ambitions went well beyond the commercial as he added that "through the medium of the Banks acting through a Central Bank, the whole system of intelligence could be built up... in any case an entirely British control could be arranged. In addition to this intelligence scheme, organised through the Central Bank control of the press could be secured and maintained. Further a propaganda service could be established. In this way, Great Britain would have secured...an intelligence service for political and economic purposes, control of the press, an organ for propaganda and a call on influential persons." He must have foreseen that this was tantamount to making Russia an economic satrapy of the British Empire as he rather lamely added that "a great benefit which Russia could obtain through this understanding with Great Britain would be through the employment of British colonial experts in the colonisation of Siberia."[360]

It is quite clear that what Picton Bagge intended was the wholesale British domination of Russian political and commercial life. No doubt in recommending this course, he not only had in mind British economic interests but foreign policy ones as well since British influence in Russian political activities would have neutralised any long term threat to India. It is however difficult not to marvel at the scope of Picton Bagge's ambition which, if successful, would have made Britain truly the preponderant global power. On the other hand, the naiveté underlying the hubris is also apparent as the idea that Russia would pliantly acquiesce in becoming a bigger and more sophisticated version of Egypt where British rule was inadequately hidden behind protectorate status is wholly implausible. At best, the scheme would have held together whilst some kind of alternative government to the Bolsheviks established itself. After that, it could only have ended in bitterness and acrimony.

There is no evidence that Picton Bagge's recommendations were treated seriously in London and the Foreign Office in particular was unimpressed. The whole scheme bears the hallmarks of Picton Bagge being caught up in one of Reilly's overly clever schemes to kill several birds with one stone. However, should Denikin's advance in the summer of 1919 actually have achieved its goal and led to the overthrow of the Bolshevik government, then there is every chance that it would have been dusted off to ensure that any reconstruction bore the hallmarks of British influence. However, like many alliances, the chances are that the conflicting and fundamentally selfish motivations underpinning Allied support would have led to yet more uncertainty and possible conflict with a new regime that ultimately lacked any legitimacy other than military force and whose own component parts were only just held together by a shared hatred of the Bolsheviks.

Chapter 21:

South Russia 1919-20: Victory into Defeat

By the autumn of 1919, Denikin's armies were less than two hundred miles from Moscow and had control of most of the Ukraine including the important cities of Kiev and Kharkiv. There was widespread optimism that the Bolsheviks were finally beaten and Denikin boasted of being in Moscow for Christmas. In Britain, Churchill believed his strategy to be vindicated and reported as much to the Cabinet.

The Bolsheviks in Moscow were panicked and many destroyed their party membership cards and sought to establish better relations with the bourgeoisie. At the same time, Elena Stasova, the Party Secretary, scurried about organising money and fake identities for the Central Committee so that they would be able to escape if, as was widely feared, Moscow fell.[361] The immediate next objective for the Volunteer Army was to advance from Orel which was at the tip of the salient created by Denikin's advance on towards Tula which was not only on the direct route to Moscow but was the Bolsheviks' main munitions base. Trotsky claimed that "the surrender of Tula would have been a catastrophe" and its "loss would be more dangerous than that of Moscow."[362] As a result, the local Bolshevik commander, Dmitry Os'kin, was ordered to take whatever steps he deemed necessary to avoid its fall. Os'kin did this with characteristic ruthlessness, establishing work parties of thousands of citizens to build defences and taking hostages to ensure their diligence. He also conscripted twenty thousand troops who were to fight alongside reinforcements hurriedly rushed from Moscow.

By October, the Bolshevik forces in and around Tula totalled two hundred thousand, more than twice the White forces which were also spread very thinly. They counter-attacked and successfully pushed the Volunteer Army forces back towards Orel. Shortly afterwards, the Red Cavalry led by Semyon Budenny attacked the Don Cossack force which formed the eastern flank of the White advance, pushing it back in disarray beyond Voronezh towards its Don homeland. Critically, following the Bolshevik capture of the vital railway junction at Kastornoe, the Volunteer Army and Don Cossacks were split and exposed to encirclement. As a result, they had no option but to retreat. On 18 November, after protracted and heavy fighting, Kursk fell to the Bolsheviks and with it control of much of the Ukraine. After that, the Whites retreated headlong towards the South and inevitable but drawn out defeat.

The causes of this sudden reversal of fortunes are varied and complicated. Militarily, Wrangel's concerns about Denikin's order for a lunge towards Moscow during the summer look to have been vindicated. The three constituent parts of the White forces, the Volunteer Army, the Don Cossacks and the Kuban Cossack army had been ordered to advance on too wide a front with the inevitable thinning of resources and attendant difficulties of supply. As a corollary, the more the Whites advanced upon Moscow, the more the Bolsheviks were driven towards their own equipment depots and the easier it became for them to supply their own forces.

Equally, by advancing on a wide front, the Whites were never able to concentrate sufficient force to overwhelm the Bolsheviks facing them. The available forces were further weakened by the need to meet raiding by Makhno's anarchists who increasingly threatened the lines of communication in the Ukraine particularly in October, at the time when all resources were required to meet the Bolshevik counter-attack in Tula. Makhno also made a concerted attack on the crucial White base and supply depot in Taganrog resulting in the diversion of large numbers of troops from the front to meet this threat. Interestingly, some British observers believed that Makhno had German military advisers who trained his men to utilise the tactics they had adopted during the 1918 offensives on the Western Front and fight in small packets bypassing and isolating White strongpoints and gradually infiltrating White territory.

Makhno's success was largely attributable to the fundamental political incoherence inherent in both Denikin's Armies and the White movement in general. Each of Denikin's armies had divergent background and aims. The Volunteer Army was top heavy with former Imperial Army officers who reflected an unreconstructed wish to return to the past. They also looked down upon the much larger but less sophisticated Cossack armies whose principal motivation was defence of their home territories and a wish to take revenge on conquered territories in terms of blood and loot.

Denikin was never really in a position to control or prevent looting by any of his forces including the one most directly under his control, the Volunteer Army. As a result, conquered towns were given over to three days' looting and grain was extorted from the countryside either forcibly or by taxation. The Bolsheviks were equally as guilty in this regard but the peasantry were particularly suspicious of a White victory for the very good reason that it would mean the restoration of land to its previous owners. Accordingly, the White forces were never able to exploit the natural peasant resentment against the Bolsheviks and when it came to the point, the peasants rallied to them rather than risk the fall of Moscow and a White government.

Another fundamental White failing was the absolute refusal to countenance the creation of breakaway states. Denikin was probably the most farsighted of the White leaders but he was explicit that Ukraine would remain part of a reconstituted post-revolutionary Russia. His views were emphasised by his invariable custom of referring to the Ukraine as "Little Russia." Inevitably, this guaranteed overwhelming Ukrainian support either for Makhno or Petliura's Nationalists. By late 1919, the Kuban Cossacks were indicating that they would only continue to fight for the Whites if they were guaranteed independence which again was something Denikin could never concede whilst retaining the loyalty of the Volunteer Army.

An even more damaging example of this was Yudenich's refusal to guarantee Finnish independence. This had deprived his North

Western Army of one hundred thousand trained troops who Mannerheim was eager to supply. As it was, Yudenich's poorly equipped army of approximately eighteen thousand men narrowly failed to capture Petrograd in October 1919. Their approach had caused panic amongst the Petrograd Bolsheviks and Lenin, thinking it doomed, wanted to evacuate the city so as to free up reinforcements to send south to fight the Whites there. However, in the end, Trotsky was sent to the city to replace Zinoviev who had given up all hope and spent his time supine on a sofa in the Smolny Institute. Trotsky galvanised resistance and even though Yudenich's army advanced as far as the outer suburbs, they were turned back at Gatchina which was renamed "Trotsk" in his honour.[363]

It is almost inconceivable that Yudenich would have failed to take the city if he had been supported by the Finns but it could not be countenanced. Kolchak, as officially recognised leader of the White forces had declared that "history will never forgive me if I surrender what Peter the Great won" and, whilst both arrogant and unrealistic, it reflects one of the few strands that unified at least the Greater Russian portions of the White forces other than a visceral hatred of Bolshevism.[364] As such, concessions of this type could not be made by the White commanders however much they would have assisted their cause.

In contrast, the Bolsheviks continued to make pragmatic concessions wherever necessary to ensure survival as they had done at Brest-Litovsk. Thus, whilst Kolchak and Yudenich were wedded to wholly unrealistic concepts of the sanctity of the Imperial boundaries, the Bolsheviks reached agreements with the Finns, Estonians and Poles whenever was necessary. One of the reasons why Denikin's advance on Moscow was held back was that the Russians agreed a truce with the Poles which allowed them to transfer desperately needed reinforcements to meet the threat. None of these pacts prevented later moves to recover lost territories either in the immediate future such as the Russo-Polish war or later so that much of Stalin's foreign policy was directed at regaining control of former Russian territories along the western borders.

Another factor particularly in South Russia was the Whites' attitude to Jews. Almost all the White commanders were anti-Semitic to some degree and, to a greater or lesser extent tolerated pogroms. Although not violent, many members of the British Military Mission were also reflexively anti-Semitic as can be illustrated by the report on the political and economic situation in South Russia prepared by Major Pinder of the Military Mission in which he sniffily states that "an outstanding fact is that most big Russian companies and organisations are either largely controlled by Jews or have Jewish participants some of course, being of quite good character but without such knowledge and study there can never be any certainty."[365]

Denikin himself was scarcely philo-Semitic but appreciated the damage that was done to the White cause by the attacks upon the many Jewish settlements particularly in the old Jewish Pale of Settlement. The Whites however were far from alone and Makhno and Petliura's forces were equally culpable. Indeed, Denikin emphasised their outrages as a way of minimising those of his own troops. Jews also suffered under the Bolsheviks chiefly because they were seen as class enemies.

The Military Mission was well aware of the damage that was done to the White cause by these atrocities and sought to prevent them so far as was possible but with limited effect. The main culprits were the Cossacks but pogroms were also explicitly sanctioned by Generals in the Volunteer Army including Mae-Maevsky and Mamontov. One of the worst was in Kiev between 1-6 October when the city was under the control of the Volunteer Army General, Vladimir Dragomirov. It is uncertain how many Jews were killed as the official number of just over thirty one thousand is manifestly too low and more realistic estimates vary from sixty to one hundred thousand. It is equally unclear how many of these were killed by White forces as opposed to others including the Bolsheviks but the answer must be very many indeed.

Unsurprisingly, the White actions in this regard reinforced the perceptions in the West, particularly the United States and Britain, that they were scarcely to be distinguished in their barbarity from the Bolsheviks. This no doubt increased the political moves, principally by Lloyd George, for Britain to extricate itself from supporting the Whites and that a rapprochement with the Bolsheviks represented a better albeit unpalatable alternative.

Whilst many of the White officers had always been innately anti-Semitic to some degree, Jewish officers had felt able to serve with the Volunteer Army in the early days. This was, in many ways natural, since there were many Jews involved in trade, finance and banking and their existence was directly threatened by the Bolshevik actions. However, by 1919, the position had completely changed and the Volunteer Army had become institutionally anti-Semitic and the Cossacks overtly so. The cause of this was twofold; first, as Denikin's forces advanced they took control of more of what had been the Pale of Settlement so that there were more Jews on hand to persecute. Secondly and far more importantly, the belief took hold that the Bolsheviks were a largely Jewish organisation.

Jews made up just over four percent of the total Russian population and five percent of European Russia but they were very heavily represented amongst the leading Bolsheviks.[366] A number of the leading Bolsheviks were Jewish including Trotsky, Sverdlov, Zinoviev, Litvinov and Karl Radek. This gave the Whites the impression that the Bolsheviks were a Jewish front organisation. Yet more importantly, the Cheka had a particularly high representation of people of Jewish origin. This was not only at the pinnacle of the organisation where, for example, both Moisei Uritsky and Jakov Peters were influential but more tellingly at a junior level so that, for example, three quarters of the Cheka employees at Kiev were Jewish.[367]

No one seems to have considered why, in the openly anti-Semitic Tsarist state, a revolutionary organisation dedicated to its overthrow might have appealed to a better educated but thwarted section of that society but what they did notice was that once the Red Terror was unleashed, many of its most prominent exponents were Jewish. The effect of this was to fuel an already incipient dislike as well as to provide an easy justification for terror. The result was that Jews were blamed for the undoubted Bolshevik outrages and wholly unconnected people and places bore the brunt of a thirst for revenge to the extent that it was common for the victims of White pogroms to have the Red Star carved into their bodies before execution. It also fed into conspiracy theories about a worldwide Jewish conspiracy to overthrow the West.

Having said all that, there is ample evidence of vicious cruelty being perpetrated by the Cheka. The head of the Cheka in Kharkiv was Stepan Saenko, a bloodthirsty maniac as well as being a cocaine addict, who presided over the murder of up to three thousand hostages. Many of the Whites' preoccupation about Jewish involvement with the Bolsheviks and the Cheka in particular, were shared by members of the Military Mission. It was a theme that Keyes himself returned to again and again. He describes how in Kharkiv "the most vicious torturer here, as in Kiev, was a young Jewess" adding how "from Kharkov I was sent a parcel of gloves by the Investigating Committee. These gloves were the skin off women's hands got by putting their arms alternately in boiling and cold water. They were nailed around the walls of a room in the Cherezvychaika [Cheka offices] like rats' tails on a barn door."[368] The process was seemingly a speciality of the Cheka in that area and was known as "the glove trick."

He reported in a similar vein to Lord Curzon that "the evidence of wholesale executions, without enquiry, carried out by brutal and clumsy ways, by Chinese experts and the revolting sadism of the young Jewesses is irrefutable... the aim of Bolshevism [is] to induce revolution in all countries in order to destroy the very roots of Christian civilisation."[369] He continued the theme on his return to England in 1920.[370]

This obsession with the extent to which Jewish influence governed Bolshevik actions confirmed a pre-existing prejudice with both the White forces and the British although clearly to varying degrees of viciousness. It ultimately proved to be self-defeating as it poisoned White relations with Jews in South Russia and the Ukraine so that cooperation became almost impossible even though there was much common ground as many Jews were as fearful of Bolshevik actions - not least the all out assault on commerce and property - as were the predominantly bourgeois and landowning Whites. The paradox was neatly summarised by the Chief Rabbi of Moscow who wrote that "it was the Trotskys who made the revolution but it was the Bronsteins who paid the bills."

Another critical factor in the collapse of the Whites in South Russia was attributable to the decision by the War Cabinet on 7 September to cease to support Denikin following the despatch of one last "packet" of military aid with a value of £15m and that the Military Mission was to be withdrawn by spring 1920. This represented Lloyd George's triumph over Churchill who wanted to continue to offer support to Denikin. Lloyd George later went public with the decision declaring in a speech at the Guildhall in November 1919 that Britain had supplied arms and materiel to the value of £100m to Denikin and had thereby repaid "the debt of honour" owed to its Russian allies. From then on, whatever attempts were made by Churchill or indeed the men on the ground in Russia, particularly General Holman, it was only a question of time as to when the Military Mission would come to an end.

Up until then, Denikin had been, if anything, oversupplied with arms and equipment and so the decision to cease further shipments should not have impacted on his ability to continue offensive operations. However, the loss of the British advisers was highly significant not only psychologically but also in direct military terms, such as 47 Squadron (which by October 1919, had been renamed A

Detachment to distance it from claims of active British involvement) or the tank training crews. Denikin's forces had, by December 1919, been forced back to the lands between the Dnieper and the Don and the dreams of taking Moscow were long gone. Further, by then the other White threats to the Bolsheviks were effectively over which meant that they could focus their forces on South Russia. Bearing in mind the fundamental incoherence of Denikin's political strategy, it is reasonable to conclude that Lloyd George was correct to fear that by continuing to bankroll the White resistance, the British were, in reality, merely prolonging the suffering.

There was also the issue of the cost of continuing support. Britain, like almost all the other belligerents, was practically bankrupt and so was desperate to embark upon an urgent scaling back of its military spending. The continued funding of White counterrevolution was therefore under very close scrutiny. Nevertheless, the figure of £100m quoted by Lloyd George was highly misleading. The equipment already existed, having been manufactured in fulfilment of wartime orders and a large proportion of it was mouldering in the large British supply bases at Salonika and also in Egypt. As all the major nations were demobilising their conscript armies, there was no realistic possibility of finding a purchaser. It is likely therefore that the true value of the unwanted equipment supplied was nearer to £5-10m.

By Christmas, the situation in South Russia had become critical. The Volunteer Army was still at its headquarters in Taganrog but only just having, as Keyes put it, fallen back from Kursk "pell mell."[371] The Don Cossacks were back in their own territories facing a Bolshevik attack and the Kuban Cossack Army had retreated from Tsaritsyn to its homelands in the North Caucasus. Wrangel had reported to Denikin that the Kuban Army had ceased to exist as an effective fighting force.

Economic collapse followed in the wake of military retreat so that "the Denikin rouble went from 26 to the pound to 11,000."[372] As Keyes put it, "the real reason for the debacle was the complete moral collapse of the educated classes."[373] Moral collapse was equally evident amongst the component parts of Denikin's forces and by January, there was increasing tension between the Volunteer Army and the two Cossack hordes. This exacerbated an already evident sense of panic as troops fled back towards Novorossiysk. The retreat also brought to the fore the lack of cohesion between the White officers and their men. It was not unknown for units to defect wholesale on both sides in the Civil War and be welcomed by the opposing side whether White or Bolshevik. However, in such instances, it was common for the officers to be killed either by the deserting troops or their new masters. White officers knew this and therefore took pains to ensure their escape route whenever possible.

Another factor was the White officers' insistence on shipping their personal belongings, including looted items by train and leaving their troops to make their own way by foot. This meant that military equipment was frequently abandoned either because there was no space on the trains or because the men left to retreat on foot could or would not carry it. The lack of esprit de corps was regularly lamented by members of the Military Mission not least because it worsened an already strained relationship between officers and enlisted men. It also led to tensions between the Whites and the British not least when senior White officers fled leaving junior officers and members of the Military Mission to sort out a controlled evacuation. This happened repeatedly, often in major cities such as Rostov, Odessa and Novocherkassk. In the former, two British officers failed to escape and were captured and murdered by the Bolsheviks.

The same thing happened at Christmas 1919 when Denikin's headquarters abandoned Taganrog. The British only received an indication that this was going to happen at the last moment which limited their ability to coordinate the withdrawal of men and equipment particularly the remaining tanks and 'A' Detachment (formerly 47 Squadron). It also took the direct intervention of General Holman to overrule a White General's insistence that only

British officers could travel by train and that the NCOs and men would have to walk.

It was clear that the Denikin's position was doomed and that the only viable option was to evacuate Ekaterinodar and ship the remaining forces to the Crimea which remained defensible and where they could regroup. By then, his command was limited to the rump of the Volunteer Army and there was considerable dissatisfaction amongst his remaining Generals. At the prompting of Holman and others of the Military Mission including Keyes, he was persuaded to offer considerable concessions including recognition of the Cossack areas as autonomous regions as well as promising land reforms. However, this was too late to gain widespread support not least because the lands under his command had shrunk to the area around Ekaterinodar and Novorossiysk and it is arguable that the hostility his promises engendered with the ultras in the White movement accelerated his enforced resignation. It is indicative of the wooden headedness of the Whites that these obvious concessions were resisted even as the Bolshevik forces were closing in on them.

The political situation had changed with the collapse of the hopes of the White forces in South Russia. In November 1919, the British had finally acceded to the longstanding request of the Military Mission and sent out Sir Halford Mackinder as High Commissioner of South Russia. Mackinder was an eminent political geographer and Liberal MP. His role however was, to all practical purposes impossible as he was to take steps to ensure the establishment of a constitutional government of Russia which meant supporting the Whites whilst at the same time encouraging new states in the Caucasus which Denikin's forces opposed. This fundamental tension between the aims of the War Office and Foreign Office was a reflection of the divergent approach within Government.

Mackinder was also given the task of securing better relations between the White government in South Russia and those of Ukraine and Poland. Once again, there was an inconsistency in Foreign Office (and French) ambition to establish a cordon sanitaire between the Bolsheviks and the rest of Europe and White ambitions to reconstitute the Tsarist Empire. Keyes was appointed as Mackinder's deputy and travelled with him to Warsaw in December to hold discussions with the Polish Government. They, together with Sir Horace Rumbold, the British Ambassador to Poland, had meetings both with the Polish premier and international pianist, Ignacy Paderewski, and Marshal Pilsudski who Keyes described as "chief of the state" as well as a military leader. Their intention was to build bridges between the newly independent Poles and Denikin's Whites. This was never going to be easy but the Whites' willingness to compromise increased as their military position worsened and the potential for mounting a coordinated assault on the Bolsheviks alongside the Poles was a prize worth having.

Their discussions were encouraging and Keyes clearly was very impressed by Paderewski writing to Edith that "I fell a victim to him in a moment. He's the most sympathetic man I've ever come across - loves England but really sore about the way he's been treated [by the Allies]." On the other hand, he was rather less impressed by Mrs Paderewski who he ungallantly described as "a managing wife - a monstrous woman." He was also sceptical about Pilsudski who he considered "a strong man who has suffered greatly from Russians and Germans, a straightforward man but I think ignorant and illogical."[374] By the end, however, they had achieved agreement and were optimistic for a White revival in the spring.

They visited Constantinople on the way back where the evident failure of the Whites was causing tensions amongst the British as Keyes wrote that "things are going very badly and it almost seems that what we have effected in Poland is too late." He also remarked how he had been told by an unnamed General "I always thought it was a mistake to back Denikin there was never any chance of him winning." Keyes was furious at this backsliding adding "I am very miserable and lonely and out of sympathy with the rest of the Mission." In reality, he had lost perspective in his determination that "we must save these people; they cannot save themselves." This was unachievable without a much more robust military commitment which, as Keyes, well knew was never going to happen and certainly not at that late stage.[375]

Keyes travelled back to Novorossiysk in January where the seriousness of the situation became increasingly obvious. He noted that "there was little panic but a leaden helplessness which, to me, is worse."[376] From there, he and Mackinder travelled to confer with Denikin at his headquarters somewhere beyond Ekaterinodar described by Keyes as Tukhorntzskaya which is probably present day Timashevsk. It took them three days to return even though it cannot have been much more than one hundred miles and Keyes noted how "there were twenty thousand people living in carriages at Ekaterinodar station." Unsurprisingly, bearing in mind the overcrowding and lack of heat, many died of cold and the situation was made worse when typhus broke out.

Keyes stayed in Ekaterinodar before moving to Novorossiysk in February ahead of the final evacuation of Ekaterinodar by Denikin in March. The chaos that was enveloping South Russia clearly deeply affected him as he was to write to Edith:

"I feel very guilty and contemptuous of myself for having made such a mess of things and just for the moment [am] angry with myself for having written to you when I was feeling hurt and sore. This business into which I have put my heart into [for] two and a half years is going to hell and I see now how many mistakes I've made.

I believe I've done more harm to Russia and I haven't helped the British Empire at all, you and my country. I'm so bitter being such a damned failure."[377]

The evacuation to the Crimea was long foreseen and Holman had made certain that this time the British were effectively in control of it. He had made plans for equipment to be detained at Novorossiysk in readiness for shipment and had ordered the diversion of supplies so that they did not worsen an already chaotic position. Holman also ensured that members of the Military Mission supervised the preparation of defensive trenches so as to give time for the orderly evacuation.

In the meantime, Keyes and Mackinder were in agreement that however desperate things were, it was incumbent upon the British to foster an alliance of anti-Bolshevik nations to encourage the ongoing resistance to Bolshevik rule. Mackinder was to write, doubtless with Keyes' support, that otherwise "out of such a welter history might produce again, as so often before from these very plains, some great leader of nomads who would gather the bands together and fall now on this region and now on that. Asia and Europe alike would have to maintain military borders'.[378] This gloomy prognostication was to go unheeded in London where moves were already afoot to normalise relations with the Bolshevik regime.

In fact, Mackinder returned to England in January and Keyes was appointed Acting High Commissioner in his place. He must have appreciated that whilst this represented a further sign of how valued he had become, it also meant that he would have to take a greater share of responsibility for the failure of British policy which was by now readily apparent.

Keyes could appreciate how bad things were becoming but remained convinced that the biggest threat to Denikin was the withdrawal of British support. His anger was exacerbated by the fact that he was not kept fully informed and so he wrote to the Foreign Office on 19 January deploring the fact that he had discovered from US press reports of the decision by the British to "reopen trade with the Bolsheviks and recognition of Georgia." He added with some asperity "I trust that I may be sent clear the line official instructions on the subject and that in future not be reduced to learning of the actions of HMG affecting Russia from global press reports… News of the intention to reopen trade relations with the Bolsheviks will cancel good done and give the impression of ill faith of HMG."[379]

Keyes must have known that such intemperate language would have gone down badly particularly with the notoriously prickly Curzon but he does not seem to have been able to help himself and continued to protest at the change in British policy. On 9 February, he urged Curzon to support a joint offensive by the Poles and Denikin's forces although by then, he must have been aware that this was completely unrealistic. Initially, there was sympathy for his position and the practical difficulties he faced but by 25 February, these had turned to concern when Curzon was to write "I feel after your arduous work of last year, you will be glad of a rest and will welcome to return home on leave."[380] Even this hinted reproach failed to prevent further expressions of dismay at British conduct. By March, Curzon's patience was at an end and he wrote a sharp telegram to Keyes pointing out that "Russian policies through this difficult transition period are necessarily decided by HMG in London and valuable though your information and advice as regards local developments are, you are in the position to envisage the Russian problem at a single angle. You must conform to your direct affairs on the spot to the lines of this telegram and bear in mind that you remain in Russia in a political and not military capacity and are subject to my authority in all relations."[381]

Taking into account the polite and diplomatic language usually used in communications between government officials, this was an explicit demonstration of disapproval and Keyes must have realised that he had crossed a line. He thereafter wrote in more measured terms but it is clear that he had lost all heart in his role which in any event was increasingly concentrated upon trying to do what he could to limit the loss of life attendant upon the collapse of the White position in South Russia.

The moral turmoil that Keyes was undergoing at that time is even more explicit from his correspondence with Edith where there was a marked change of tone from the breezily informative to heartfelt anguish and the sense of someone struggling to maintain any sense of purpose in both his professional and personal life. On 12 February, he wrote explaining how "the incompetence of the FO and of the dirty intrigues at home [had meant that] Denikin is naturally a little sulky with us" and adding that "I am in the most humiliating position but mean to see things through. I really believe that the Bolsheviks are beat." A week later he wrote the most revealing of his surviving letters beginning by telling how "177 people died of cold in a train [left] standing in the station" and how this had come about by administrative disorder. He then went on "I have just received the papers from England up to January 26 with the account of our betrayal of Russia. I'm too sick and ashamed to do anything. I hit out hard at the time and [sent] a heartfelt 'secret and personal' to Curzon... It's dreadful to think of two ex-Viceroys taking it lying down for that dirty little Welsh attorney."[382] As well as feeling abandoned and betrayed by London, he clearly also felt the same personally as he added a bitter coda "Rory and Rosemary seem to have inherited your dislike of letter writing."

It is clear that by now Keyes was at the end of his tether and by acting in the way that he did, must have known that he was irreparably damaging his career as indeed proved to be the case. This is evident from a comment in a letter to Edith where he indicated that "I am very unhappy at the way things are going and the prospect of going back to India when this thing breaks up. It means more separation when I had hoped that this was the last."[383] As events were to prove, his fears were borne out and whilst he might once have hoped for postings either in Europe or at home, this was no longer realistic.

Having spent so much time with Denikin, for whom he had great personal respect, he had must have felt the policy shift from London very deeply. He was not alone in this, as many officers with the Military Mission had come to identify closely with the White cause. Keyes more than most had personal experience of Bolshevik rule and his dislike of it was visceral. Nevertheless, whilst Keyes still believed that, with continuing support, Denikin could succeed in overthrowing the Bolsheviks, it is hard to resist the conclusion that Curzon was correct in concluding that he had become far too involved and had lost sight of the strategic picture. By early, 1920, the Bolsheviks had defeated Kolchak and Yudenich and the

British had withdrawn from Murmansk and Archangel. Whilst the Allies remained in Vladivostok, the justification for being there had evaporated with Kolchak's failure and subsequent execution and they were planning the evacuation that was to take place that summer.[384] This meant that the Bolsheviks could, for the first time, concentrate practically all their forces against South Russia. The White forces were therefore heavily outnumbered and it was only a matter of time before they collapsed.

The final stages of the White collapse in South Russia were extremely difficult for Keyes as he felt personally compromised by the actions of his superiors. The remains of Denikin's forces converged on Novorossiysk and the evacuation to Crimea anticipated by Holman became the only viable option and also one strongly recommended by Admiral de Robeck, the Commander in Chief of the Mediterranean Fleet and High Commissioner to Turkey. De Robeck's support was vital as the evacuation was largely carried out by the Royal Navy. Mackinder and Keyes were extremely concerned about the likely fate of the large number of women and children who would be trapped in Novorossiysk. They therefore ordered the evacuation of the families of White officers 'as to be caught by the Bolsheviks means for them death if not torture'.[385] They also took the view that by doing this it "would improve the morale" of the Whites so that they might continue the struggle without worrying about the safety of the their families.[386]

Following Mackinder's departure, Keyes as Acting High Commissioner, worked alongside General Holman in organising the evacuation. This not only required considerable administrative and political effort in organising the embarkation of the departing troops and such equipment as could be saved but also the destruction of what remained. At the same time, he had to undertake the delicate task of representing British interests in the manoeuvrings that led to Denikin's resignation and his replacement by Wrangel. These were particularly fraught since the Whites were a non-democratic organisation and so Denikin had to be persuaded to resign and agree to Wrangel succeeding him even though relations between them were by then exteremely frosty.

On 14 March, Keyes confirmed that Denikin was to embark for the Crimea and from there on to exile. He later passed on Denikin's request that the British transport "as well as the sick, wounded, women and children such males as would be liable to be murdered."[387] His attitude by now appears to be contradictory; at one moment beseeching the Foreign Office that "we cannot divest ourselves of responsibility for these people" in their ongoing struggle against the Bolsheviks, at another reporting that he was "convinced that Denikin realises that the game is up."[388]

As was probably inevitable, the evacuation was chaotic with the inhabitants of the massively overcrowded town desperately trying to get on board the waiting ships as they were only too aware what awaited them if they remained. Whilst this was going on, Bolshevik and Green forces were held up just outside the town. From time to time, the Navy was called upon to shell forces that tried to advance. On 16 March, Keyes himself landed at Gelendzhik a few miles south of Novorossiysk "under a white flag and informed the Green commander that any further advance would... render them liable to be fired on by our ships." It is not clear whether his warnings were heeded.[389] Later, on 28 March, at Denikin's request, *HMS Emperor of India* shelled Bolshevik forces six miles from the town so as to delay their "attack by several hours to allow the Military Mission to embark. Keyes was amongst the last to leave and he walked the deserted town receiving looks from the remaining population "as if [he] were mad to be out in such conditions."[390] As for those who could not flee, Keyes had comforted himself that "we should have to take a guarantee from the Bolsheviks not to molest or persecute those that are left behind; this I think, they will do as they are so anxious to be recognised by the rest of the world that they would forego their desire to kill them."[391] It is not clear to what extent he really believed that this was so.

The Military Mission, along with the fleeing Whites, landed at Theodosia in the Crimea and Keyes then went on to Constantinople feeling "as Wrangel [had] said to me at Sevastopol as if I had been burying a friend." On his arrival, he discovered that "a very important telegram" had been sent and "that the commanders in chief, Milne and de Robeck had acted on it in what seems to me to be an insupportable manner...and would not listen." The telegram contained an order by the War Cabinet that Denikin be pressurised to resign and be replaced by Wrangel. Although this was far from unexpected, it clearly affected Keyes deeply not least because the telegram also ordered him to return to the Crimea taking Wrangel with him before returning with Denikin. This was a manifestly delicate mission requiring tact on everyone's part. However, it got off to a bad start when Wrangel was taken seriously ill with what turned out to be Angina. Keyes related how he ended up acting as medical adviser to the ailing General as "the only man on board with any medical training, the sick bay attendant, was too in a funk to do anything."[392] The ship had to return to Constantinople for Wrangel to receive medical attention before setting off again.

On arrival at Sebastopol on 4 April, Wrangel took command of what remained of the Volunteer Army. Shortly afterwards, Denikin, and his Chief of Staff, Romanovski, left Theodosia for Constantinople along with General Holman who had been ordered to return to England. Romanovski "was murdered within an hour of arriving at the Russian Embassy" and there was then a final emotional meeting with Denikin at which Keyes was presented by Denikin with "his sword with a crusader blade."[393] Denikin then left that evening for England. Possibly touched by the romance of the occasion, Keyes wrote that "this business has broken my heart. If our government will play the game, I'm going back to Sevastopol to help Wrangel start things and then come straight home. I'm worn out."[394] He did indeed return and was impressed noting that Wrangel "had infused new life into the Army." This optimistic view needs to be balanced against his more realistic assessment to the Foreign Office of a few days earlier that "the Remnants of the Russian Army can no longer be considered as normal. Horrors of last two years has so demoralised them that they should be treated as suffering from a complete nervous breakdown. If the League of Nations is not to start its existence as cruel farce, it must intervene."[395] Keyes then, along with a number of other senior British officers who were regarded in London as being in need of "a change" ostensibly because of the stresses of the preceding months but also because of their increasing disenchantment with the instructions that they were receiving from the War Office, was ordered to travel back to England.

At this point, British policy becomes confused as support continued to be given to Wrangel whilst at the same time negotiations began with the Bolsheviks to agree a normalisation of relations. The Military Mission was now led by Brigadier General Percy and remained significant with one hundred and seventy one officers and four hundred and fifty eight other ranks. Further, although over four hundred tons of stores had been lost at Novorossiysk, a large amount of equipment including artillery had been safely delivered to the Crimea and shipments of supplies continued to arrive until June. The DH9s of A Detachment were also handed over giving Wrangel a functioning air force. The Military Mission established training bases at Theodosia and Sebastopol and also played a prominent part in organising the supply and distribution chain. Wrangel was therefore swiftly able to reconstitute a new army from the remnants of the White forces. He was given the space to do this by the Bolsheviks because the British continued to provide naval support, including that of an aircraft carrier, which regularly bombed Bolshevik positions. This combined with the readily defensible geography of the Crimea gave him a solid, if temporary base. In the meantime, he was put under pressure by the British to come to terms with the Bolsheviks as the continued existence of the sole remaining White force was an obvious block on achieving a negotiated peace.

The critical question is what was Wrangel seeking to achieve. Even with the assistance of the Military Mission and the supplies that continued to arrive, he could not hope to succeed in overthrowing the Bolsheviks militarily as he had at most fifty thousand men at his disposal. The answer to this and indeed Keyes' continued hope for the success of the White cause was the belief that the Bolsheviks would be ousted by a long predicted internal convulsion. More importantly however, great faith was placed in the Poles following the meetings that had taken place in December 1919. These discussions in which, of course, Keyes played a vital role had resulted in a full scale military attack on the Ukraine by the Poles commencing in February 1920. The Poles had reached an accord with Petliura's Ukrainian nationalists and intended to take control of the Ukraine and create a new state there under Polish protection. Wrangel therefore had much to gain by playing for time since, if the advance was successful and an independent Ukraine was created, then the White forces would be freed from the immediate Bolshevik threat. It is a measure of how far the Whites had come in their political thinking that not only could they contemplate the independence of much of former Russia but also that they looked on it as a source of salvation. If a similarly realistic approach had been taken earlier particularly by Kolchak and Yudenich, then a White victory, albeit a temporary one, might easily have been achieved.

The Poles enjoyed tacit support from the Allies and the French in particular. Initially, all went well and on 7 May, the joint forces took Kiev. However, the Poles were viewed as unlikely saviours by the Ukrainians and the armies had advanced far beyond their supply base. Accordingly, they were extremely vulnerable when the Bolsheviks began a series of counterattacks in late May that culminated in the Poles being forced back to the outskirts of Warsaw.

Probably with the intention of supporting the Polish advance, Wrangel's forces advanced north from the Crimea on 8 June. His advance was initially successful but, once the Bolsheviks had agreed a peace with the Poles in October, they were able to concentrate all their forces against him and his position was doomed as he faced Bolshevik forces of up to one hundred and thirty thousand men.

Eventually, in November 1920, Wrangel and one hundred and forty six thousand Whites, both military and civilian, evacuated the Crimea for exile.

Viewed against this background, Wrangel's policy appears far more coherent. If the Poles had been successful, then he would have been in a position at least to carve out an area of South Russia as White territory and the possibility of encouraging an internal rebellion against the Bolsheviks remained a realistic prospect. It also to some extent explains the decision by the British to continue support until June when all forces were withdrawn. Although, by then, Keyes was back in England, he would have sympathised with the position of the British instructors who very closely identified with the White cause. This was so much so that Brigadier General Percy had serious doubts about their willingness to obey orders and so tricked the instructors into attending a conference in Sebastopol at which they discovered an armed detachment of Royal Marine Military Police who disarmed them and then marched them straight to waiting ships for evacuation.[396]

Thereafter the breach with the White cause was irrevocable and they received no further British support although British and French ships assisted in the November evacuation. Of those who remained, many had been convinced by Bolshevik leaflets that they would be welcomed into a new branch of the Red Army under General Brusilov. In fact both Brusilov and they had been tricked and as many as eighty thousand soldiers and civilians were murdered. Brusilov was haunted by this for the rest of his life.[397]

Afterword

It would be easy to dismiss Keyes' career after his departure from South Russia in 1921 as one of failure and increasing irrelevance and, in contrast with his activities during the preceding three years, his later life certainly followed a more predictable path. However, that is in many ways a false comparison and it makes more sense to view his career under the aegis of the India Office as a whole and regard the wartime interlude as being exceptional.

That being said, Keyes was haunted by the failure of British policy in Russia and the triumph of Bolshevism and, even if he had wanted to put it behind him, which must have been the case, he was repeatedly drawn back into the entanglements of the Bank Schemes until shortly before his death. This largely came about as various former shareholders of the Russian Banks tried their luck with litigation against the British Government. As a consequence, Keyes was repeatedly asked to provide evidence or answer questions about his activities in 1918 even though for much of the time he was posted at the extremities of the North West Frontier so that, on one occasion in 1928, he justified his delay in providing an Affidavit to the Treasury Solicitor until he had reached the relative sophistication of Quetta on the grounds that until then, he was the only properly qualified person before whom it could be sworn.[398]

On his return to England in April 1920, Keyes finally enjoyed a relatively long home leave. If he had retained any hopes of a European posting, he was swiftly disabused of them and it was made clear that neither the Foreign or War Office continued to require his services and that therefore a return to the Indian Political Service was inevitable. This came as a blow as it revived the likelihood of long term absences from Edith and his family which he had so much hoped to avoid. He was also caught up in the aftermath of the collapse of the British policy of supporting the White forces and must have watched with dismay as Lloyd George pursued a policy of détente with the Bolsheviks in conjunction with the withdrawal of financial and political support for the White regime now entirely émigré.

As well as having to accept the inevitability of a return to the Indian Political Service, Keyes also had to accept the loss of military rank. By the time of his departure from Russia, he had been promoted to acting Brigadier General on the General Staff and acting High Commissioner. Both posts did not survive his return and he was to go back to India as brevet Lieutenant Colonel with the consequent loss of status and, perhaps even more germane, pay.

There is scant evidence as to how Keyes spent his time in England during 1920. He was manifestly exhausted both physically and mentally from his exertions in Russia and in need of recuperation. He would also have been busy finalising details of his return to India particularly since Edith and the younger members of his family were to accompany him. His return would not only be a personal disappointment but would require his re-entry into the relatively closed world that he had left in 1917.

Having long been the predominant priority in British foreign policy, India had become something of a strategic backwater during the war. This was in large part a tribute to the success of the Indian Government and Political Service in preventing any large scale disruption and heading off the various attempts, principally of German origin, at fomenting rebellion. There was however a change in political temperature during the war with increased radicalism by the Indian Nationalists. The British were hampered in dealing with this because wartime demands, particularly in Mesopotamia, had led to garrisons being reduced to the barest minimum. This was compounded by the inevitable demand that first line regiments to be transferred abroad on active service and so what remained was frequently not of the highest calibre.

A further consequence was that the quality of intelligence received by the British dipped with the reduction of resources which in turn meant that the authorities were increasingly taken by surprise by events which then led to hasty and often counterproductive decisions being made. This, together with a fear of matters becoming out of control, contributed significantly to Colonel Dyer's ill judged overreaction at Amritsar in 1919 which led to the massacre and political unrest.[399]

Unsurprisingly, the British in India at the time of Keyes' return had lost considerable self-belief and felt under increasing threat. Their vulnerability was exacerbated by the marked reduction in military spending following the end of the war which increasingly led to the Government of India being permanently underfunded and with insufficient resources to meet a rising instability. This soon fed into a sense of impermanence about British rule that had certainly not existed before 1914. For many, like Keyes and indeed Dyer, although they called it "home" their connection with Britain was attenuated and so the impending loss of the Imperial world must have been extremely unsettling.

On his return to Quetta, Keyes was met on the steps of the Residency by Lieutenant Colonel Sir Armine Dew who was Chief Commissioner of Baluchistan and therefore his new superior with the far from encouraging words, "good afternoon Terence and I don't want to hear a word about Russia." This reflected the weary views of those who had remained performing dull duties in backwaters whilst Keyes had been actively engaged at the centre of events. Whether or not these words were serious, Keyes did not pay them close attention as one of the first things that he was to do was to deliver a detailed lecture to the staff at Quetta entitled "Bolshevism and British Aid to the Anti-Bolshevik Forces of South Russia."[400] As mentioned in Chapter 18, the lecture explored Keyes' principal obsessions with the murderous nature of the Bolshevik class war and the tragedy of the Whites' failure. It also dealt in some detail with the threat posed to British India with Keyes concentrating on the activities of the Bolshevik propaganda school in Bokhara.[401] Keyes was in no doubt that the Bolsheviks posed a far more potent threat to British rule in India than the Tsarist regime ever had stating that "their policy in the East using with great subtlety as it does, the psychological current of various races is infinitely more dangerous and insidious than was the hostility of the old regime."[402]

Keyes' principal role upon his return was as Political Agent based in Sibi, Baluchistan and he was therefore preoccupied with the same issues as he had been back in 1913 prior to his posting to Bahrain. He continued to have difficulties preventing the local tribes from violent raiding and gun-running and as well as trying to persuade them to abandon some of their more recherché customs such as the blood feud and wife murder. Keyes played a significant role in ensuring that the parts of Baluchistan under his control remained peaceful and that relations with the local chieftains were generally harmonious. The problem was and continued to be that peace was bought at the price of lack of progress and so Baluchistan remained backward and insular.

In 1928, Keyes was given a new role as British Envoy to Nepal which represented promotion as well as a new set of challenges. However, he was only in post for a little over six months before being unexpectedly posted to Gwalior as British Resident. This posting too was of short duration as was his next, as Agent to the Governor General in the States of Western India. His final official post was as Resident in Hyderabad between 1930 and 1933. Hyderabad was the most important of the princely states with a population of approximately sixteen million. Although preponderantly Hindu, it was ruled by the Muslim Nizam, Asaf Jah VII, who was reputed to be the richest man in the world whilst being at the same time notoriously penny pinching. Keyes' predecessor as Envoy, Sir William Barton, had chivvied the Nizam to accept British help in reorganising the state's governance and, in particular, its finances. The changes may have been necessary but they failed to endear the Nizam to British influence and so Keyes had a difficult role to play.

Keyes succeeded in improving relations with the Nizam to such an extent that he became his primary adviser. He also became a partisan supporter of the Princely States and a strong advocate for them being included in a federated solution to the governance of India. This idea had much to commend it and might have avoided the cataclysm of partition and the subsequent poor relations between India and Pakistan. However, notwithstanding three round table conferences between 1930 and 1932 consisting of the Princely States, representatives of Congress and other Indian political parties and the British, no progress was made and the prospect of a federated India with Dominion status faded.

Keyes had by then come once again to the attention of his superiors in a less than positive way not least because of his strong advocacy of federation. He was to write opposing the stance of the Indian Political Department (in other words, his direct superiors) and their determination to maintain a clear distinction between British and Princely India stating "to me this is the madness that the gods send before destruction...What Butler calls British India is just that part of India that is trying to repudiate all that is British ...what he calls Indian India is that part that wants to retain the British connection."[403] This outspokenness caused the Viceroy, Lord Willingdon, to describe him "as one of those people who rather like spreading themselves and has to be watched pretty closely."

At the same time, he and Edith were active in encouraging improvements to Hyderabad and the surrounding areas. Perhaps inspired by his commitment to the evangelical Oxford Movement and teetotalism, they were instrumental both in the creation of a model village under the control of the local temperance society and educational developments so that the Keyes Girls High School in Secunderabad still exists. They also fully participated in the various social activities required of a Resident and Keyes became an enthusiastic pig sticker being described "as a very short sighted man of well over fifty [who] was to go at it as if he had a dozen necks to break."[404]

Generally, retirement from the Indian Political Service took place at fifty five. However, Keyes was permitted to stay on a further year until the end of his tour of duty on 1 July 1933. Unfortunately, retirement also meant confronting his considerable debts arising not least from the expenses incurred as Resident at Hyderabad. Keyes found that he was unable to find sufficiently remunerative employment on his return to England and therefore decided to return to India once again, this time as tutor to the seventeen year old George Jivajirao, Maharajah Scindia of Gwalior. To save expense, he returned alone leaving Edith and his family in England. The role was always going to be difficult to fulfil, as there was an inevitable rivalry with the British Resident at Gwalior who understandably resented Keyes' access to the Maharajah. To make matters worse, Keyes was unable to distance himself from internal politics and he came into conflict with the Senior Maharani who was acting as Regent. Matters came to a head with the death of the Maharajah's sister in a road accident in March 1934. Keyes was suspicious and openly maintained that the steering gear of her car had been partially cut through with the intention of causing her death. Although he did not specifically allege as much, the obvious imputation was that he believed that the Maharani's supporters were responsible which made his position untenable. Soon afterwards, the British defused what was becoming an intractable problem by arranging for the Maharajah to take over the running of Bangalore as preparation for taking over full responsibility for Gwalior. Keyes may very well have encouraged in this decision but with it came the end of his role as tutor and he finally left India in the summer of 1934.

Keyes' final years were spent coping with rapidly declining health and, following a heart attack in 1938, he was either in hospital or convalescing at his home in Ninfield, East Sussex. During this time, he wrote the series of stories referred to throughout this book. They were intended for broadcast on the BBC as part of a series to be entitled "Tight Corners" but his final illness prevented this occurring. He died on 26 February 1939 aged sixty one.

Appendix:

Charles Patton Keyes

The Keyes' connection with India dated back to 1820 when Doctor Thomas Keys (sic.) was appointed an Assistant Surgeon in the Honourable East India Company ("HEIC").[405] He had been brought up at Longvale in Clonfade (now Glenfade) near Lifford in County Donegal. Shortly before he left, he married Mary Anne who was the only child of William Patton of Croghan, Mulroy Bay, Northern Donegal. They were therefore near neighbours and would have known each other from childhood. However, it was only upon his appointment to the HEIC that Thomas was in a position to propose. This delay meant that Mary Anne was thirty two at the date of her marriage which was unusually old for the time and indicates that although both the Keys and Pattons were well established Ulster families, financial resources must have been restricted. The Keys had been in Ulster since the Elizabethan plantations principally as landowners and this heritage continued to be important to the family for several generations. It may even have informed the Low Church tendency which certainly carried through to Terence Keyes.

Dr Thomas Keys must have known the risks in enlisting in the HEIC. Surgeons had a less than thirty per cent chance of completing their eight year tour of duty, principally because of what was then known as Hospital Fever, a louse borne form of Typhus common in the insanitary conditions then prevalent in hospitals. Weighed against that was the opportunity to acquire substantial wealth either through promotion or private trading.[406] The HEIC was by then fully established and expanding its influence both by trade and conquest.

Dr Keys was posted to the Madras Army and not long after his arrival in Madras his first son, Thomas was born. Subsequently, he was posted to Trichinopoly with the 24th Regiment and then to Dindigul where their second son, Charles Patton, was born in

300

December 1822. The 24th was moved north to Bellary and then during May and June 1823 it marched through the hottest part of the Deccan to Julna. Travel was slow and difficult in the absence of roads and the baggage train would have travelled at two miles an hour at most. Mary Anne and her children would have travelled by *palki*, a form of palanquin or sedan chair. The regiment stayed at Julna where their third son, William, was born before travelling back to Kamptee (originally, Camp T) which had been founded in 1821 as a military cantonment. On 25 March 1825, Dr Keys died of fever leaving Mary Anne, then aged thirty seven with three children under five.

Without her husband, Mary Anne decided to return to Donegal and began a seven hundred mile journey retracing her steps back to Madras which would have taken more than six weeks. In 1931, Terence Keyes was to visit Jalna "where my father was as a baby... my poor grandmother had to bring three small boys...from Bellary which is the hottest place in the South of India in May and June. It is over six hundred miles and there were no regular roads."[407]

She sailed back to England in autumn 1825 and returned to her parents in Donegal remaining there until 1829 when she rented a small house in Harrow so that Thomas and Charles could be enrolled as dayboys at the school. In 1833, the Royal Naval School in Camberwell opened with the specific aim of providing education to the sons of officers in the Royal Navy and Royal Marines.[408] Mary Anne managed to obtain foundation scholarships for both Charles and William.[409] Thomas remained at Harrow for the remainder of his education.

Charles and William later moved back to Ulster where they were enrolled at Foyle College which then had a reputation for providing soldiers and administrators to India. Whilst this was taking place, Mary Anne endeavoured to find cadetships for Thomas and Charles, as she was clear that both were destined for military service.[410] In this, she was initially disappointed as in 1840 Thomas went to St John's College, Cambridge. This must have placed an increased burden on

Mary Anne's strained financial resources but at least it opened the way for Charles to accept a cadetship without delay - there being a difficulty in two cadetships being granted to one family in two consecutive years. Whilst Charles seems never to have been in doubt about his future career, his hopes failed when, after a year, Thomas decided to leave Cambridge and accept his offer of a cadetship in the Madras Army after all.

There is scant evidence as to how Charles spent the next two years but presumably he remained in Ulster either in Londonderry or at Croghan.[411] Eventually, he left for India arriving in 1843. At twenty, he was old for a cadet - the more usual age being sixteen which must have caused him frustration and, no doubt, some self-consciousness. It is in the HEIC records that both Thomas and Charles' names are first recorded as "Keyes" rather than "Keys." This could be a tribute to the Thomas Keyes who settled in Derry in or about 1623.

Thomas Keyes' military career was successful but unspectacular. He remained in Madras for the entirety of his career and by the time of his retirement, had risen to the rank of Lieutenant Colonel.[412] Whilst in Madras, he married Jane Merry and had two sons, Charles and Alfred. Both in turn, rose to be Lieutenant Colonels, one in the Royal Marines and the other in the Royal Artillery. Both were childless.

Charles Keyes' military career could not have been more different from that of his brother. He joined the 30th Madras Native Infantry in 1843 but apparently was soon restless at being confined to a military backwater whilst so much was taking place in the Punjab. Following the death in 1839 of Ranjit Singh, the founder of the Sikh Empire, the British began to create a base for operations in Ferozepur as it was clear that the territory was plagued by internal dissension. This presented both an opportunity and threat to the British as the Sikh Empire represented the sole remaining challenge to British domination of Northern India and was noted for its wealth and military power.

There is continuing debate as to whether the British intentions were primarily defensive or aggressive. It is probable that they were merely opportunistic but either way, the First Sikh War commenced in late 1845 and battles were fought at Mudki in December and then Aliwal in January 1846 culminating in a crushing defeat of the Sikhs at Sobraon in February. The peace established at the Treaty of Lahore did not last and the Second Sikh War lasted for three further years resulting the annexation of Punjab by the British.

Charles Keyes would no doubt have followed the progression of both wars with close interest not least because of the involvement of several former pupils of Foyle College - notably the Lawrence brothers, George, Henry and John.[413] His connection with Ulster was close and he acquired the lifelong nickname of "North" as a result. Nevertheless, he failed to obtain a transfer to Northern India until 1849 although, as some compensation, he had been promoted Adjutant of 30th Madras Infantry. On arrival at Peshawar, he was appointed Adjutant to the 1st Punjab Infantry under Captain John Coke. Although Keyes' senior by almost twenty years, Coke had only received his captaincy in 1848 which was a reflection on the slow pace of promotion in the HEIC armies. This regiment was formed on 18 May at the direction of Lord Dalhousie who was then Governor General. It was one of five regiments raised by Henry Lawrence who was then Agent to the Governor General of the North West Frontier and Agent at Lahore to form the infantry element of the trans frontier brigade. Like the other regiments, its men were recruited from the disbanded forces that had opposed British annexation of the Punjab.

It was a challenge for Coke and Keyes to weld together a fighting unit from former enemies particularly as they comprised Sikhs, Dogras, Punjabi Muslims and Pathans. They clearly succeeded as on 23 February 1850, the regiment was reviewed by the Commander in Chief, Sir Charles Napier, who reported to Henry Lawrence that:

"As to Coke's regiment, I have seen nothing superior to it in drill – it is admirable; both you and I saw how this brave corps fought under its excellent leader in our five days' campaign in the Kohat Pass. I am more pleased with this young commander than I can express."

This esprit de corps led to the regiment becoming known as the "Kukis" after the Pathan pronunciation of their commanding officer's name.[414]

In 1850, the Regiment participated in the Kohat Pass Expedition which was led by Sir Colin Campbell. The purpose of the expedition was to punish the Afridis for attacking a British force which was constructing a road through the Pass even though they had been paid a subsidy by the British to keep it open. It was successful and the Afridis submitted and paid an indemnity. In 1851, the Regiment was re-named the 1st Regiment of Infantry, Punjab Irregular Force when the Brigade was given the challenging role of policing the North West Frontier. In time, they became known as "Piffers."

Over the following years, Charles Keyes participated in a number of expeditions against the hill tribes on the Dera Ghazi Khan border, principally the Shiranis and the Kasranis. During these expeditions, he was twice mentioned in despatches for crowning the heights during an advance and then covering a withdrawal. Also, in 1853, he was given command of the 6th Punjab Infantry even though he was still only a Lieutenant. This regiment was originally the Scinde Camel Corps and consisted of camel mounted infantry with particular responsibility for policing the Scinde/Punjab border.

In 1856, he returned to England on sick leave and did not return to India until 1858. He therefore missed the Mutiny and the numerous opportunities that it gave for action and promotion. He was, however, gazetted Captain in that year. On his return, he took over command of the 1st Punjab Infantry after John Coke had been given command of a brigade at Rohilcund. In 1860, he led the 1st Regiment of Infantry in an expedition against the Mahsud Waziris. This was precipitated by acts of brigandage by the Waziris chiefly against the caravans of the Powindahs a nomadic tribe who traditionally carried trade between India and Central Asia.

Powindahs would congregate each autumn near Chazni where caravans often consisting of several thousand travellers would set off towards the British area of Dera Ghazi Khan. Once there, they would disperse either to sell the produce that they had brought from Central Asia or to offer their services as labourers - often on road or irrigation works. Neville Bowles Chamberlain, then commander of the Punjab Frontier Force as well as John Lawrence were keen to mount a punitive operation but failed to obtain the support of the Governor General, Charles Canning who was given the derisive nickname, "Clemency" by his British Indian contemporaries.[415] Some time later, a force of some three thousand Waziris raided British territory even laying siege to the town of Tonk. As a result, an expedition became inevitable.

The expedition, some five thousand strong was led by Chamberlain and moved cautiously into the Waziri hills which were then practically unmapped. The Waziris retreated towards one of their principal villages, Palosin from which they launched a dawn attack with a force of three thousand. Five hundred swordsmen broke through the transport lines killing camp followers and other servants and hamstringing horses and camels. As it became lighter, they were driven back by bayonet some three miles. Sixty three soldiers were killed and as many as one hundred and fifty Waziris.[416]

On 2 May 1860, a further skirmish took place at Barari Tangi which was a narrow gorge which the Waziris had blocked with fallen timber and boulders. The left hand companies of the First Regiment were in reserve. At one point, it looked like the guns might be lost but, before the Mahsud forces could reach them, Charles Keyes rushed out and single handedly cut down the foremost Mahsud who was a tribal leader. Then utilising his right company he struck the attacking Mahsud force in the flank, drove it back and captured the breastwork which had previously held the British back. The Mahsud force then withdrew. Following on, the British force destroyed the Shingi settlement of Jaljal but spared Khanigurum on payment of a fine probably because its inhabitants were mainly Urmars who had not taken part in raiding of British territory.

The Mahsuds still declined to make peace with the British and so the expedition continued to Makin which was one of the Mahsud's principal settlements. On 11 May, the British destroyed the houses of the Mahsud leaders in Makin causing damage to the value of just under one hundred and fifty thousand Rupees - a substantial sum for the time. The value of the expedition should be questioned as, whilst it opened up South Waziristan to the British for the first time and reinforced their authority in the frontier region, no settlement with the Waziri Mahsuds was achieved. In particular, Bartle Frere who was Governor of Bombay wrote a critical minute in which he challenged the Punjab authorities' policy of destroying crops and property to deter raiding.[417]

Charles Keyes was recommended for a Victoria Cross for his actions at Barari Tangi but the despatches were delayed and he received no official recognition. In one account, the recommendation was turned down on the curious grounds that as a commanding officer he should not have needlessly exposed himself to danger. Some three years' later, a clasp was awarded for the expedition and Neville Chamberlain was awarded the KCB.

The First Regiment was again in action in 1863 during the Ambela Expedition which was another attempt to quell raiding and lawlessness; the target this time being Pashtuns of Jusufzai tribes who were grouped around the mountain stronghold of Malka. The expedition consisted of six thousand troops again under the command of Neville Chamberlain and its intention was to capture Malka.

Charles Keyes had by then been promoted to Major and with the main body of the expeditionary force reached Ambela pass on or shortly after 20 October 1863. By this time, it was clear that Chamberlain's information about the friendly intentions of the local Bunerwal tribes was incorrect and the camp was surrounded and outnumbered by hostile forces. These were a combination of

Bunerwals, Pashtuns and their allies and numbered fifteen thousand men. Chamberlain therefore fortified the camp based upon two strong points Crag Picquet and Eagles' Nest. The problem was that whilst both strong points dominated the area, they could only hold a limited number of men. Charles Keyes was responsible for Crag Picquet which was on the right hand side.

Before dawn on 30 October, the Pashtuns attacked and overwhelmed the small force on Crag Picquet before continuing down the reverse slope to attack the facing British. Keyes had assembled a group of twenty picked men to provide support to Crag Picquet when it was overrun. He remained in place out of sight of the Pashtuns until dawn broke, then, together with two other officers led the regiment up the three paths to the summit of Crag Picquet. After fierce fighting, it was cleared of Pashtuns but Keyes was wounded in the left hand and also by a ball which struck him on his cross belt, penetrated it and then ran around his body before exiting opposite where it had struck. His sword was also struck by a pistol bullet which temporarily paralysed his right hand. Chamberlain stated in his despatch that "Major Keyes led the assault with a perseverance and intepredity seldom surpassed."

Lieutenant Fosbery who was first to reach Crag Picquet was awarded the Victoria Cross as was Lieutenant George Pitcher for his role in subsequent attacks whilst Charles Keyes received a Brevet Lieutenant Colonelcy. The failure to award the Victoria Cross to Keyes and another Major (Sir Charles Brownlow) whilst giving it to two Lieutenants caused discussion in military circles. However, the Commander in Chief explained in a letter;

"personal gallantry.... during a hard fought campaign on the part of certain majors in command of regiments is no more than their duty and should be recognised by awards other than the Victoria Cross. ...A Captain or Subaltern can stake his life and lose it, for the sake of a decoration, without playing with the lives of others; but a field officer in command risks not only his own life but possibly the success of the operation devolving to him by an unnecessary display of personal valour."[418]

Over the next few weeks, Crag Picquet fell to the Pashtuns three times but was retaken by the British. On 20 November, Chamberlain was seriously wounded and was replaced by Sir John Garvock on 6 December. At the same time, the position was reinforced principally by the 11th Bengal Cavalry led by Colonel Dighton Probyn VC.[419] The Pashtuns were pushed back and on 17 December surrendered to Garvock. He then went on to burn Malka in fulfilment of his mission but at a cost of in excess of one thousand casualties.

Later, in 1869, Charles Keyes was instructed to mount a raid on the tribes in the Kohat Pass following an attack on a police station in which three men were captured by Oorukzais and one killed.[420] A few weeks following this, when visiting Simla, Keyes learned that he had been promoted to full Colonel with command of the Guides which consisted of three squadrons of cavalry as well as a battalion of infantry. The Guides were based at Hoti Mardan on the Yusufzai Plain, a strategic point near the gateway of several passes from the tribally controlled hills.

Whilst at Simla, he spent time with his friend Major General Sir Henry Norman who was also a distinguished soldier having been mentioned in despatches on twenty three occasions during the Mutiny.[421] Norman introduced Keyes to his much younger sister, Kate. She was twenty two and he was forty seven. At their marriage in January 1870, the Governor General, Lord Mayo proposed the toast with the words "now that the families of Keyes and Norman are united, what fighters their youngsters ought to be"

In May 1870, Charles Keyes was given command of the Punjab Frontier Force with the rank of Brigadier General. He and Kate therefore left the comparative sophistication of Simla, for a fort in Peshawar. It was there that their eldest son, Norman was born in autumn 1870.

The Punjab Frontier Force controlled a chain of posts from the Sind Frontier to Black Mountain and over the next eight years,

Charles Keyes moved between them from time to time taking Kate with him.[422] It therefore came about that his second son, Roger John Brownlow was born at Tundiani Fort.[423]

In the southern section of his command, Charles Keyes worked closely with the Political Officer, Major Robert Sandeman, who was, from 1877, Agent to the Governor General in Baluchistan.[424] Sandeman's approach was to foster close relationships with the border tribes and this was particularly successful when he was able to broker an agreement between the Khan of Khalat and his tribesmen who had been in dispute for the previous twenty years. The benefits of this agreement led to the establishment of a British presence at Quetta and the opening of the Bolan Pass as a result of which, when the Second Afghan War broke out in 1878, the Pass was freely available whereas it had had to be forced with considerable losses during the First Afghan War. This more nuanced approach to border control gradually became standard and reflected an increasingly sophisticated appreciation of the relationship between the British and the Hill Tribes.

The northern section of Charles Keyes' command presented greater problems and it was not possible to establish a unified approach when confronted by many disunited tribes who spent much of their time engaged in internecine conflict. Keyes sought to address this issue by the construction of forts along the border but the problem persisted.[425]

On 18 July 1874, Dorothea Agnes was born in Murree and was baptised on 26 September in the same year. Murree is some seven thousand feet high and was the summer capital of Punjab until 1864. It remained popular as a hill station and no doubt was a cooler and more comfortable place for Kate's confinement. Muree had been established in 1851 by Sir Henry Lawrence shortly after the conquest of the Punjab. The land it was built then enjoying the imaginative name of "Sunnybank." It was the original home of the Murree Brewery which is now Pakistan's leading alcohol producer and which continues to prosper even though its products are prohibited to ninety seven percent of the population. The brewery was founded by Edward Dyer whose son, Reginald was to acquire notoriety as "the Butcher of Amritsar."

More children followed with Charles Valentine being born at Abbottabad on 14 February 1876 and Terence Humphrey in the same town on 28 May 1877. In the meanwhile, Charles Keyes commanded the expedition against the Jowaki Afridis between 30 August 1877 and 30 January 1878. This followed a smaller expeditionary force of fifteen hundred men led by Colonel Mocatta which had punished the Jowaki Afridis for cutting the telegraph wires. The unrest continued and Charles Keyes led a much larger force of some seven thousand four hundred men which he divided into three columns. He then occupied the Jowaki Afridis' principal villages until the tribal leaders agreed to terms which led to the Kohat Pass remaining undisturbed for some years.

Following the successful completion of the expedition, Charles Keyes was awarded the KCB which was an unusual distinction for someone of comparatively junior rank. However, he had been in India for nineteen years since his last home leave and so was ordered to hand over command of the Punjab Frontier Force to Colonel Frederick Roberts and return to England. In many ways, Charles Keyes was unfortunate in leaving at this time as the Second Afghan War commenced in the autumn of 1878. Roberts ended it as Commander of the Kabul and Kandahar Field Force and later became a Field Marshal, commanding British forces in the Second Boer War before becoming Commander of the British Army. There is every chance that should Charles Keyes not have gone on leave, he would have had a similar career.

Charles Keyes remained in England for three years. There is limited information about how he spent his time. Presumably, he would have returned to Ulster but must have spent much of it in London as Katherine Mary was born in Kensington on 5 November 1878. Time may also have been spent in Kent as Norman was enrolled at Albion House a preparatory school in Sweyn Road, Margate run by a Mr Schimmelmann.

After three years, his leave came to an end. As mentioned in Chapter 1, this presented a problem with what to do with his children and a decision was made to leave the five eldest with a country parson. On his return Charles Keyes commanded the Hyderabad Subsidiary Force which was where he had been when an infant. Whilst there, he fathered two further children, Phyllis Marion in 1881 and Adrian St Vincent who was born on 19 December 1882. He retired in 1884 when he returned to England.

Charles Keyes had a reputation in India as an expert in mountain warfare and as a swordsman. Frederick Roberts remarked "put Tom Hughes on a hill and let North [Keyes] attack him and you'll see the finest fight ever seen on the Frontier." Equally, Sir Dighton Probyn would cover his VC in front of members of Charles Keyes' family saying "I'm ashamed to let one of North's sons see me wearing a VC."[426]

Again as mentioned in Chapter 1, Charles Keyes had originally intended to settle in Croghan but the practicalities of living in such a remote place with eight young children were overwhelming and he moved to Shorncliffe Lodge in Sandcliffe - half a mile from the castle where Thomas Keyes had been Constable during the reign of Elizabeth I.[427] He did however, spend most summers in Ulster.

In 1886, when he was aged sixty four and Kate thirty eight his last child Madeline Helen was born.[428] Although both Pine and Aspinall-Oglander refer to limited means, the 1891 census records they were still able to employ six servants.[429] Charles Keyes died on 5 February 1896.

SELECT BIBLIOGRAPHY

Primary Material
British Library: Keyes Papers (Mss. Eur. F 132)
Royal Society of Asian Affairs: Papers deposited by Michael Keyes
(RSAA\M\129) by kind permission
National Archives
London Gazette
Haileybury: Colvin House Record Book
Hansard
Mesopotamia Commission 1917: Report of the commission to enquire into
operations in Mesopotamia together with a separate report by J Wedgwood
and appendices

Secondary Material
Adochitei, Liliana *Romania and its allies during World War One* (online) 2014
Aspinall-Oglander, Cecil *Roger Keyes*. 1951, London: Hogarth Press
Bainton, Roy *Honoured by Strangers: Captain Cromie's Extraordinary First World
    War* 2002, London: Constable & Robinson
Beattie, Hugh *Imperial Frontier: Tribe and State in Waziristan* 2013, London:
    Curzon
Bosher, JF in *Imperial Vancouver Island: Who was Who* 2012, Vancouver: Berry
    Books
Bruce Lockhart, RH *Memoirs of a British Agent* 1932, London: Putnam
Bruce Lockhart, Sir Robert *Diaries of Sir Robert Bruce Lockhart* 1973, London:
    Macmillan
Chenevix Trench, Charles, *The Frontier Scouts* 1985, London: Cape
Collett, Nigel *The Butcher of Amritsar: General Reginald Dyer* 2005, London:
    Hambledon Continuum
Crowe Eyre *Memorandum on the Present State of British Relations with France and
    Germany* 1907, 2013, Newcastle: Cambridge Scholars Publishing
Crowley, Patrick T *Kut 1916: Courage and Failure in Iraq* 2009, Stroud: History
    Press
Davies, Norman *White Eagle Red Star* London. 1972: Macdonald &Co
Dunn, Jeffery Stephen *The Crowe Memorandum: Sir Eyre Crowe and Foreign
    Office Perceptions of Germany* 2013, Newcastle: Cambridge Scholars
    Publishing
Figes, Orlando *A People's Tragedy* London 1996, London: Pimlico

Footman, David *Civil War in Russia* 1961, London: Faber & Faber

Gato, Conrad *The Navy Everywhere* 1919, London: Contstable

Gazdar, Haris, Khakar, Ahmad and Khan, Irfan *Buffer Zone: Colonial Enclave or Urban Hub? Quetta: Between Four Regions and Two War* 2010, London: LSE Crisis States Working Papers No 2

Hill, George Alexander *Go Spy the Land: Being the Adventures of IK8 of the British Secret Service* 1932, London: Cassell & Co

Hughes, Michael *Inside the Enigma* 1997, London: Hambledon Press

Jeffery, Keith *Field Marshal Sir Henry Wilson: a Political Soldier* 2006, Oxford:OUP

Jwaideh, Wadie *The Kurdish National Movement, its Origins and Development* 2006, New York: Syracuse University Press

Kettle, Michael *The Allies and the Russian Collapse* 1981, London: Andre Deutch

Kettle, Michael *The Road to Intervention* 1988, London: Routledge

Kettle, Michael *Churchill and the Archangel Fiasco: November 1918 – July 1919* 1992, London: Routledge

Keyes, Lavender *The Lavender Diaries* 2006, London: FreeHand Publishing

Kinvig, Clifford *Churchill's Crusade: The British Invasion of Russia 1918-20* 2006, London Bloomsbury

Lazarski Christopher *The Lost Opportunity: Attempts at Unification of the Anti-Bolsheviks 1917-19* 2008, Lanham: University Press of America

Lieven, Dominic *Towards the Flame* 2015, London: Allen Lane

Martin, Lt. Gen LG *Sunset on the Main* 1951, London: Museum Press

Occleshaw, Michael *Dances in Deep Shadows* 2006, London: Constable

Pine, LG *The Family of Keyes* 1961, London: (unpublished)

Pipes, Richard *The Russian Revolution* 1990, New York: AA Knopf

Prasad, Shankar *The Gallant Dogras: An Illustrated History of the Dogra Regiment* 2005, New Delhi: Lancer Publications PVT Limited

Reilly, Sidney *Britain's Master Spy* London 1985: Dorset Press

Repington, Charles à Court *Imperial Strategy* 1906, London: John Murray

Rich, Paul *Creating the Arabian Gulf: The British Raj and the Invasions of the Gulf* 2009, Lanham: Lexington Books

Service, Robert *Spies and Commissars: The Early Years of the Russian Revolution* 2011, London: Macmillan

Service, Robert *The Last of the Tsars: Nicholas II and the Russian Revolution* 2017, London: Macmillan

Sluglett, Peter *Britain in Iraq; Contriving King and Country* 2007, London: IB Tauris & Co Limited

Smith, Douglas *Former People: The Last Days of the Russian Aristocracy* 2012, New York; Farrar, Strauss & Giroux

Sykes, Sir Percy *History of Persia* 1921, London: Macmillan

Trotsky, Leon *My Life: An Attempt at an Autobiography* 1930, New York: Scribner

Trotsky, Leon *History of the Russian Revolution* 1932, Michigan: University of Michigan Press

Tolczyk, Darius *See No Evil: Literary Cover ups and Discoveries of the Soviet Camp Experience* 1999, New Haven: Yale University Press

Townshend, Charles *When God made Hell: The British Invasion of Mesopotamia and the Creation of Iraq* 2010, London: Faber & Faber

Tyson, Joseph Howard *Fifty Seven Years of Russian Madness* 2015, Bloomington:iUniverse

Volodarsky Boris *Stalin's Agent: the Life and Death of Alexander Orlov* 2015, Oxford: OUP

Private Papers and Academic Theses

Keyes Michael *Provisional Biography*

Kopisto Lauri *The British in South Russia* 2011, Academic Dissertation presented at the University of Helsinki 29 April 2011

Roe, A (Major) *British Governance of the North West Frontier 1919-47: A Blueprint for Contemporary Afghanistan* 2005, Kansas: Thesis presented to the Faculty of US Army Command and Staff College

ENDNOTES

Chapter 1

1   *Abbotabad* written by its eponymous founder, James Abbott, Deputy Commissioner of Hazara 1849-53. It has been described as "one of the worst poems ever written."

2   It was also the last residence of Osama bin Laden.

3   Shelwin: *Thanet's Private Schools Nineteenth and early Twentieth Century.*

4   Haileybury: Colvin House Record Book.

5   Michael Keyes provisional biography ("M Keyes") p.5.

6   Aspinall-Oglander *Roger Keyes* p.8.

7   The idea of Terence Keyes as a pioneering member of CHERUB has great appeal.

8   See the 1878 Music Hall song, "We don't want to fight but by Jingo if we do, we've got the ships, we've got the men, we've got the money too. We've fought the bear before and while we're Britons through, The Russians shall not have Constantinople"

9   Charles à Court Repington. *Imperial Strategy* 1906, London: John Murray.

10   M Keyes, pp. 6 and 65.

11   M Keyes pp.2 and 8. He had wished to join his brother Charles in the Punjab Frontier Force but this had become a fashionable regiment with an expensive mess. Following his father's death in 1896, Terence could not expect an allowance to top up his military salary. The expense of being in the PFF eventually led to Charles' leaving.

12   Shankar Prasad *The Gallant Dogras: An Illustrated History of the Dogra Regiment,* 2005.

13   Ibid.

14   *The Advertiser*, Adelaide South Australia.

15   There is a memorial to his memory at St Alban's Church, Mardan, Nigeria.

Chapter 2

16   Charles Chenevix Trench, *The Frontier Scouts* (1985), p.135.

17   See in particular *British Governance of the North West Frontier 1919-47: A Blueprint for Contemporary Afghanistan* Major A Roe 2005.

18   Seistan and Sistan were interchangeable terms. Baluchistan is now known as Balochistan.

19   Keyes refers in his story *The Patriach* to leaving in the Spring and that during his return "the seed heads of grass shone white as they bent in the breeze" which points to a return in late summer (M Keyes p.19).

20   M Keyes p.16.

21 M Keyes *Additional Stories of Sir Terence Keyes.*

22 M Keyes *Additional Stories, The Book on Carpet*s.

23 Now Torbat e Heydarieh and Sistan.

24 M Keyes pp.16-23.

25 The same Indo-European term lies behind the final syllable in Ona*ger*.

26 Nikolay Prejevalsky (1839-88) was a Russian geographer and explorer and at one time rumoured to be Stalin's father.

27 List of Fellows and Honorary Foreign Members and Medallists to May 1910.

28 For this and following see M Keyes *Bye-Bye the Persian Spy.*

29 Ibid.

30 M Keyes *The Babu at Turbat i Haidari: The Answer to Everything can be found in the Government of India Regulations* - seven days for striking camp in Torbat i Haidari, a further seven for pitching camp on arrival, plus travel time between stations calculated by reference to the speed of a baggage camel (twelve miles a day) and then two days train travel to Quetta.

Chapter 3

31 Principally, the Khyber and the lesser known, at least in this context, Khojak.

32 *Buffer Zone: Colonial Enclave or Urban Hub? Quetta: Between Four Regions and Two Wars* Haris Gazdar, Sobia Ahmad Kaker, Irfan Khan LSE Crisis States Working Papers No 2 2010. The population of Quetta is now 565,137. The European population is negligible. Sadly, much of old Quetta was destroyed in an earthquake in 1935.

33 Sir Robert Sandeman, 1835-92, Chief Commissioner of Baluchistan 1889-91 and 1891-2.

34 Hugh Beattie *Imperial Frontier: Tribe and State in Waziristan* 2002.

35 Wadie Jwaideh *The Kurdish National Movement, its Origins and Development, 1960.*

36 He received the 18 Degree (Sovereign Prince of Rose Croix de Herodem and Knight of the Eagle and Pelican) in McMahon Chapter No 161 in 1923. Paul J Rich, *Creating the Arabian Gulf: The British Raj and the Invasions of the Gulf,* Lexington Books 2009.

37 Ibid.

38 Much more should be written about the role of Freemasonry in British India but this should be done by a writer who knows whereof he speaks which, as is readily apparent, is not the case here.

39 Keyes Papers Mss Eur F 131/44.

40 Ibid.

41 Ibid.

42 M Keyes p.26. It is likely that Peshin in now known as "Pishin." There are two

possible candidates; either Pishin on the Baluchistan/Iran border or Pishin near Quetta. On balance the latter seems most likely.

43   Rory subsequently went to Charterhouse and Worcester College Oxford. During the Second World War, he was a Captain in the Royal Sussex Regiment and Intelligence Corps. He later lived in Brook Green, Hammersmith and died unmarried on 16 March 1952.

44   In adult life, Rosemary lived as a single woman in Chatsworth Court, South Kensington in 1939. She joined the Women's Royal Naval Service in April 1941 (could this be through her Uncle, Roger Keyes' influence?) where she became a Second Officer. She married Lieutenant Colonel (later Major General) Halford David Fellowes in January 1942.

45   Budget Debate of the Indian Legislative Council cited in *The Campaign in Mesopotamia 1914-18* Volume 1 Imperial War Museum 1927.

46   Cited in *The Ideals of Empire: Political and Economic Thought 1903-13*, Ewen Green, 1998 p.667.

47   It is also the case that the German economy was struggling to fund both military and naval expansion programmes of the type envisaged by the Kaiser.

48   *Memorandum on the Present State of British Relations with France and Germany* Eyre Crowe 1907.

49   Quite how this counterfactual would have worked out is well beyond the scope of this book but it is surely unlikely that Russia would have had the resources or inclination to cause trouble in Central Asia whilst facing the German and Austro-Hungarian threat. The consequences for the Middle East are difficult to fathom.

50   Keyes Papers Mss Eur F 131/44.

Chapter 4

51   John Gordon Lorimer was an official of the Indian Civil Service who had spent much of his career on the North West Frontier. He compiled the Gazette over ten years commencing in 1903. It was published between 1908 -15. It is likely that he would have known Keyes personally.

52   Paul J Rich, *Creating the Arabian Gulf: the British Raj and the Invasions of the Gulf.*

53   Keyes Papers Mss Eur F 131/44.

54   The Al Khalifas are still the rulers now but with far more substantive powers.

55   M Keyes pp. 27-44.

56   During its mission, the *Emden* had sunk fifteen ships, one Russian cruiser and a French destroyer.

57   Keyes to Knox 4 November 1914 BL IOR L/PS/11/86/P4923/1914.

58   *Pearl Island or Mahbruk's Ramazan* was published in Chamber's Journal June 1952 (M Keyes pp.34-44).

59   M Keyes p.27.

60 A regular feature in literature about the Empire; it continues today in practically anything involving Ireland or France.

61 M Keyes p.34.

62 It is assumed that Keyes' professional staff such as clerks might have lived out. However, the ones mentioned such as the *chaprassi* (waiter) and *khitmutgar* (manservant) would surely have lived in.

63 M Keyes p.40.

64 Probably worth in excess of £1.2m in 2019

65 M Keyes p.43.

66 Ibid.

67 Keyes Papers Mss Eur F 131/44.

68 Ibid.

69 Ibid.

Chapter 5

70 Peter Sluglett, *Britain in Iraq; Contriving King and Country*, IB Tauris 2007.

71 HMS Agincourt was actually originally commissioned by Brazil but the sale fell through when the Brazilian economy underwent one of its periodic collapses precipitated this time by a recession in the rubber industry.

72 Colonel Patrick T Crowley, *Kut 1916: Courage and Failure in Iraq*, 2009.

73 The concern about threats to the loyalty of the Empire's Muslim population was a real and continuing one.

74 Charles Townshend, *When God made Hell: The British Invasion of Mesopotamia and the Creation of Iraq*, 2010.

75 Report of the Commission to Enquire into Operations in Mesopotamia Together with a Separate Report by J Wedgwood and Appendices, Mesopotamia Commission 1917 p.167.

76 M Keyes pp.45-56.

77 For various reasons, there are now only approximately four million trees.

78 M Keyes p.55. To be fair, this line is attributed to the subaltern.

79 Keyes Papers Mss Eur F131 - also see Chapter 4.

80 Ibid.

81 Conrad Gato, *The Navy Everywhere*, 1919.

82 Ibid.

83 Keyes Papers Mss Eur F131.

84 Isaiah Friedman,*The Question of Palestine; British-Jewish-Arab Relations 1914-18*, 1992.

85 Lt Gen HG Martin, *Sunset From the Main*, 1951, p.76.

86 Keyes Papers Mss Eur F131. Quite who the sickly Romanian was and why he

was in Bahrain is unclear.

87 Now Al Qatif, a suburb of Damman, the nearest Saudi town to Bahrain.

88 Keyes Papers Mss Eur F131/44.

89 Henry McMahon wrote to him from Egypt hoping that the meeting had taken place.

Chapter 6

90 The Hindu-German Conspiracy caused a series of mutinies, rioting and protests between 1914-17 including an attempt to cause the Indian Army to mutiny in February 1915 which failed when the plot was uncovered by the Punjab CID as well as another failed mutiny in 1915 by the 5th Light Infantry and a small contingent of the Malay Straits Guides in Singapore. Subsequent plots were substantially compromised by the intelligence services.

91 Paragraph 9 of the purported will of Peter the Great states that Russia should "push on to the Persian Gulf...and force our way to the Indies." This is now regarded as an Eighteenth Century forgery by Michael Sokolniki - a Polish General but remains in many ways a template for Russian expansionism.

92 Von der Goltz was a widely respected military academic as well as being a serving officer. Whilst he issued orders sanctioning reprisals against civilians when he was Military Governor of Belgium in 1914, he managed to obtain a temporary block on the Turkish annihilation of the Armenians in 1915.

93 Sir Percy Sykes, *History of Persia Vol 2*, Macmillan

94 *The Times History of the War*, p. 96

95 *The Times*, 17 August 1916.

96 Colonel Reginald Dyer, 1864-1927, was born in Murree where his father managed the local brewery. He was educated in India and Ireland before attending RMC Sandhurst. Much of his career was spent in India and effectively came to a conclusion following the Amritsar Massacre. He remained unrepentant and justified his actions as necessary for the preservation of good order.

97 *London Gazette*, 31 October 1917.

98 Keyes Papers Mss Eur F131 cf Sir Percy Sykes, *History of Persia volume 2*, (1921).

99 See Chapter 6.

100 Nigel Collett , *The Butcher of Amritsar: General Reginald Dyer*, 2005.

101 Keyes Papers Mss Eur F 131/8.

102 Collett, *The Butcher of Amritsar.*

103 *London Gazette* 31 October 1917.

104 Keyes Papers Mss Eur F 131/8.

105 Keyes Papers Mss Eur F 131/10.

106 *London Gazette* 1 June 1917.

Chapter 7

107   Christopher Thomson, 1875-1930, was later equally far-sighted when he condemned the Versailles treaty as "containing the seeds of another war." He was a prominent Socialist and was made Baron Thomson of Cardington by Ramsay Macdonald in 1924. In his role as Secretary of State for Air, he was responsible for the development of the R101 and was killed on its maiden flight in October 1930.

108   Liliana Adochitei, *Romania and its allies during World War One*, 2014.

109   *London Gazette*, 13 January 1920, p.706.

110   See Chapter 1.

111   The timing would certainly fit with raspberry leaves being out (M Keyes p.64).

112   An Ovis Erskini is almost certainly a Urial (a type of wild sheep native to the hills of western central Asia). Kopet Dagh is a mountain range between Turkmenistan and Iran. It is interesting to speculate how and when Keyes found himself hunting there.

113   See HG Martin, *Sunset on the Main*, supra.

114   M Keyes Mss Eur F131 p.65.

115   Keyes Papers Mss Eur F 131/44.

116   Keyes Papers Mss Eur F 131/12.

117   Ibid.

118   Michael Occleshaw, *Dances in Deep Shadows: Britain's Clandestine War in Russia 1917-20*, 2006.

119   Keyes Papers Mss Eur F131. The Grand Duchess and her husband, Grand Duke Kiril Vladimirovich fled Petrograd in June 1917.

Chapter 8

120   Michael Kettle, *The Allies and the Russian Collapse*, 1981.

121   RH Bruce Lockhart, *Memoirs of a British Agent*, 1932.

Chapter 9

122   Michael Hughes, *Inside the Enigma: British Officials in Russia 1900-39*, 1997.

123   Robert Bruce Lockhart, *The Memoirs of a British Agent*, p.60.

124   Bruce Lockhart, *The Memoirs of a British Agent*, p.64.

125   Bruce Lockhart emphasises his Scottishness at every turn writing at one point that "There is no drop of English blood in my veins."

126   Michael Kettle, *The Allies and the Russian Collapse*, p.80.

127   Keith Jeffery, *Field Marshal Sir Henry Wilson: a Political Soldier*, OUP 2006, p.140.

128 Kettle is adamant that Keyes was part of Poole's mission but this is contradicted by Keyes' own account as well as that of Michael Hughes in *Inside the Enigma*.

129 Bruce Lockhart, *Memoirs of a British Agent*, p.163.

130 Felix Dzerhinsky 1877-1926, a professional revolutionary and, as head of the Cheka, was responsible for thousands of executions. He took the lessons which he had learned from the Tsarist secret police - the Okhrana - to new levels of brutality but was also a talented head of counter-intelligence setting up front organisations that entrapped opponents. Both Bruce Lockhart and Sidney Reilly became ensnared in his scheming.

131 Keyes Papers Mss Eur F131/44.

Chapter 10

132 Discussed in more detail in Chapter 12.

133 Orlando Figes, *A People's Tragedy: The Russian Revolution 1891-1924* p.493. He goes on to quote a 1930s survey conducted by the party which claimed that forty six thousand were involved.

134 Keyes Papers Mss Eur F 131/11.

135 Leon Trotsky, *History of the Russian Revolution*, 1930.

136 Cited in Kettle, *The Road to Intervention*.

137 Keyes Papers Mss Eur F132/11.

138 Keyes Papers Mss Eur F131/44.

139 These primarily involved the Swedish Nya Banken which had been set up in 1912 as the first Swedish bank for trades unions and cooperatives. Its founder Olof Aschberg later assisted the Bolsheviks in evading sanctions on the trading of Russian gold seized after the revolution.

140 See for example, poor Mr Weinberg of Mendelsohn & Co.

141 Sinclair later succeeded Maxwell Cumming as head of the Secret Intelligence Service and was in part responsible for the publicity given to the Zinoviev Letter in 1924.

142 M Keyes pp.67-74.

143 Ibid.

144 The Women's Battalion of Death had been formed for the Kerensky government by Maria Bochkareva in an attempt to shame their male counterparts into fighting with more vigour. They played their part in the Kerensky Offensive with some success but, with its collapse, they became less significant. Figes gives an account of the formidable Bochkareva coming across one of her troops having sexual intercourse with a male soldier in a shell-hole and bayoneting her on the spot. Figes *A Peoples' Tragedy*, p.419.

145 M Keyes supra.

146 The Frenchman was Diderot although the line is also attributed to Peter the Great.

Chapter 11

147   FO 371/2999, Buchanan to Foreign Office 6 November 1917.

148   Kettle, *The Allies and the Russian Collapse*, p.122.

149   CAB 23/4 War Cabinet 295 10 December 1917 cited in Hughes *Inside the Enigma* p.121.

150   Keyes Papers Mss Eur F 131/11.

151   Ibid.

152   Keyes Papers Mss Eur F131/44.

153   Ibid.

154   Ibid.

155   Ibid.

156   Ibid.

157   See Chapter 13 for more details.

158   Keyes Papers Mss Eur F131/44.

159   Ibid.

160   Ibid.

161   Ibid.

Chapter 12

162   Figes, *A Peoples' Tragedy*, p.556.

163   NA FO371/3018 B to FO 23/11.

164   NA FO175/16, British Economic Mission to Russia Report No III, Report on the Banking Schemes negotiated by Colonel Keyes pp. 2-3.

165   Keyes Papers Mss Eur F131.

166   Keyes Papers Mss Eur F 131/12.

167   War Cabinet 294 cited in Kettle *The Allies and the Russian Collapse*, p.156.

168   NA CAB23/4, 289th meeting of War Cabinet.

169   NA FO371/3018, telegram dated 26 November 1917.

170   Keyes Papers Mss Eur F 131/44.

171   Keyes Papers Mss Eur F 131/12.

172   Keyes Papers Mss Eur F 131/21 *Loans to Russian Banks.*

173   Ibid.

174   Kettle, *The Allies and the Russian Collapse*

175   Ibid, p.135

176   Keyes Papers Mss Eur F 131 17/19

177   NA FO3071/3019 no 243216 and NA FO371/3238 NO 2143

178 Keyes Papers Mss Eur F 131/21

179 Kettle, *The Allies and the Russian Collapse*, p.136 states that he "acquired a good deal of money." However, in his second volume *The Road to Intervention* ("Volume 2), he quotes a member of the British Economic Mission named Armistead informing Lindley that Leech "was regarded completely as a man of straw before the war".

180 Keyes Papers Mss Eur F131/44.

181 Keyes Papers Mss Eur F131.

182 Ibid.

183 Keyes Papers Mss Eur F131/21.

184 There is a conflict between what Keyes wrote in one of his reports and the detailed letter of advice given by Robert Chalmers to the Treasury on 11 April 1918.

185 Keyes Papers Mss F 131/21, p.24.

186 Keyes Papers Mss F 131/21.

187 Ibid.

188 Ibid.

189 NA FO 175 5B355.

190 NA Papers of Sir Arthur Steel-Maitland GD193/328 Appendix Mr Karol Iaroshinski p 39, cited in Occleshaw, *Dances in Deep Shadows*. p.6.

191 Keyes Papers Mss Eur F 131 Russian Bank Scheme p.4.

Chapter 13

192 Keyes Papers Mss Eur F131/22.

193 Keyes Papers Mss Eur F131/21.

194 NA FO371/3283 No 12745 17 January 1918 Keyes to Foreign Office.

195 Keyes Papers Mss Eur F131/21.

196 Ibid.

197 See Kettle Vol 1 *The Allies and the Russian Collapse*, p.206.

198 Ibid.

199 Keyes Papers Mss Eur F 131/22.

200 Kettle in Vol 1 *The Allies and the Russian Collapse*, p.206 believes that Yaroshinski asked for £5m and was beaten down to £500,000 by Poliakov. This, although plausible, is not apparent from Keyes' own report.

201 Keyes Papers Mss Eur F131/21.

202 Keyes Papers Mss Eur F131/22.

203 NA FO 175 5B 355.

204 NA FO371/3283 No 118 and as referred to in Chapter 13.

205　Ibid.

206　NA FO95/802.

207　Kettle *The Allies and the Russian Collapse*, p.247.

208　Keyes Papers Mss Eur F131/12.

209　Bruce Lockhart, *Memoirs of a British Agent* pp.164-6. Bruce Lockhart's memoirs are not always reliable and sometimes vary significantly from his contemporary diaries. However, there is no reason to doubt the veracity of this account.

Chapter 14

210　See in particular Sir John Picton Bagge's report discussed in Chapter 20. Mss Eur F 131/19.

211　PRO FO 175/16/60212.

212　Ibid.

213　Ibid.

214　Ibid.

215　Keyes Papers Mss Eur F131/12.

216　IPRO FO 175/16/60212 telegram L411.

217　Keyes Papers Mss Eur F131/12.

218　IPRO FO 175/16/60212.

219　Ibid.

220　Ibid.

221　Keyes Papers Mss Eur F 131.

222　See Chapter10 for details and in particular the involvement of Helphand (Parvus).

223　PRO FO 175/16/60212.

224　Burton, Richard (1 of 10) National Life Story Collection: Architects' Lives, British Library Sounds; Shelf mark C467/117.

225　See Chapter 22.

226　Robert Service, *The Last of the Tsars*, (Macmillan 2017) pp. 132-135.

227　Ibid. Solovëv was a fanatical Monarchist who had married Rasputin's daughter.

228　Joseph Howard Tyson *Fifty Seven Years of Russian Madness*, Bloomington 2015. In a very Russian way, Krasin was the son of a police chief who became a revolutionary bomb maker before becoming a millionaire electrical engineer. He returned to Russia in 1917 and was Commissar for Foreign Trade 1920-24.

Chapter 15

229　Keyes Papers Mss Eur F131.

230   Keyes Papers Mss Eur F131/21, p.15-16.

231   Keyes Papers Mss Eur F131/21.

232   Ibid.

233   Ibid.

234   Keyes Papers Mss Eur F131, quoted in detail in Chapter 14

235   Kettle, *The Road to Intervention*, p.25.

236   *The Diaries of Sir Robert Bruce Lockhart Volume 1*, but compare with his *Memoirs of a British Agent* (p.163) where the Foreign Office is replaced by Lloyd George and the focus is far more upon documents which purported to prove that Trotsky and Lenin were German agents. Trotsky was infuriated that the Allies (principally the Americans, the British were far more circumspect) gave credence to them. There is a definite sense that Bruce Lockhart's Memoirs were written with a great deal of hindsight.

237   NA FO371/3286 No 116763.

238   Ibid.

239   *The City of Marseilles* was to have an eventful life having been completed in 1913. She suffered considerable damage from a mine on 6 January 1940 just off the east coast of Scotland. Having been repaired, she was later stranded in Batticaloa, Ceylon before being refloated and was scrapped in 1947.

240   Kettle *The Road to Intervention*, p.200.

241   Edward Dominick Spring Rice 1889-1940 a writer on financial matters and friend of Virginia Woolf.

242   M Keyes, *The Hush Ship*.

243   Ibid.

244   The British and French were active in bribing groups of workmen to sabotage large sections of the Ukrainian economy so as to prevent resources falling into German hands.

Chapter 16

245   David Footman, *Civil War in Russia*, Faber and Faber 1961.

246   Dunsterville, as a schoolboy, was the inspiration behind Kipling's Stalky.

247   Savinkov left Russia soon afterwards and returned to France where he served as Admiral Kolchak's diplomatic representative. After a spell in Poland during the Russo-Polish war of 1919-20, he became caught up in a scheme with Sidney Reilly and together with him was captured on his return to Russia and allegedly died when he fell from a window in the Lubyanka. The more likely scenario is that he was murdered by OGPU as the Cheka had then become.

248   The Japanese were one of the few net beneficiaries of World War 1 as they were later able to acquire much the German empire in the Pacific as well as the base at Tsingtao for minimal military commitment.

249   NA FO371/3286.

250   Kettle *The Road to Intervention*, p.204.

251   Ibid.

252   The assassins, Andreev and Jacov Blumkin, were both Left SRs but it is noteworthy that Blumkin worked for the Cheka both before and after the assassination attempt and that after a brief spell in the Ukraine, he was to return and join the Bolsheviks.

253   Kettle *The Road to Intervention*, p.270.

254   Ibid pp. 266-7.

255   Ibid.

256   Ibid.

257   Ibid.

258   Keyes Papers Mss Eur F131.

259   McGrath was awarded the Military Cross for his services.

260   Bruce Lockhart *Memoirs of a British Agent*, p.211.

261   Ibid p.213.

262   Keyes Papers Mss Eur F131/22, Witness Statement paragraph 18.

263   Ibid.

264   Ibid paragraph 10.

265   Cited in Kettle *The Road to Intervention*, p.280.

266   Ibid pp.280-1.

267   Keyes Papers Mss Eur F131, Report entitled *Loans to Russian Banks* p.78

268   His and Keyes' paths therefore crossed again. Struvé later fled to Paris where he died in 1944.

269   NA FO371/3287.

270   Bruce Lockhart *Memoirs*, p.216

271   NA FO371/3287.

272   Vasily Vasilevich Shulgin (1878-1976) was a leading monarchist and member of the Duma from 1907 until 1914 when he joined the army. He, together with Alexander Guchkov was active in persuading Nicholas II to abdicate. He later worked alongside the Whites in South Russia before fleeing to Yugoslavia where he lived in exile before being captured by the Russian forces in 1944.

273   Keyes Papers Mss Eur F 131/12.

274   Ibid.

275   Christopher Lazarski, *The Lost Opportunity: Attempts at Unification of the Anti-Bolsheviks 1917-19*, University Press of America 2008, p.80.

276   Keyes Papers Mss Eur F131/12.

277   M Keyes pp.84-89.

278   It is likely that this was the Igor Lebedinsky who was an OGPU agent

working undercover as a Resident in Vienna in 1932. See Boris Volodarsky, *Stalin's Agent: The Life and Death of Alexander Orlov*, OUP 2014.

279   Keyes Papers Mss Eur F131, Loans to Russian Banks p.78.

280   Keyes Papers Mss Eur F131/12.

281   RNSM A1990/73.

282   Trotsky's *Diary in Exile* 1935 translated from the Russian by Elena Zarudnaya. Faber and Faber 1959 p.81.

283   Keyes Papers Mss Eur F131/44.

284   NA FO337/87 8 August 1918.

285   Clifford Kinvig, *Churchill's Crusade: the British Invasion of Russia 1918-20*, Bloomsbury, 2006 p.25.

Chapter 17

286   Kettle *The Road to Intervention*, p.314.

287   Von Ungern-Sternberg continued to fight the Bolsheviks until 1921 when his brigade fell apart. He was captured and, following a six hour show trial, executed.

288   Keyes Papers Mss 131/44.

289   William Gerhardi would have been twenty three at the time and based his first novel, *Futility* on this experiences in North Russia and at this time.

290   Adm 137/1371 cited in Kettle *The Road to Intervention*, p.313.

291   Sidney Reilly, *Britain's Master Spy: His Own Story*, Dorset Press, 1985.

292   Or possibly Kherson also in the Ukraine.

293   Sidney Reilly, *Britain's Own Master Spy* p.32.

294   Ibid.

295   Ibid p.35

296   Darius Tolczyk *See No Evil: Literary Cover ups and Discoveries of the Soviet Camp Experience*, Yale University Press, 1999 p .9.

297   Bruce Lockhart *Memoirs*, p.240.

298   Ibid p.241.

299   This near blindness has caused some to question whether it was really her who pulled the trigger.

300   Keyes Papers Mss Eur F 131/12.

301   George Alexander Hill *Go Spy the Land: Being the Adventures of IK8 of the British Secret Service*.

302   Hansard July 7 1924.

303   Roy Bainton, *Honoured by Strangers: Captain Cromie's Extraordinary First World War*, Constable & Robinson, 2002 Chapter 24.

304   Kettle, *The Road to Intervention*, p.324. British involvement is not generally

accepted although far from impossible.

305 *The Mercury,* Hobart 6 September 1918.

306 Bruce Lockhart, *Memoirs,* p.243.

307 Robert Service, *Spies and Commissars: The Early Years of the Russian Revolution.*

308 John Maclean had himself been a celebrated victim of DORA in 1915. Possibly encouraged by Litvinov, not that he needed any; he was arrested again in April 1918 and imprisoned for sedition.

309 Reilly *Memoirs* covers much of this.

310 Bruce Lockhart *Memoirs* p.266.

311 Keyes Papers Mss F131/12.

312 M Keyes.

Chapter 18

313 Keyes Papers Mss Eur F131/12.

314 Keyes Papers Mss Eur F131.

315 No, not that one.

316 Keyes Papers F131/18.

317 Ibid.

318 Kettle *Churchill and the Archangel Fiasco: Russia and the Allies 1917-1920.*

319 Ibid.

320 It remained a sore point and was resolved by Soviet occupation in 1940 following the Nazi-Soviet Pact.

321 Ibid.

322 Kettle *Churchill and the Archangel Fiasco.*

323 Keyes Papers Mss F 131/12.

324 Ibid.

325 *London Gazette,* 26 April 1920.

326 Kettle *Churchill and the Archangel Fiasco.*

Chapter 19

327 See Norman Davies, *White Eagle Red Star,* 1972 p.94 et seq. for details of this paladin.

328 Ibid p.94.

329 Lloyd George Papers F89/2/16.

330 Martin Gilbert, *Winston S Churchill Volume IV World in Torment,* p.235.

331 Kettle, *Churchill and the Archangel Fiasco.*

332 Ibid.

333   Keyes Papers Mss Eur F131/23, *Lecture delivered to the Staff College Quetta 10 August 1921.*

334   Kettle certainly thinks so, *Churchill and the Archangel Fiasco.*

335   Cabinet Office briefing on Sidney Reilly personal file CX 2616 cited in Occleshaw, *Dances in Deep Shadows* p.292.

336   Keyes Papers Mss Eur F131.

337   Keyes Papers Mss Eur F131/44.

338   *Hansard,* 9 April (HC Deb 5s Vol 114)

339   Kettle, *Churchill and the Archangel Fiasco.*

340   Ibid.

341   Where they remain.

342   Cameron Bruce's subsequent career was less glorious. He joined the Black and Tans in 1920 and was dismissed following a scandal and conviction for theft from a dairy. He died still protesting his innocence in 1925.

343   Keyes Papers 131F/23.

344   Keyes Papers Mss Eur F 131/44.

345   Keyes Papers Mss Eur F 131/23 and 44.

346   Keyes Papers Mss F 131/23.

347   Report on the British Military Mission to South Russia by General Holman WO 33/971.

348   Lauri Kopisto, *The British in South Russia* dissertation, Helsinki 2012   p.118

349   Kettle, *Churchill and the Archangel Fiasco.*

350   Ibid.

Chapter 20

351   War Cabinet 532A, WO 0149/6324.

352   Keyes Papers Mss Eur F 131/17.

353   Keyes Papers Mss Eur F 131/17.

354   Keyes Papers Mss Eur F 131/17. Graham was then at the Eastern Department of the Foreign Office.

355   Ibid.

356   NA FO 175 5B355.

357   Ibid.

358   Keyes Papers Mss Eur F131/17.

359   Ibid.

360   Ibid.

Chapter 21

361 Orlando Figes, *A Peoples' Tragedy*, p.664.

362 Trotsky, *My Life* Chapter XXXVII.

363 Orlando Figes , *A Peoples' Tragedy*, p.673.

364 Ibid p.672

365 Keyes Papers Mss Eur F131/17.

366 David Vital, *A People Apart: A Political History of the Jews in Europe 1789-1939*, p.29, OUP 1999.

367 R. Pipes, *The Russian Revolution*, p.824, 1984.

368 Keyes Papers Mss Eur F131/23.

369 British Documents on Foreign Affairs ("BDFA") 2A Vol3.

370 See Keyes' comments to Leonard Cohen referred to in Chapter 19.

371 Keyes Papers Mss F131/23.

372 Ibid.

373 Ibid.

374 Keyes Papers Mss Eur F131/44.

375 Ibid.

376 Ibid.

377 Ibid.

378 BFDA 2A Vol 2 *Report on the situation in South Russia by Sir H Mackinder* cited in Hughes, *Inside the Enigma*. p.179.

379 Keyes Papers F Eur 131/15.

380 Keyes Papers F Eur 131/14.

381 Ibid.

382 Keyes Papers F Eur 131/44. The two ex Viceroys were Curzon and Lord Hardinge.

383 Ibid.

384 The Czechs left at the same time as the Allies leaving the Japanese who did not leave until 1922.

385 Keyes Papers F Eur 131/44.

386 Ibid.

387 Keyes Papers Mss Eur F131/15.

388 Ibid.

389 Ibid.

390 Ibid.

391 Ibid.

392 Keyes Papers Mss Eur F131/44.

393   Ibid.

394   Ibid.

395   Keyes Papers Mss Eur F131/15.

396   Kapisto, *The British in South Russia* p.177.

397   Orlando Figes, *A Peoples' Tragedy*, p.720.

Chapter 22

398   Keyes Papers Mss Eur F131. The Affidavit was finally sworn in Quetta on 5 March 1928.

399   Reginald Dyer was well known to Keyes (see Chapter 7). Although he had been temporarily promoted to Brigadier General on 12 March 1918, Dyer had reverted to his Colonelcy by the time of the massacre. Following the ensuing furore, Dyer retired from the Army and returned to Britain.

400   Mss Eur F131/23. The lecture was delivered on 10 August 1921.

401   Ibid.

402   Ibid.

403   Paul Rich, *Creating the Arabian Gulf*, letter Keyes to Bray dated 21 July 1930. The "Butler" referred to was RA Butler then Parliamentary Private Secretary to the India Secretary, Samuel Hoare.

404   Lt. Gen HG Martin, *Sunset on the Main*, Museum Press 1951.

Appendix

405   *The Family of Keyes* Terence Keyes' papers as edited by LG Pine in 1961. He was the Editor of Burke's Peerage.

406   Such people were known as "nabobs" see for example Jos Sedley in Vanity Fair.

407   M Keyes, RSAA/M/129.

408   Alumni include the Arctic explorer, Admiral Sir George Nares.

409   Pine has them starting at the Royal Naval college in 1830 which must be incorrect.

410   William's fate is unclear. Pine states that he died before the move to Harrow in 1829 but this too must be incorrect.

411   Aspinall-Oglander in *Roger Keyes*, Hogarth Press 1951, writes that he spent the time studying English Literature for a year before going to India. There is no other evidence for this and, as he did not arrive in India until 1843, it is more likely that this period of enforced idleness was nearer two years.

412   Pine states that he became a Colonel in the Indian Staff Corps. By this, he may well mean a position in the Madras Army.

413   The Lawrences could be regarded as one of the archetypal Anglo-Indian families. John was described as "the Saviour of the Punjab" for his work in establishing good government after the Second Sikh War. He was also

Viceroy and Governor General. Henry was a gifted administrator who also founded four educational establishments which are still in existence. He died at the Siege of Lucknow in 1857. George Lawrence served forty three years in India retiring as a Major General.

414 Pine is the only source for this nickname.

415 There is no connection between Neville Bowles Chamberlain and his prime ministerial namesake.

416 For this and what follows, see Hugh Beattie, *Imperial Frontier: Tribe and State in Waziristan*, 2013

417 Bartle Frere, 1815-84, was Governor of Bombay in 1860 but later became High Commissioner for Southern Africa. He is credited with the introduction of the Indian postal service.

418 This comment can be viewed as a moue of official disapproval for what might be regarded as recklessness on Keyes' part.

419 Probyn had won the Victoria Cross for gallantry during the Mutiny. He subsequently became secretary to the Prince of Wales prior to his becoming Edward VII

420 Hansard Questions 3 March 1869.

421 Later Field Marshal and Governor General of Jamaica. He was also appointed Viceroy of India but turned it down on the basis that he had insufficient funds to fulfil the obligations of the post.

422 Now known as Tor Ghar of which it is a direct translation.

423 Roger Keyes was later to become an Admiral, Commander of the Mediterranean Fleet and Baron Keyes of Dover and Zeebrugge.

424 Later Colonel Sir Robert Sandeman. He advocated a policy of involvement with the border tribes which was in contradistinction to that previously advocated by Lord John Lawrence and his supporters. The DNB records that his methods were disapproved of by the Chief Officer of the Sind Frontier. Bearing in mind Pine's account of the close relationship between Sandeman and Charles Keyes, this is presumably his predecessor.

425 And persists today. Casey Connor, a journalist covering the Tor Ghar (Black Mountain) earthquake in 2005 wrote "Tor Ghar has a poor reputation among the military and the country in general of being a violent, backwards place"

426 Pine.

427 Shorncliffe Lodge is a substantial Victorian property with views overlooking the Channel.

428 She remained single and died in 1964.

429 Nurse, Ladies Maid, Cook, Parlour Maid and two housemaids. There is however, no record of Charles, Roger or Terence.

Index

Kiev Private Bank, The 140
Kitchener, Horatio Herbert, First
  Earl Kitchener 18, 44, 50, 69
Klyshko, Nicolai 227
Knox, General Alfred William
  Fortescue 90, 108, 132, 237
Knox, Stuart, British Resident in
  Bushire 32, 317
Kohat Pass 304, 308, 310
Kolchak, Admiral Alexander
  Vasilyevich 208, 209, 237, 241,
  245, 249, 251, 252, 255, 256, 258,
  260, 262, 275, 288, 292, 325
Komuch 209
Kon, Isidore 132
Kornilov, General Lavr Georgyevich
  91, 101, 117, 120, 121, 145, 146,
  175, 177
Krasin, Leonid Borisovich 158, 324
Krasnov, General Pyotr Nikolayevich
  175, 176, 182, 205, 218, 236, 247,
  249, 259
Krivoshein, Alexander Vasilyevich
  132, 138, 144, 192, 193
Kursk 273, 280
Kut 46, 49, 57, 312, 318
Kun, Bela 252
Kuwait 41, 52

Lagutin 145
Lahore 15, 19, 20, 303
Lahore, Treaty of 303
Lake Onega 193, 199
Latsis, Martin 221
Lawrence, George 332
Lawrence, Sir Henry 303, 309
Lawrence John Laird Mair, First
  Baron Lawrence 305, 332
Lebedinski, Igor 197, 327
Leech, Hugh Ansdell Farran 128-
  132, 134-136, 138, 140, 141, 146,
  161, 162, 164, 184-188, 190, 191,
  256, 266, 323, 333
Lessing, Edward 130, 131, 156,
  191, 225
Lied, Jonas 158
Lindley, Sir Francis Oswald 96,
  184, 238

Litvinoff, Maxim 226, 227, 277,
  328
Lloyd George, David 50, 90,91,
  124, 130,131, 156,157, 165, 169,
  171, 178, 191, 195, 207, 229, 239,
  241, 245,247, 250, 253, 277, 279,
  280, 294, 325, 329
Locker Lampson, Oliver 75, 76,
  91, 102
Lorimer, John Gordon 28, 317
Ludendorff, General Erich Friedrich
  113, 164, 180,182, 202, 205,206,
  230
Lugansk 253
Lutsky, Alexei 147
Lvov, Prince Georgi Yevgenyevich
  193

Macdonagh, Lieutenanat General
  George 127, 128
Mackensen, Field Marshall August
  von 71
Mackinder, Sir Halford John 282,
  285, 288, 330
Maclean, John 227, 328
Macmillan, Maurice Harold, First
  Earl of Stockton 312, 314, 319,
  324
Mae-Maevsky, General Vladimir
  Zenonovich 259, 276
Mahsuds 8, 306
Makhno, Nestor 240, 254, 258,
  273, 274, 276
Makin 306
Maliki System 17
Malleson, General Sir Wilfrid 210,
  231, 236
Mamontov, General Konstantin
  Konstantinovich 276
Mannerheim, Baron Carl Gustav
  Emil 138, 166, 275
Marchand, René 218, 220
Mardan 315
Markov, Nikolai E 158
Masaryk, Thomas 168
Maude, General Frederick Stanley
  58
Maynard, Major General Sir C M
  211

Index

BV - #0025 - 200919 - C0 - 229/152/24 - PB - 9781912419586